# Theatrical Space

## *A Guide for Directors and Designers*

## William Faricy Condee

The Scarecrow Press, Inc.
Lanham, Maryland, and London
2001

# SCARECROW PRESS, INC.

Published in the United States of America
by Scarecrow Press, Inc.
4720 Boston Way, Lanham, Maryland 20706
www.scarecrowpress.com

4 Pleydell Gardens, Folkestone
Kent CT20 2DN, England

Copyright © 1995 by William Faricy Condee/Scarecrow Press
First paperback edition 2001

British Library Cataloguing in Publication Information Available

The hardback edition of this book was previously cataloged by the Library of
Congress as follows:

Condee, William Faricy
Theatrical space : a guide for directors and designers / by William Faricy
Condee.
p.    cm.
Includes index.
1.    Theatres—Stage-setting and scenery. 2.  Theater—Production and
       direction. I. Title.
PN 2091.S8C615 1995 792'.025—dc20  95-3311

ISBN: 0-8108-4211-4     (paper)

Manufactured in the United States of America.

⊖™ The paper used in this publication meets the minimum requirements of
American National Standard for Information Sciences—Permanence of
Paper for Printed Library Materials, ANSI/NISO Z39.48-1992.

For Kathleen

# CONTENTS

Introduction vii

Acknowledgments xii

Descriptions of Directors, Designers, and Actors in the Book xv

1. Examining the Theatre Space 1

2. The Performance's Relationship to the Architecture 9

3. Using the Architecture of the Theatre 20

4. Involving the Audience 33

5. The Proscenium Arch's Effect on Performance 46

6. Comparing Performance on Open and Proscenium Stages 58

7. Designing for the Open Stage: Problems and Solutions 69

8. Using the Portal on a Thrust Stage 92

9. The Open Stage's Effect on Staging 103

10. Director-Designer Collaboration on the Open Stage 115

11. Stage Up or Stage Down? The Vertical Relationship of Audience and Performance 127

12. Engaging the Stage Volume 140

13. Flexible Theatres 154

14. Environmental and Promenade Theatre 169

15. Transferring a Production 185

16. Two Planks and a Passion 195

Index 201

About the Author 207

# INTRODUCTION

Theatre space can make an active, positive contribution to the art of theatre. Too often, theatre artists decry the space in which they must work: "If only . . ." "If we had . . ." "If we could get rid of . . ." "If this weren't like that . . ." Directors and designers who work in a small, cramped, irregular space yearn for the rich amenities of a new, regularized theatre. Theatre artists who work in fancy, new theatres nostalgically recall the rough-and-ready spaces they started out in.

Directors and designers are trained to examine a text and to conceive a performance for it, but the space in which the play will be performed is often an afterthought. This approach leads to viewing the theatre space as an unfortunate condition that must be overcome or accommodated.

This book is a plea to accept—even embrace—the place of the performance. Directors and designers can conceive the production as a performance that happens in a given space, imbued with the character and attributes of that space. Instead of viewing the architecture as an impediment to be conquered, the theatre space can be exploited and used creatively, contributing to the overall success of the production.

A few terms need to be defined to ensure clarity. A "proscenium" theatre has two specialized, dedicated spaces: a stage for the performance and an auditorium for the audience. These spaces are joined by the proscenium arch, a large hole through which the audience views the performance. The auditorium and stage may be entirely separate and distinct, as in a picture-frame theatre, or joined by an apron, a stage extension that extends past the proscenium arch and partially into the auditorium. Whichever the case, the audience views the performance from roughly one direction.

In an "open-stage" theatre, the audience and performance share a common volume, rather than having two separate spaces. The walls and ceiling of the unified space are continuous, not inter-

1. Theatre forms:
Proscenium stage
Theatre-in-the-round, or arena stage
Three-sided thrust stage
Semi-thrust stage
Two-sided, or transverse, stage
Illustrations by Ming Cho Lee. Reprinted from American Theatre Planning Board, *Theatre Check List* (1969), Wesleyan University Press, xii–xiii. Reproduced with permission of University Press of New England.

rupted by a proscenium arch. The audience in an open stage theatre usually encircles the stage, to a greater or lesser degree.

The fullest degree of encirclement is the "arena," or "theatre-in-the-round," in which the audience completely surrounds the stage. An arena stage may be square, rectangular or round.

In a "thrust theatre," the audience encircles the stage to a lesser degree. One side of the stage is backed by a wall or portal, which may provide a background for the action. The degree of encirclement in thrust theatres varies. In a "three-quarter thrust," the audience is on three sides of the stage, which juts into the middle of the auditorium. A "semi-thrust," or "modified thrust," is somewhere between three-quarter thrust and an apron proscenium; the stage thrusts into the audience, but most of the spectators are gathered near the center. At the back of the semi-thrust stage there is usually a portal, a de-emphasized arch, that delimits a specialized area that may be used for scenic effects. The semi-thrust maintains much of the frontality of the proscenium, in that most of the spectators view the stage from essentially one direction, but the theatre has the unity of the open stage, in that the action occurs in the same space that the audience occupies.

A rarer form of the open stage is the "two-sided," or "transverse," theatre. The audience is seated on two sides of the stage, similar to a stadium.

The "end-stage theatre" straddles the distinction between the open stage and proscenium theatre. An end-stage is essentially a proscenium theatre with the arch removed: the audience sits in parallel rows facing a stage at one end of the space. It is a form of open stage in that the audience and performance share a single, unified volume. But the audience views the performance from essentially one direction, as in a proscenium theatre. Except as noted, the term "open stage" is used here to refer to theatres in which the audience partially or completely encircles the stage, including arena, thrust and two-sided. The end stage is included only where the attributes of the open stage specifically pertain to it.

In open stage theatres, the actors often make their entrances and exits through "vomitories," or "voms" (the term is derived from the Latin "vomitorium," in the Roman theatre). Voms are tunnels under the auditorium that open onto the edge of the stage.

This book is not meant to represent just my views on the

creative use of theatre space. The book is based primarily on hundreds of interviews with prominent American and British directors, designers and actors conducted over roughly a ten-year period. The quotes included here represent a tiny fraction of the total interviews, and the selection and organization process was arduous. When a given theatre artist is quoted offering a given point of view, this quote does not mean that he or she does not hold other alternative views, or that he or she disagrees with other views presented. I have simply chosen representative quotations that promote each approach to a given situation.

There is no right or wrong in theatrical production, and there are no rules. Instead there is an almost infinite variety of choices. I have therefore organized each chapter into a series of problems and ways of addressing these problems. Some of these approaches are complementary, others are mutually exclusive. It would be counterproductive to my goal to suggest that any method is right. My aim is to gather and clarify the views of distinguished, experienced theatre artists who have used theatre space creatively, in order that others may learn from, or even be inspired by, their ideas and practice.

# ACKNOWLEDGMENTS

Portions of this book have appeared in earlier versions in *Theatre Design and Technology* 31 (1995): 9–15; and *Theatre Insight* 2 (1990): 3–7.

Foremost I wish to thank Dr. Bernard Beckerman of Columbia University, who first suggested that I examine theatre architecture. But my debt to him is far greater: he remains persistently over my shoulder as I write, prodding and cajoling. After Dr. Beckerman's untimely death, my research was wisely guided by Dr. Martin Meisel and Prof. Howard Stein, who continue to this day to advise and support my work as a scholar and theatre artist.

Two individuals in the practice of theatre architecture have inspired me to forge ahead with this project: Dennis Sharp, who first taught me theatre architecture at Columbia, and Iain Mackintosh of Theatre Projects Consultants, who always makes me think and question.

This book would not exist without the many individuals who took the time from their busy schedules to be interviewed. In many ways, this book is theirs, and I cannot thank them enough. In addition, much of the research was undertaken at the Lincoln Center Library for the Performing Arts, and I wish to thank the staff of the Theatre Collection.

At Ohio University, this research was supported by a generous grant from the Ohio University Research Committee. Chris Pealer assisted on the preparation of the manuscript, supported by a grant from Honors Tutorial College at Ohio University. The School of Theater has also been strongly supportive of this project, providing time and money for me to continue this work. In particular, I wish to thank the two Directors of the School, Dr. Kathleen F. Conlin and Prof. Toni Dorfman, for their unflagging patience and support.

Most of all, I wish to thank my family: My parents provided me with a sense of the ideals and principles of scholarship, and offered their unbounded love. My wife and son have borne the brunt of this enterprise, and I am eternally in their debt. While all the faults in the writing are mine, Kathleen unerringly caught my inaccuracies, infelicities and mistakes. She has patiently waited for the completion of this project, and she richly deserves all the thanks and love I can provide.

# DESCRIPTIONS OF DIRECTORS, DESIGNERS, AND ACTORS IN THE BOOK

Brief descriptions of directors, designers, and actors referred to in the text (Please note that these descriptions are highly selective):

JASON BARNES is production manager of the Royal National Theatre's Cottesloe Theatre in London, where he has supervised the production of over 200 plays.

JOHN LEE BEATTY designed sets for the Circle Rep (New York City) and Broadway productions of *Talley's Folly* and *The 5th of July,* as well as over twenty other productions at Circle Rep. In addition, he designed New York productions of *The Water Engine, Ain't Misbehavin', Crimes of the Heart, Burn This, The Sisters Rosensweig, Penn and Teller, The Miss Firecracker Contest, The Road to Mecca, A Life in the Theatre,* and *Lips Together, Teeth Apart.* In addition, he has designed at Yale Repertory Theatre (New Haven, Conn.), Joseph Papp Public Theatre (New York City), Manhattan Theatre Club (New York City), Goodman Theatre (Chicago), McCarter Theatre (Princeton, N.J.), Folger Theatre (Washington, D.C.), Hartford Stage (Conn.), Guthrie Theatre (Minneapolis), Mark Taper Forum (Los Angeles), Goodspeed Opera House (New Haddam, Conn.) and Long Wharf Theatre (New Haven, Conn.).

MELVIN BERNHARDT directed New York productions of *The Effect of Gamma Rays on Man-in-the-Moon Marigolds, And Miss Reardon Drinks a Little, Da,* and *Crimes of the Heart.* In addition, he has directed at the Cincinnati Playhouse in the Park, Hartford Stage Company, and La Mama ETC (New York City).

HERBERT BLAU was co-director and co-founder of the Actor's Workshop of San Francisco, and was later co-director, with Jules Irving, of the Repertory Theatre of Lincoln Center. At the Vivian

Beaumont, he directed *Danton's Death* and *The Condemned of Altona*. He is currently a distinguished professor of English and comparative literature at the University of Wisconsin, Milwaukee. He is also the author of *The Impossible Theatre, A Manifesto, Take Up the Bodies: Theatre at the Vanishing Point* and *The Eye of the Prey: Subversions of the Postmodern*.

PHILIP BOSCO has been a member of the companies of Arena Stage (Washington, D.C.), American Shakespeare Festival Theatre (Stratford, Conn.), and Lincoln Center Repertory Company. His New York productions include *Whose Life Is It, Anyway?, Hedda Gabler, Misalliance, Ah, Wilderness!, A Man for All Seasons, Lend Me a Tenor,* and *Breaking Legs.* He has appeared at New York's Circle in the Square in *St Joan, Man and Superman, Major Barbara, The Bacchae, Eminent Domain, The Caine Mutiny Court-Martial, Heartbreak House, The Loves of Anatol, You Never Can Tell,* and *The Devil's Disciple.*

PETER BROOK is former co-artistic director of the Royal Shakespeare Company and later formed the International Center of Theatre Research in Paris. He has directed productions of *King Lear, Titus Andronicus, Marat/Sade, A Midsummer Night's Dream, Orghast at Persepolis, The Conference of the Birds, The Cherry Orchard, The Tragedy of Carmen, The Mahabarata, The Tempest,* and *The Man Who.* He is the author of numerous books, including *The Empty Space.*

ARVIN BROWN is artistic director of the Long Wharf Theatre, where he directed *The Indian Wants the Bronx, Hay Fever, Ah, Wilderness, American Buffalo, A View from the Bridge, Requiem for a Heavyweight, A Day in the Death of Joe Egg,* and *All My Sons,* many of which have been moved to Broadway.

PAUL BROWN designed the Royal Court Theatre productions of *Our Selves Alone, A Lie of the Mind, Greenland* and *The North Season.* At the LaMama ETC Annex, he designed the Lincoln Center Theatre production of *Road.*

ZACK BROWN designed sets for the Circle in the Square productions of *The Importance of Being Earnest, Tartuffe, 13 Rue de l'Amour,*

*Man and Superman, Loose Ends, The Man Who Came to Dinner, Major Barbara, The Night of the Iguana, The Devil's Disciple,* and *Salome.* He also designed the Broadway production of *On Your Toes.* In addition, he has designed sets at Williamstown Theatre Festival (Mass.), Guthrie Theatre, Arena Stage and Yale Repertory Theatre.

RENE BUCH is co-founder of Repertorio Español in New York City, where he has directed plays from the Spanish Golden Age, as well as modern Spanish and Latin American plays. He has also directed at Milwaukee Repertory Theatre, Folger Theatre, and Juilliard Drama Theatre (New York City).

MICHAEL CACOYANNIS directed *The Bacchae* at Circle in the Square, and New York productions of *The Trojan Women, And Things That Go Bump in the Night, The Devils, Iphigenia in Aulis, Lysistrata* and *Zorba,* in addition to the films *Stella, A Girl in Black, A Matter of Dignity, Electra, Zorba the Greek, The Trojan Women,* and *Iphigenia.*

JOHN CAIRD is an associate director of the Royal Shakespeare Company, where he has directed *As You Like It, A Midsummer Night's Dream, Twelfth Night, Romeo and Juliet, Antony and Cleopatra,* as well as plays by Shaw, Jonson, and premieres of new works. With Trevor Nunn, he co-directed *Peter Pan, Nicholas Nickleby,* and *Les Miserables.* In London's West End, he directed Andrew Lloyd Webber's *Song and Dance.*

SARAH CALDWELL is artistic director and conductor of the Opera Company of Boston.

LIVIU CIULEI directed *Leonce and Lena* at Arena Stage, *Spring's Awakening* at Juilliard Drama Theatre, and was later appointed artistic director of the Guthrie Theatre. He has also directed at the McCarter Theatre and the American Repertory Theatre (Cambridge, Mass.).

JOHN CONKLIN designed sets for New York productions of *The Au Pair Man, Cat on a Hot Tin Roof, Leaf People, Rex, Philadelphia Story, Awake and Sing,* and *A Streetcar Named Desire.*

RICHMOND CRINKLEY produced plays for the Folger Theatre Group and the Kennedy Center for the Performing Arts, and was later executive director of the Lincoln Center Theatre Company at the Vivian Beaumont Theatre, where he produced *The Philadelphia Story, The Floating Light Bulb,* and *Macbeth.*

SIMON CURTIS directed the Broadway production of *Rise and Fall of Little Voice* and the Lincoln Center Theatre production of *Road,* which was performed at the LaMama ETC Annex. He is director of the Royal Court Theatre in London, where he has directed *Our Selves Alone, A Lie of the Mind, Greenland,* and *The North Season.*

F. MITCHELL DANA designed lights for the Circle in the Square productions of *Man and Superman, The Inspector General,* and *Once in a Lifetime,* as well as the Broadway productions of *The Suicide, Mass Appeal, Monday After the Miracle,* and *The Babe.* He has also designed at the Ahmanson (Los Angeles), Cincinnati Playhouse in the Park, Syracuse Stage, Seattle Repertory Theatre, Mark Taper Forum, McCarter Theatre, and the American Conservatory Theatre (San Francisco).

LOWELL DETWEILER designed sets for the Off–Broadway productions of *More than You Deserve, A Thousand and One Nights, Black Hole in Space, The Yellow Wallpaper,* and *Come Back, Little Sheba.* He has also designed in regional theatres, including the Hartford Stage, Guthrie Theatre, the McCarter Theatre, Actor's Theatre of Louisville, Goodspeed Opera House, Denver Theatre Center, and Cincinnati Playhouse in the Park.

KARL EIGSTI designed sets for the Circle in the Square production of *Once in a Lifetime.* In addition, he designed the New York productions of *The House of Blue Leaves, Yentl, Wings, Sweet Bird of Youth, Eubie!, The American Clock, Joseph and the Amazing Technicolor Dreamcoat, The World of Sholom Aleichem, Richard II,* and *Accidental Death of an Anarchist.* He has also designed at the Long Wharf Theatre, Arena Stage, Cincinnati Playhouse in the Park, Actor's Theatre of Louisville, and the Milwaukee Repertory Theatre.

ELDON ELDER's Broadway designs include *Fallen Angels, Venus Observed, The Young and the Beautiful, Of Love Remembered, The Affair, Legend of Lovers, Take a Giant Step, Shinbone Alley,* and *Will Rogers' U.S.A.* He has also designed for the New York Shakespeare Festival, American Shakespeare Festival, Baltimore Center Stage, PAF Playhouse (Huntington Station, N.Y.), Syracuse Stage, Queens Playhouse, Seattle Repertory Company, and Ford's Theatre (Washington, D.C.). He served as a designer and theatre consultant for the Delacourt Theatre (New York City), as well as many others across the country.

ALVIN EPSTEIN is former artistic director of the Guthrie Theatre and associate director of the Yale Repertory Theatre. At the American Repertory Theatre he directed *A Midsummer Night's Dream, The Seven Deadly Sins, The Marriage of Figaro, Boys from Syracuse,* and *Macbeth,* and performed in twenty-four other productions.

JOHN FALABELLA designed sets for the Circle in the Square production of *The Caine Mutiny Court-Martial,* as well as New York productions of *Perfectly Frank, Baseball Wives, The Middle Ages, Blues in the Night, Tallulah, The Guys in the Truck, Sullivan and Gilbert,* and *Home Front.* He also designed at the Hartford Stage Company and the Goodspeed Opera House.

GEORGE FERENCZ founded and was director and co-producer of the Impossible Ragtime Theatre (New York City). He has directed many productions at the LaMama ETC, including *The Tooth of Crime, Angel City, Back Bog Beast Bait,* and *Suicide in B Flat.* He has also directed extensively at other Off–Broadway theatres, including INTAR, American Place Theater, St. Clement's and Theater for a New City, as well as San Diego Repertory Theatre, Cleveland Play House, Pittsburgh Public Theatre, and Actor's Theatre of Louisville.

JULES FISHER has designed lights for over one hundred Broadway and Off–Broadway productions, including *Hair, Butterflies Are Free, No, No Nanette, Jesus Christ Superstar, Pippin, Chicago, American Buffalo, Beatlemania, Dancin', La Cage aux Folles, Song and Dance, Grand Hotel, The Will Rogers Follies, Jelly's Last Jam,* and *Angels In America.* He is also a theatre consultant.

RICHARD FOREMAN founded the Ontological-Hysteric Theatre (New York City), for which he has written, designed, and directed over thirty original productions in the U.S. and throughout Europe, including *PAIN(T)*, *Egyptology*, *Penguin Touquet*, *Film Is Evil, Radio Is Good* and *Miss Universal Happiness*. He has also directed and designed works by Brecht, Buechner, Molière, Gertrude Stein, Botho Strauss, Philip Glass, Vaclav Havel, and Arthur Kopit.

KENNETH FOY designed *Candida* at Circle in the Square, as well as New York productions of *Styne after Styne* and *Wind in the Willows*. He has also designed at Long Wharf Theatre and Buffalo Studio Arena.

GERALD FREEDMAN has served as artistic director of the New York Shakespeare Festival, American Shakespeare Theatre, and the Great Lakes Theatre Festival (Cleveland). He directed *King Lear* and *The Au Pair Man* at the Vivian Beaumont Theater, and *An American Millionaire* at Circle in the Square, as well as New York productions of *Hair, The Creation of the World and Other Business, The Robber Bridegroom,* and *West Side Story*.

JACK GARFEIN is artistic director of the Harold Clurman Theatre in New York. He directed *Shadow of a Gunman* on Broadway, and was producer for international and New York productions of *The Price, The American Clock, All Strange Away, Avner the Eccentric, Endgame, Rockaby,* and *The Beckett Plays*.

JACK GELBER wrote *The Connection, The Apple, Square in the Eye, The Cuban Thing, Sleep, Barbary Shore,* and *Jack Gelber's New Play: Rehearsal*. He also directed the New York productions of *The Kitchen, Indians, Kool Aid, The Kid,* and *Seduced*.

BERNARD GERSTEN is executive producer of the Lincoln Center Theater at the Vivian Beaumont Theater. Formerly he was associate producer, with Joseph Papp, of the New York Shakespeare Festival.

ROBYN GOODMAN is co-founder and artistic director of Second Stage (New York City), where she produced fifty plays.

ANDRE GREGORY co-founded and was artistic director of the Seattle Repertory Company, and then was artistic director of the Theatre of the Living Arts in Philadelphia. Gregory formed the Manhattan Project, where he directed *Alice in Wonderland.* He also co-wrote and appeared in the film *My Dinner with Andre.*

ULU GROSBARD directed Broadway productions of *The Subject Was Roses, A View from the Bridge, The Price, American Buffalo* and, at the Vivian Beaumont Theater, *The Floating Light Bulb.*

THOMAS GRUENEWALD has directed plays, musicals, and operas on Broadway, Off–Broadway and in regional theatres across America. He directed *Oh, Boy* at the Goodspeed Opera House.

JOHN GUNTER served as resident designer at the Royal National Theatre, where he designed sets for *Guys and Dolls, The Rivals, The Beggar's Opera, Wild Honey* (also produced at the Ahmanson Theatre and on Broadway), *The Government Inspector, Mrs. Klein,* and *The Secret Rapture.* His set designs in London's West End include *Comedians, Stevie, The Old Country, Rose* (also on Broadway), *High Society,* and *Timon of Athens.* He has also designed frequently on Broadway and in London's West End, Royal Court Theatre, Royal Shakespeare Company, Broadway, and opera companies throughout the world.

TYRONE GUTHRIE provided the main impetus for thrust staging in the post-World War II era. He was responsible for the creation of the Stratford Festival Theatre (Canada) and the Guthrie Theatre. Prior to that he directed an innovative production of *The Satire of Three Estates* at the Edinburgh Festival, and was a leading director of the Old Vic in London.

ADRIAN HALL served as artistic director of the Trinity Square Repertory Company (Providence, R.I.) and the Dallas Theatre Center.

HUGH HARDY, an architect, is the founding partner of Hardy Holzman Pfeiffer Associates. He was the architect for the renovation of the BAM Majestic Theatre (New York City) and Broadway's Biltmore Theatre, as well as the new Alice Busch Opera Theatre for the Glimmerglass Opera Company (Cooperstown, N.Y.) and the original design and expansion of Dance Theatre of Harlem.

BILL HART is dramaturg and director at the New York Shakespeare Festival. He directed *Cuba and his Teddy Bear* on Broadway and the premier of Sam Shepard's *States of Shock*.

JULES IRVING co-founded and was co-producing director (with Herbert Blau) of the San Francisco Actor's Workshop. He was appointed co-director (again with Blau) of the Repertory Theatre of Lincoln Center (Vivian Beaumont Theater), and was sole director from 1967 to 1973.

BILL IRWIN's theatre pieces include *Largely/New York, The Courtroom,* and *The Regard of Flight.* He has appeared in *Waiting for Godot* at the Vivian Beaumont Theater, and on Broadway in *Accidental Death of an Anarchist.*

DANA IVEY appeared in the New York productions of *Driving Miss Daisy, Quartermain's Terms* and *Sunday in the Park with George.* Productions at Circle in the Square include *Heartbreak House, Present Laughter,* and *The Marriage of Figaro.* At the Joseph Papp Public Theater, she has appeared in *Wenceslas Square* and *Hamlet.*

GEORGE IZENOUR is Professor Emeritus of Theater Design and Technology and Director Emeritus of the Electro-Mechanical Laboratory of the Yale University School of Drama. He is the author of *Theatre Design* and *Theatre Technology.* He has contributed many inventions to the technology of the theatre and has served as consultant for the design of many theatres.

ANDREW JACKNESS designed the Broadway production of *Wings, The Little Foxes, Grownups, Beyond Therapy, Whodunnit,* and *Precious Sons.* At Circle in the Square, he designed *John Gabriel Borkman.* For Playwrights Horizons (New York City), he designed *Geniuses* and *Isn't It Romantic,* and *Cinders* and *Salonika* at the Joseph Papp Public Theater. At Second Stage, he designed *The Adventures of Kathy and Mo* and *Little Murders,* and at Roundabout Theatre (New York City) he designed *Mrs. Warren's Profession.* He has also designed at Yale Repertory Theatre, Williamstown Theatre Festival, American Repertory Theatre, Spoleto Festival U.S.A. (Charleston, S.C.), Long Wharf Theatre, Mark Taper Forum, Hartford Stage Company and American Shakespeare Festival.

DAVID JENKINS designed New York productions of *Rodgers and Hart, The Elephant Man, Piaf, Preppies, Stepping Out, Quarter-main's Terms, And a Nightingale Sang . . ., The Common Pursuit,* and *Other People's Money.* At Circle in the Square, he designed *Saint Joan.* He designed *Mary Stuart* and *Hamlet* at Circle Rep, *The Art of Dining, Talk Radio,* and *Lullaby and Goodnight* at the Joseph Papp Public Theatre and at Second Stage he designed *Short Eyes.* He has also designed for the McCarter Theatre, Trinity Square Repertory, Long Wharf Theatre, Goodman Theatre, Arena Stage, Baltimore Center Stage and the Mark Taper Forum.

JOHN JENSEN designed sets for many productions at the Guthrie Theatre, including *Ceremonies in Dark Old Men, Cyrano de Bergerac, Taming of the Shrew, A Touch of the Poet, The Diary of a Scoundrel, A Midsummer Night's Dream, The Government Inspector,* and *King Lear.* He has also designed at the Actor's Theatre of Louisville, American Conservatory Theatre, Goodman Theatre, Pittsburgh Public Theatre, Milwaukee Repertory Theatre, Long Wharf Theatre, McCarter Theatre, Hartford Stage, Goodspeed Opera House, Williamstown Theatre Festival, Cincinnati Playhouse in the Park, and the Goodman Theatre.

MICHAEL KAHN has served as artistic director of the American Shakespeare Festival Theatre, McCarter Theatre, Acting Company, and the Shakespeare Theatre at the Folger. He directed the Off–Broadway production of *America Hurrah,* at the Delacourt Theatre he directed *Measure for Measure* and his production of *Cat on a Hot Tin Roof* at the Kennedy Center was also performed on Broadway. He has also directed at the Goodman Theatre, Cincinnati Playhouse in the Park, and the Guthrie Theatre.

ROBERT KALFIN is the founder and artistic director of New York's Chelsea Theater Center. His Broadway productions include *Happy End, Strider,* and *Yentl.* He also co-produced *Candide* on Broadway. He was artistic director of the Cincinnati Playhouse in the Park, and has also directed at the Hartford Stage Company, Seattle Repertory Theatre and Cleveland Play House.

MARJORIE BRADLEY KELLOGG is the resident designer for Tony Randall's National Actor's Theatre in New York. She has also designed Broadway productions of *Arsenic and Old Lace, A Day in the Death of Joe Egg, Requiem for a Heavyweight, American Buffalo, Steaming, Da, The Best Little Whorehouse in Texas,* and the infamous *Moose Murders.* Circle in the Square productions include *Borrowed Time, Heartbreak House, The Marriage of Figaro,* and *Present Laughter.*

RON LAGOMARSINO directed New York productions of *My Favorite Year, Driving Miss Daisy, Laughing Wild, Abundance, Women of Manhattan,* and *Digby.* He has also directed at Hartford Stage, Arena Stage, and Cincinnati Playhouse in the Park.

MARK LAMOS is artistic director of the Hartford Stage Company, where he has directed *Hamlet, Pericles, Twelfth Night, The Greeks, Peer Gynt, Cymbeline, Undiscovered Country, Anatol, The Tempest, A Midsummer Night's Dream, The Illusion,* and *Master Builder.* He directed the Broadway production of *Our Country's Good.* He has also directed at the Guthrie Theatre, Stratford Festival Theatre and the Mitzi Newhouse Theater.

HEIDI LANDESMAN designed sets for the New York productions of *Table Settings, A Midsummer Night's Dream, 'Night Mother, Painting Churches, Big River, Hunting Cockroaches,* and *The Secret Garden.* At the Joseph Papp Public Theater, she designed *Leave It to Beaver Is Dead, How It All Began, Penguin Touquet, Twelve Dreams,* and *Romeo and Juliet.* She has also designed at the Mark Taper Forum.

HUGH LANDWEHR designed New York productions *All My Sons, A View from the Bridge, The Baby Dance* and *Candide.* He has also designed at Long Wharf Theatre, Alley Theatre, Guthrie Theatre, and Baltimore Center Stage.

MICHAEL LANGHAM was artistic director of the Birmingham Repertory Company and the Glasgow Citizen's Theatre, Stratford Festival Theatre and Guthrie Theatre, and directed for the Royal Shakespeare Company and Old Vic. He is known for his productions of *Hamlet, Love's Labour's Lost, Cyrano de Bergerac, The Prime of Miss Jean Brodie, Peccadillo, Merchant of Venice,* and *Timon of Athens.*

BASIL LANGTON has directed at the Arena Stage, Cleveland Play House, GeVa Theatre (Rochester, N.Y.), and Birmingham Repertory. He directed the Circle in the Square production of *13 Rue de l'Amour.*

WILFORD LEACH directed at LaMama ETC, as well as over twenty productions at the New York Shakespeare Festival, including *The Mandrake, The Taming of the Shrew, All's Well That Ends Well, Othello, Marie and Bruce, Mother Courage, The Pirates of Penzance, Non Pasquale, The Human Comedy, La Bohême,* and *The Mystery of Edwin Drood.*

ELIZABETH LECOMPTE is director of the Wooster Group, which performs at the Performing Garage (New York City). She has directed *Sakonnet Point, Rumstick Road, Nayatt School, Point Judith, Route 1 & 9, L.S.D. ( . . . Just the High Points . . .)* and *St. Anthony.*

EUGENE LEE designed the New York productions of *Slave Ship, Saved, Dude, Candide, The Skin of Our Teeth, Agnes of God,* and *Sweeney Todd.* At the Joseph Papp Public Theater he designed *The Ballad of Soapy Smith* and *The Normal Heart.* He also designed many productions for Theater of the Living Arts in Philadelphia, Buffalo Studio Arena Theatre, Trinity Square Repertory Company, and Dallas Theater Center.

MING CHO LEE designed sets for the New York productions of *Mother Courage, Little Murders, Caesar and Cleopatra, The*

*Shadow Box, Angel, The Grand Tour, For Colored Girls . . . , K2,* and *The Glass Menagerie.* He was principal designer for the New York Shakespeare Festival, where he designed over forty productions. At the Vivian Beaumont Theatre he designed *King Lear,* and at Circle in the Square he designed *All God's Chillun Got Wings, The Glass Menagerie,* and *Romeo and Juliet.* He has also designed at Arena Stage and the Ahmanson Theatre.

EUGENE LESSER directed *The Beggar's Opera* Off–Broadway, and has directed at the Goodman Theatre and the Milwaukee Repertory Theatre.

JACQUES LEVY directed plays for LaMama ETC, the Open Theatre, including Sam Shepard's first Off–Broadway plays and the original production of *America Hurrah.* He also directed *Oh, Calcutta!, Scuba Duba,* and *Doonesbury.*

SANTO LOQUASTO designed the Broadway productions of *Sticks and Bones, That Championship Season, Kennedy's Children, Legend, Miss Margarida's Way, Golda, American Buffalo, The Goodbye People, Bent, The Suicide, Singin' in the Rain, Cafe Crown, Grand Hotel, Lost in Yonkers,* and *Jake's Women.* At the Vivian Beaumont Theater, he designed *In the Boom Boom Room, What the Wine-Sellers Buy, Mert and Phil, The Dance of Death, A Doll's House, Hamlet, The Floating Light Bulb,* and *The Cherry Orchard.* For the New York Shakespeare Festival he designed over twenty-five productions. He has also designed at the Hartford Stage Company, Long Wharf Theatre, Yale Repertory Theatre, Williamstown Theatre Festival, Arena Stage, Mark Taper Forum, Guthrie Theatre, and Hartford Stage Company.

THOMAS LYNCH designed the New York productions of *Driving Miss Daisy* and *Tintypes,* and at Circle in the Square he designed *Design for Living, Arms and the Man,* and *You Never Can Tell.* He has also designed at Arena Stage, Goodman Theatre, Guthrie Theatre, Mark Taper Forum and the La Jolla Playhouse.

IAIN MACKINTOSH is design director of Theatre Projects Consultants and was co-founder and producer of Prospect, a theatrical touring company.

ALINE MACMAHON appeared at the Vivian Beaumont in *Trelawny of the 'Wells', The Crucible, Mary Stuart, Cyrano de Bergerac, Tiger at the Gates, Galileo, The East Wind, Yerma,* and *The Alchemist.* She also acted in many productions at the American Shakespeare Festival and on Broadway.

JUDITH MALINA is co-founder, with Julian Beck, of the Living Theatre, whose productions included *The Connection, The Marrying Maiden, The Brig, Frankenstein, Paradise Now,* and *I and I.*

THEODORE MANN is co-founder and producer of Circle in the Square, where he produced *Dark of the Moon, Summer and Smoke, The Girl on the Via Flaminia, The Iceman Cometh,* and *Desire Under the Elms.* He also directed *A Moon for the Misbegotten, Mourning Becomes Electra, The Iceman Cometh, The Glass Menagerie* and *Awake and Sing.*

JONATHAN MILLER was a member of the satirical revue *Beyond the Fringe* and served as artistic director of the Old Vic Theatre. He has directed many operatic productions, and was producer and director for several of the BBC's "Shakespeare Plays." He has directed *The Merchant of Venice, Long Day's Journey into Night,* and *Candide.*

DAVID MITCHELL designed sets for the Vivian Beaumont Theater productions of *Short Eyes, Little Black Sheep,* and *Trelawny of the 'Wells'.* His Broadway productions include *Annie, The Gin Game, Working, I Remember Mama, Barnum, Can-Can, Foxfire, Brighton Beach Memoirs, Dance a Little Closer, Private Lives, La Cage aux Folles, Harrigan 'n Hart* and *Biloxi Blues.* He has also designed many productions for the New York Shakespeare Festival, as well as for the Goodman Theatre and the Long Wharf Theatre.

BENI MONTRESOR designed sets for Broadway productions of *Marco Millions* and *Do I Hear a Waltz?,* and has designed sets, lights, and costumes for operatic productions at La Scala, Metropolitan Opera, San Francisco Opera, and New York City Opera.

ROGER MORGAN is a lighting designer and has served as theatre consultant for the American Place Theatre (New York City), Baltimore Center Stage, and Ford's Theatre.

GREGORY MOSHER has served as director of the Lincoln Center Theatre and the Goodman Theatre. As a director, he is most closely associated with the work of David Mamet, most of whose plays have been produced or directed by Mosher since *American Buffalo* in 1975. Other writers with whom Mosher has worked closely include Samuel Beckett, John Guare, Arthur Miller, Richard Nelson, David Rabe, Wole Soyinka, and Tennessee Williams.

BRIAN MURRAY is an actor and director. He directed New York productions of *Blithe Spirit, Hay Fever, Tartuffe, Stevie,* and *Enter a Free Man.* At Circle in the Square he directed *The Waltz of the Toreadors,* and he has also directed at the Goodman Theater and Cincinnati Playhouse in the Park.

JOHN NAPIER designed *Cats, Les Miserables, Miss Saigon, Sunset Boulevard, Starlight Express, Time,* and *Children of Eden.* He is an associate designer of the Royal Shakespeare Company, for whom he has designed *Macbeth, The Comedy of Errors, King Lear, Once in a Lifetime, Nicholas Nickleby, Hedda Gabler, Peter Pan,* and *Mother Courage.* His productions for the Royal National Theatre include *Equus* and *Trelawny of the 'Wells'.*

TED OHL is former production manager of the Juilliard Drama Theatre.

JOSEPH PAPP was founder and artistic director of the New York Shakespeare Festival, producing and directing plays for the Public Theater, Delacourt Theater, Vivian Beaumont Theater, and Mitzi Newhouse Theater.

AUSTIN PENDLETON, an actor and director, directed the New York productions of *Shelter, The Runner Stumbles, Say Goodnight, Gracie, The Little Foxes,* and *Mass Appeal.* He has directed plays at the Long Wharf Theatre, Manhattan Theatre Club, and Williamstown Theatre Festival.

CAREY PERLOFF is artistic director of the American Conservatory Theater (A.C.T.) in San Francisco, and prior to that was artistic director of CSC Repertory (New York City). At CSC she directed *Mountain Language, The Skin of Our Teeth, Elektra, The Birthday Party, Phaedra Britannica, Don Juan of Seville, Happy Days, The Resistable Rise of Arturo Ui, Creditors,* and *Candide.*

HELEN POND AND HERBERT SENN designed New York productions of *What Makes Sammy Run, Showboat* and *Oh Coward.* They have also designed 37 seasons of summer stock, including approximately 350 productions, at the Cape Playhouse in Dennis, Mass. They have designed over 60 operas for Sarah Caldwell in Boston and elsewhere.

STEPHEN PORTER has divided his time as director between such proscenium theatres as APA-Phoenix at the Lyceum (New York City), Kennedy Center, Ahmanson, A.C.T., American Shakespeare Festival, and the McCarter Theater, and such open stages as Circle in the Square, Guthrie Theatre, Mark Taper Forum, Milwaukee Repertory Theatre, Stratford Festival Theatre, Cincinnati Playhouse in the Park, and Buffalo Studio Arena. At Circle in the Square he directed *The Importance of Being Earnest, Tartuffe, Man and Superman, Major Barbara, The Man Who Came to Dinner,* and *The Misanthrope.*

DAVID POTTS designed New York productions of *Born Yesterday, The Musical Comedy Murders of 1940, The Seahorse, The Boys Next Door, Album,* and *Goodnight Grandpa.* His designs at Circle Rep include *Threads, Childe Byron, Winter Signs, The Runner Stumbles, Exiles, My Life, Full Hook Up,* and *As Is.* He has also designed at Cincinnati Playhouse in the Park and the Hartford Stage Company.

JOSÉ QUINTERO, co-founder of Circle in the Square, directed New York productions of *Summer and Smoke, The Iceman Cometh, Long Day's Journey into Night, A Moon for the Misbegotten, Camino Real, Marco Millions,* and *More Stately Mansions.*

DAVID SAVRAN is Associate Professor of English at Brown University and author of *Breaking the Rules: The Wooster Group.*

RICHARD SCHECHNER founded the Performance Group, where he directed *Dionysus in 69, Commune, The Tooth of Crime, Mother Courage, The Marilyn Project* and Seneca's *Oedipus.* He is University Professor at the Tisch School of the Arts, New York University.

DOUGLAS W. SCHMIDT designed the Broadway productions of *Grease, Over Here!, Fame, The Robber Bridegroom, Angel Street, Let My People Come, Runaways, They're Playing Our Song, Most Happy Fella, Romantic Comedy, Frankenstein, Smile,* and *Nick and Nora.* His productions at the Vivian Beaumont Theater include *The Time of Your Life, Operation Sidewinder, The Good Woman of Setzuan, The Playboy of the Western World, Antigone, Mary Stuart, Narrow Road to the Deep North, Twelfth Night, Enemies, The Plough and the Stars, A Streetcar Named Desire, The Three-Penny Opera,* and *Agamemnon.* At the Joseph Papp Public Theater, he designed many productions, including *The Memorandum* and *The Death of Von Richtofen as Witnessed from Earth.* His designs at Circle in the Square include *An American Millionaire.* He has also designed at Cincinnati Playhouse in the Park, Baltimore Center Stage, Arena Stage, Guthrie Theatre, Mark Taper Forum, Ahmanson Theatre, Old Globe Theatre (San Diego), and Seattle Repertory.

KAREN SCHULZ designed sets for New York productions of *Sister Mary Ignatius Explains It All for You, The Foreigner, The Dance and the Railroad,* and *Only Kidding.*

ANDREI SERBAN has directed numerous productions at LaMama ETC, including *Fragments of a Trilogy* and *The Good Woman of Setzuan.* At the Vivian Beaumont Theater he directed *The Cherry Orchard* and *Agamemnon,* and at the Joseph Papp Public Theater, *The Master and Margarita, The Umbrellas of Cherbourg, Happy Days,* and *The Seagull.* At Yale Rep he directed *The Ghost Sonata* and *Sganarelle: An Evening of Moliere Farces.* At the American Repertory Theatre he directed *The King Stag, The Love of Three Oranges,* and *The Juniper Tree.* At Circle in the Square, he directed *Orpheus Descending* and *The Marriage of Figaro.*

MEL SHAPIRO directed the New York Shakespeare Festival production of *Two Gentlemen of Verona.* He was resident director at

Arena Stage, and has directed at Pittsburgh Public Theatre, Hartford Stage Company, and the Old Globe Theatre.

ROBERT SHAW designed the New York Shakespeare Festival productions of *The Pirates of Penzance, The Human Comedy,* and *The Mystery of Edwin Drood,* as well as *Coastal Disturbances.*

LOREN SHERMAN designed the Broadway productions of *Shogun: The Musical, Private Lives, Crazy He Calls Me, Sleight of Hand* and *Shakespeare on Broadway.* Off–Broadway productions include *Assassins, Romance Language, The Dining Room, The Harvesting, That's It Folks!, Baby with the Bathwater, Coming of Age in Soho, The Marriage of Bette and Boo, The Nest of the Wood Grouse, Wenceslas Square, Forbidden City,* and *Personals.* He has also designed at Yale Rep, Arena Stage, Actor's Theatre of Louisville, Seattle Rep, Williamstown Theatre Festival, Long Wharf Theatre, Mark Taper Forum, Walnut Street Theatre (Philadelphia), Goodman Theatre, Baltimore Center Stage, Pittsburgh Public Theatre, and American Repertory Theatre.

THOMAS SKELTON is associate director and resident lighting designer of the Ohio Ballet. His Broadway lighting credits include *A Few Good Men, Lillian, The Kingfisher, A Matter of Gravity, Absurd Person Singular, Coco, Shenandoah, Peter Pan, Oklahoma!, Brigadoon, The King and I, Carousel, The Iceman Cometh, All God's Chillun Got Wings, Death of a Salesman, The Glass Menagerie, A Matter of Gravity, Guys and Dolls, Camelot, Show Boat,* and *Mame.*

BILL STABILE designed sets for the Broadway production of *Torch Song Trilogy,* as well as *Mass* at the Kennedy Center. Off–Broadway productions include *States of Shock, Remembrance* and twenty-four productions at LaMama ETC.

TONY STRAIGES designed sets for New York productions of *A History of American Film, Gertrude Stein Gertrude Stein Gertrude Stein, Harold and Maude, Talking With, Sunday in the Park with George, Diamonds, Long Day's Journey into Night, Into the Woods, Coastal Disturbances, Rumors,* and *I Hate Hamlet.* He has also designed at the American Repertory Theatre, Hartford Stage Company, and Arena Stage.

ROBERT SYMONDS, an actor and director, is former associate director of the Repertory Theatre of Lincoln Center, and directed the Vivian Beaumont productions of *The Country Wife, Bananas, Amphitryon, The Good Woman of Setzuan,* and *The Playboy of the Western World.*

TONY TANNER, an actor and director, directed New York productions of *Something's Afoot, A Taste of Honey, Joseph and the Amazing Technicolor Dreamcoat, Preppies, Springtime for Henry, Professionally Speaking,* and *Class Enemy.*

JOHN TILLINGER has directed many productions at the Long Wharf Theatre, and New York productions of *Solomon's Child, Entertaining Mr. Sloane, The Golden Age, Serenading Louie, After the Fall, Total Eclipse, The Lisbon Traviata, Corpse!, Loot,* and *Sweet Sue.*

ROBIN WAGNER's New York set designs include *Angels in America, Putting it Together, Jelly's Last Jam, Crazy for You, City of Angels, Jerome Robbins' Broadway, Chess, A Chorus Line, Dreamgirls, 42nd Street, Song and Dance, On the Twentieth Century, Jesus Christ Superstar, Lenny, Promises Promises, The Great White Hope,* and *Hair.* His designs at the Vivian Beaumont Theater include *The Condemned of Altona* and *Galileo.* He has also designed many productions at Arena Stage.

TONY WALTON designed sets for the Broadway productions of *A Funny Thing Happened on the Way to the Forum, Golden Boy, Pippin, The Good Doctor, Chicago, The Act, Sophisticated Ladies, Woman of the Year, Little Me, The Real Thing, Hurlyburly, I'm Not Rappaport, Grand Hotel, Lend Me a Tenor, Jerome Robbins' Broadway,* and *Guys and Dolls.* At Circle in the Square, he designed *Uncle Vanya,* at the Mitzi Newhouse Theater he designed *Streamers* and *Waiting for Godot,* and at the Vivian Beaumont Theater, *House of Blue Leaves, The Front Page, Anything Goes,* and *Six Degrees of Separation.* At the Joseph Papp Public Theater, he designed *Drinks Before Dinner.* He has also designed at the Long Wharf Theatre, Mark Taper Forum, and the Goodman Theatre.

PAUL WEIDNER was producing director of the Hartford Stage Company from 1968 to 1980, where he directed *My Sister, My Sister,* which transferred to Broadway, and *All Over.* He directed *Come Back Little Sheba* at the Roundabout Theatre in New York. He has also directed at Arena Stage, Asolo Theatre (Sarasota, Fla.), Williamstown Theatre Festival, American Stage Festival, Seattle Repertory Theatre, McCarter Theatre, and Trinity Rep.

MARC B. WEISS is a lighting designer whose Broadway productions include *6 Rms Riv Vu, Find Your Way Home, Cat on a Hot Tin Roof, Words and Music, Hughie/Duet, The Eccentricities of a Nightingale, Ladies at the Alamo, Deathtrap, Once a Catholic, The First, Othello, Zorba, A Moon for the Misbegotten,* and *Rink.*

ROBERT WHITEHEAD produced many Broadway productions, including *Medea, The Member of the Wedding, Desire Under the Elms, Golden Boy, Four Saints in Three Acts, Bus Stop, Orpheus Descending, The Visit, A Touch of the Poet, A Man for All Seasons, The Prime of Miss Jean Brodie, The Price, The Creation of the World and Other Business, Old Times, Finishing Touches, A Matter of Gravity, No Man's Land, 1600 Pennsylvania Avenue, A Texas Trilogy, The Prince of Grand Street, Bedroom Farce, Betrayal, Lunch Hour, The West Side Waltz, Death of a Salesman,* and *Lillian.* As director of the Lincoln Center for the Performing Arts at the ANTA Washington Square Theatre, he produced *After the Fall, But for Whom, Charlie, The Changeling,* and *Incident at Vichy.*

MICHAEL YEARGAN designed New York productions of *Bad Habits, The Ritz, A Lesson from Aloes, It Had to Be You, Hay Fever,* and *Ah, Wilderness.*

JERRY ZAKS served as resident director of Lincoln Center Theater from 1986 to 1990, where he directed *Six Degrees of Separation, The House of Blue Leaves, Anything Goes,* and *The Front Page.* His other New York productions include *Assassins, Square One, Lend Me a Tenor, Wenceslas Square, The Foreigner, The Marriage of Bette and Boo, Baby with the Bathwater, Sister Mary Ignatius Explains It All for You, Beyond Therapy,* and the recent revival of *Guys and Dolls.*

# CHAPTER 1

# EXAMINING THE THEATRE SPACE

Perhaps the most important step in the production process—and one all too easily rushed through—is the first encounter with the theatre space. By definition, it is an experience that cannot be repeated. Preserving the first impression of the play is imperative in script analysis; by the same token, the first impression of the performance space must be carefully honored and noted. The tendency might be to rush in and check acoustics and sightlines. These aspects are important, but can be dealt with in due time.

## JUST SIT THERE

The easiest step is simply to sit in the theatre. Just relax, look around, and gather an impression from the space as a whole. Consider such questions as: How do you feel about the space? What emotions are aroused? Do you feel comfortable? Is it a pleasant space? These questions are not an intellectual checklist, but rather a series of emotional, intuitive reactions.

Many designers and directors stress the importance of the simple first step of sitting and absorbing. Eldon Elder tries to respond to the "textures, colors and shapes" of the space.* Austin Pendleton stresses that just sitting is part of the creative process: "What really turns me on and gets my juices going is simply being in the space to see what comes to me."

The best way of absorbing the space is to be alone, as Bill Stabile suggests: "I sit there in the quiet, on the empty stage, and it speaks to me." He recommends, "Let yourself loose, just remain open to it, and look at all the possibilities. Be calm, look at it, feel it, and see how you want to shape the air."

---

*All quotations are from interviews with the author, except as noted.

After gaining a general feeling for the space, examine the architectural sources. *Why* are certain emotions and reactions aroused? *What* is it that makes the space pleasant or not? *Where* in the theatre do you feel comfortable or not?

At this point, it isn't helpful to think about the particulars of the upcoming production. There will be time later to consider how the production will or won't work in the given space. Now is the time to discover what the space itself suggests, absent of any particular production. The space itself may begin to suggest ideas that would be smothered by preconceived notions. Pendleton urges that the theatre artist allow him- or herself to remain open to all possibilities:

> Every stage and auditorium has its own set of purely physical dynamics, and each of those suggests a whole other set of possibilities. The kind of relationships that people can have to each other and to the audience in every kind of space is completely different, and if you go in there and try to absorb it, it begins to suggest ideas to you.

Richard Foreman, who generally develops a performance piece for a particular space, reports, "In order to conceive the piece in this space, I will just be there to sort of 'not think,' to soak up the atmosphere, to be able to remember it when I start making the play."

## IS IT BEST TO SEE THE THEATRE EMPTY OR IN PERFORMANCE?

The advantage of seeing a theatre empty is that the space is in a more "neutral" condition, free of the impositions and colorations of any particular production. Pendleton comments, "I love it empty; it reverberates and starts to tell you."

But by seeing a performance, one can see how the theatre actually operates; what its strengths and weaknesses are in production. According to Gregory Mosher,

> You can't judge a theatre when it's empty, unless you're very, very, very experienced, and I'm not experienced enough to do it. Those

things that make a theatre seem nice when there's no show going on—lots of legroom, pretty colors—are usually the things that end up detracting from a production later.

## EXAMINE THE AUDIENCE-PERFORMANCE RELATIONSHIP

Experience the auditorium by entering the theatre as the audience does—through the front doors and lobby. In most cases, time and money do not allow alteration of these areas, but nonetheless be aware of the audience's first impressions of the theatre building.

The audience will, presumably, be perceiving the performance from the auditorium, so pay close attention to the nature and peculiarities of that space. As Karl Eigsti observes, "The stage is definitely important—obviously, that's where you're going to be working. But you have to give yourself the audience's eye. How will the audience be looking at this?"

Ming Cho Lee offers a list of questions to help investigate this audience-stage relationship:

> Is the proscenium opening too small or too big? Is it too wide? Is it too low? Is the theatre too deep? How are the sightlines? How much do you see under the balcony overhang? How does it feel? When you walk in there, do you feel it's a good theatre or a lousy theatre? What are you going to do about it?

There are actually many audience-performance relationships in any one theatre, in that there are many areas of the auditorium from which to view the performance. Moving around is especially important in an open-stage theatre, in that the audience will be viewing the stage from fundamentally different directions. Eigsti recommends, "Try to get a feeling for the space from many different points of view, so that when you're working on the model or plan, you are working out of this feeling for the space and the multiple viewpoints that the audience has."

Take special note of problematic areas of the auditorium. John Jensen asks, "What can you do for those people over there, who may not have seen anything for years?"

After examining the auditorium, move to the stage in order to experience the other end of this audience-actor relationship, especially the actor's potential to command the auditorium. Ming suggests checking to see if "the stage can somehow control the audience: Stand on the stage and feel if the auditorium is within your reach or not." Paul Weidner tries "to get a sense of how much projection is going to be necessary for this play," because everything in the production depends on "the kind of scale and size of what you're going to be able to do."

Examining the actor's relation to the audience is important not only for the actor and director, but also for the designer. Look for problems to be solved and opportunities to be exploited in order to enhance the actor's performance.

## FIND THE FOCUS

Focus is a more subtle, but still crucial, aspect of the theatre space. Marjorie Bradley Kellogg explains:

> There is a focal point where all the energies converge. It's about where the walls are. It's about where the volume of people will be when the house is filled. That empty space—without any scenery— will triangulate into a zone. It's not always one spot, but a zone where the tension is strongest.

Michael Yeargan describes the focal point in similar terms:

> There's a little imaginary area that you can define in any theatre that feels good, that's determined by the architecture, by the way that the seats are placed in relation to the stage. No matter what play you do, it is always going to feel as if *that* is where it can happen.

There are numerous methods for finding the focal point. John Conklin walks around the stage until he feels "in control of the space." Brian Murray locates the "center of gravity, the pivot upon which the space, the actors, the set, everything in it, revolves." John Lee Beatty asks the resident director, "Where do actors usually stand? Where have the most successful scenes occurred? Where do most people end up standing—even though they say they're not going to?" Mosher points out that finding the stage focus is a good reason to rehearse in the actual performance space, in that "you tend to find it during rehearsal." If this is not possible, he suggests seeing another production in the theatre.

The simple matter of sightlines is part of finding the focus. David Jenkins examines the geometry of the seating: "Is it straight across? Is it on a center point? Is there a radius to the seating?" Jerry Zaks says that in the Vivian Beaumont Theater (New York City), the focal point is the area "that almost everyone in the audience will be able to see what's going on and have access to it."

The designer can be the ally or enemy of the actor in this regard, in that the designer can creatively exploit or neglect the stage focus, or even change the focal area. Thomas Gruenewald contends that if there are problems with the focus, "then it's up to me and the designer to solve these problems so that we get the maximum use of that spot." Kellogg maintains that the designer can "manipulate" the focus "by adding seats or something, to change the volume." In one case she put extra seats into Hartford Stage, pushing the focal point upstage: "You really just man-handle it upstage, almost like catching another spot on the same line."

The director needs to use the focal point with great care. Mosher points out that one "can't stage the whole play in that little spot, but it's got to be a gravitational center." Zaks suggests that the "sweet spot" should be used for "the most important confrontation" in the play. At Long Wharf (New Haven, Conn.), Arvin Brown observes that the strongest spot for a single actor is upstage center between the columns, but it is also a "boring" place, in that it is too far from the audience and too symmetrical: "It seems to be robbing the very thing that one works for in three-quarter round."

Some theatre artists dispute the idea of an inherent focal point, suggesting that the architecture does not dictate strong and weak areas. Instead, it is up to the production, including the design and the direction, to create the visual composition. At Hartford Stage, Mark Lamos says that there is no inherent "hot spot," but that "one needs to be found in each design." Stephen Joseph argues there is no strong point on the arena stage, except that the action makes it so: "Any position on the stage can be charged with significance at the actor's choice. There is no intrinsic position of domination,

centre stage or anywhere else. Any part of the stage is capable of
supporting whatever emphasis the actors put on it."[1]

## LOOK FOR THE UNIQUE QUALITIES
## OF THE THEATRE

Examining the space more closely, certain aspects may begin to
emerge, or even pop out. There may be unique characteristics of
the theatre to exploit. Richard Schechner looks for "particular
qualities that are unique to the space, like windows, choir lofts,
nooks or crannies. What is it that makes this space different from
all other spaces?"

Foreman's approach is "to look at all the elements and start by
saying, 'How can I best explore what is there?' rather than trying
to pretend that we're somewhere else. I've always tried to really
use the room that we are performing in to make the play
reverberate with the given of that space."

## START TO ENVISION THE PRODUCTION

At some point, the director and designer begin the process of
projecting possible ideas for the play onto the space. Jack Garfein
sits in the theatre and starts "to see how the events in the play
would work in that space, and how that space would either
enhance or limit them."

Look for the range of action that the space allows, suggests, or
even encourages. Ming advises directors and designers to envi-
sion the production and space in action: not just how it looks, but
what the potential activities are. They should discover "the inner
dynamics of the space and try to have a sense of how the action
should happen in that space." He suggests asking, "Given that
theatre, what would you do, where should the action happen, and
what's the shape of the environment for the action?"

Even ask the potentially nasty question of whether the play will
actually work in the given space. According to Heidi Landesman,

"There's an ineffable atmospheric question that you must always ask yourself: Will this play be happy in this space? Is it really congenial here? Is this a space that is appropriate for the play? Will the play seem the right scale?"

The designer and the director may come into the space with a predetermined concept, and they must determine whether this approach will work. Terry Schreiber likes to visit the theatre with the designer, "because by that time we've had a number of meetings. We have pretty much conceptualized what we want to do with the play." Murray asks the designer, "Is it going to work here? Can we do what we discussed here?"

## PRACTICAL ISSUES

While all these ineffable issues are paramount, deal also with the functional, practical aspects of the theatre. For instance, Santo Loquasto examines the access: "You simply look at how people get on and off the stage."

If possible, verify that the ground plan and section are indeed accurate. While this check does entail the practicality of dimensions, look also for the intangible aspects of the theatre—the ambiance that plans or photographs cannot convey. Lowell Detweiler comments:

> Theatres have a quality that a ground plan can only hint at. There are theatres that in ground plan look huge and in fact are incredibly fun and intimate to be in. And there are theatres that look more intimate, and you find yourself in Shea Stadium when you're in them. Some theatres are cold, like the Denver Theatre Center. Some theatres are warm, like the Guthrie Theatre.

Hugh Landwehr likes to have the plans in hand when he looks at the theatre, "so you relate your emotional, spatial and instinctual response to what's on paper."

•

These are only a few suggestions. Every theatre artist should develop his or her own process for examining a theatre. Specific questions and procedures are less important than the awareness that one must observe, examine and honor the space. The memory of the space will fade and change, so the more attention that is paid to that first impression and examination, the more the production can be created in harmony with the theatre.

## NOTES

1. Stephen Joseph, *Theatre in the Round* (London: Barrie and Rockcliff, 1967) 128.

# CHAPTER 2
# THE PERFORMANCE'S RELATIONSHIP TO THE ARCHITECTURE

At a theatrical performance, the audience is, by definition, in a theatre space. The extent, however, to which the audience is aware of that theatrical environment varies enormously, according to the nature and use of the space. For a realistic production in a proscenium theatre, the goal is to diminish that awareness as much as possible during the course of the performance. On the other hand, theatrical reformers in the early decades of this century wanted to highlight the "theatrical" nature of performance, to enhance the audience's awareness that performance is artistic, artificial and theatrical. In the post-World War II era, new forms of theatre architecture, including thrust and arena, were the result. But more recently designers and directors have realized that audience awareness of the theatre space is based not only on the configuration, but also on how the theatre is used.

Some designers and directors believe that since the audience is by definition sitting in a theatre, the production should enhance the audience's awareness of that space. Others maintain that in order for the audience to become involved in the fictive realm of the drama, the awareness of the actual theatrical environment should be suppressed as much as possible.

## CAN ARCHITECTURE BE "NEUTRAL"?

Many designers and directors prefer "neutral" architecture that intrudes as little as possible into the production. According to Jules Fisher, a theatre consultant and lighting designer, "Architecture shouldn't impose itself on the drama." Fisher's preference is for a theatre space that is "neutral, that does not exert personality of its own, so you don't have to fight anything in trying to put your

9

play across. I prefer that your mind and your vision are focused on the play itself."

But opponents argue that no space can ever be neutral. Hugh Hardy, an architect, maintains that it is "madness" for a theatre space implicitly to say to an audience, "Be inside a room, whose walls and ceiling are painted black, covered with pipes and strange looking things staring at you," and to consider that space as neutral. Hardy states: "There is no such thing as a neutral room. You can't make an enclosure that's neutral. You can't make a theatre without bumping into architecture, even though you may have just a little bit of it."

Richard Schechner, director and founder of the Performance Group, agrees: "Space is never neutral; it always speaks and makes demands. Neutrality is a horrible myth. Everything is reduced to bland regularity, which is not neutral, but neutered."

Many directors and designers dislike so-called neutrality, and prefer a theatre with a more active architecture, with a deliberate character. Those who like to incorporate or use theatre architecture find would-be "neutral" theatres uncongenial to their work. Paul Weidner, a director, prefers "architectural character" and likes "to be aware of different spaces, different textures, surfaces, objects." Bill Irwin, an actor who often develops his own performance pieces, finds the tension provided by architectural character to be helpful to his work: "Sometimes you have to work against that character, or revamp your notions almost totally in order not to be against the character of the space."

Theatres with more imposing architecture create limitations for directors and designers, which is one reason why many theatre artists prefer more "neutral" architecture. But advocates of architectural character counter that all theatres impose limitations, and, in any case, limitations are helpful. Tyrone Guthrie's theatres have often been criticized for imposing limitations, but he responds, "I think that limits—tight limits—are necessary to an artist's imagination. You must not be able to feel that you can do anything. I think more great art has depended on the artist's imagination being limited."[1] David Potts suggests that the designer should

> never look at space as being limiting; that would be negative and frustrating. Instead you work with it, use it as an inspiration. You

ask, 'What does the building have to offer?' Go with the flow. 'Oh, look at that old steam pipe. What a nuisance, but you're there, we'll just have to deal with you. All right, I'll fix you up and make you something.'

Robert Shaw cites his design for *Lucky Stiff,* by Lynn Ahrens and Steven Flaherty, at Playwrights Horizons (New York City). The theatre has no entrance stage right, but the director needed one:

> The whole design was based on finding a stage-right entrance. I needed two feet offstage right. It was the easiest design, because the whole thing was a series of givens.
>
> I actually prefer it that way; when it's a totally blank slate, you can drive yourself mad saying, 'Well, it could be this, and, then again, it could be something totally different.'

## HOW SHOULD THE DESIGNER AND DIRECTOR DEAL WITH THE THEATRE SPACE?

### At the Practical Level

Designers and directors differ on when and in what way to deal with the theatre space in the creative process of mounting a production. Many recommend discovering the nature of the play first, independent of the space, and then determining on a practical level how that concept must be adapted in order to suit the given performance space. Jerry Zaks believes that the life of the play is discovered in rehearsal, and then it is the director's job to determine "how to deposit it into this space, to maximize the number of people for whom it will be an ecstatic experience."

Robin Wagner prefers not even to see the theatre before designing: "I don't want to be influenced by the architecture—not yet. I'm not interested in making the architecture look better by filling the stage full of something that corresponds to it." Instead, he wants to work with the writer and director in order to determine "what it is in that play that ticks, what it is that has to work, what it is that the audience is responding to." According to Wagner,

"Until you've solved the problem of the play, you can't begin to see the problems of the theatre. It's the theatre piece that you have to understand." He advises that the designer should look at the theatre with one question in mind: "What in this space will stop the play from happening?"

## Don't Incorporate the Theatre Architecture

Some designers and directors feel that the architecture should not be incorporated or echoed under any circumstances. Marc B. Weiss, a lighting designer, argues that the production should not be altered to fit the theatre:

> My attitude with any space is to turn the theatre into a space that serves the show, rather than the other way around. It's a matter of attitude as to whether you're willing to turn the space into something that suits the production, or turn the production into something that will fit easily into the space.

According to designer Karl Eigsti, "The whole thing about using the architecture of the space is one of these hype, PR things." He admits that when there are columns onstage the designer must deal with them, but to argue that this situation is advantageous "is making a public relations asset out of a deficit. If you don't have those things there, you could design the play also. You just deal with something that is in the way; it doesn't make the play any better or worse."

## Space Is One of the Givens

While many designers and directors do not want to incorporate or imitate the theatre architecture, they do consider it to be one of the givens that must be accounted for in the creative process; it is neither paramount nor trifling. Bill Stabile, a designer, maintains that "the space, the play, the budget and the director are all equal." According to F. Mitchell Dana,

> Anything you are designing is contingent upon the basic material you have in the first place: the play, the quality of the people involved, the money and the space in which you are doing it. To divorce our thinking from any one of those elements is foolish. You

shouldn't design it in your mind and then say, 'Oh God, I've got to change this.' You should have designed it with the idea that these are the parameters. So if you don't know the space, or if you don't deal with the space, the relationship of the audience to the space and the actors to everybody else, right from the beginning, then you're in trouble.

## Consider the Nature of the Architecture and the Play

Some designers and directors take the view that incorporating or ignoring the theatre architecture is an aesthetic decision that should be based on the nature of the performance and the architecture; in other words, is the given architecture appropriate for the given play? Designer David Jenkins' view is that "if it's there, recognize it and exploit it," but he cautions, "It's rare that you find something that suits itself to the production." The only circumstance under which Heidi Landesman uses the theatre architecture in her designs is "if it is to my advantage. If there is something wonderful architecturally about it, or really interesting or the coloration is really fun, or there is some quality about it that would be useful to echo."

## Deal with Space in the Concept

Other designers and directors believe that the theatre space should play an even greater role in the design process. Whatever the nature of the theatre, whether imposing or "neutral," the production should be responsive to the space where the performance is occurring. The designer and director should encourage the audience to be aware of the space and have a relationship to it. The space should be considered from the very beginning of the production process—at the conceptual level. The designer should allow him or herself to be inspired by the space. Jenkins suggests that the designer should "look at the theatre space for which you're going to design, and sit there for half a day if necessary. Out of that experience comes how you will approach the design, because the experience of the audience has to be taken into consideration."

Stabile's designs at the LaMama Experimental Theatre Annex (New York City) have "always respected the space." Stabile describes his process: "I often read the play in the space if I can, and try not to think about what I'm going to do at all until I've seen the space." It is important not to jump to design preconceptions, because the designer can use the architecture of each unique space: "You're going to be in that space. You start with that space, and make the design as if it were part of it."

Richard Foreman, director and founder of the Ontological-Hysteric Theater, recommends that the director and designer should

> look at all the elements and start by saying, 'How can I best explore what is there?' rather than trying to pretend that we're somewhere else. I've always tried to really use the room that we are performing in to make a design that will help make the play reverberate with the given of that space.

According to Austin Pendleton, a director, the production should begin with a respect for the space, and then develop from there:

> You're putting on a play in a room—no matter how you slice it, that's what you're doing. Sometimes it's a large room, sometimes it's a small room, and sometimes the room is designed. But it's a bunch of live people in a room and other live people are looking at them. Somehow you should never move too far from that.

Pendleton believes that theatre is "essentially a religious experience," and should therefore share religion's emphasis on place:

> The place that you are in is part of the experience, as in any church; you have to honor that, and the audience has to feel that. They have to be reminded of the particular place where they are sitting and watching that script, because it is part of their overall experience. They're not meant to be taken away from that. The place itself is supposed to lead them into the experience and to amplify the experience for them—exactly like a church.

Implicitly or explicitly incorporating the theatre architecture will then enhance the effectiveness of the particular production:

> What you want to find is the thing that this stage can accomplish that no other stage could bring out of that play for you. You try to

look at the space and say, 'What are the moments in this play that *only* this space could provide?' And then you start to organize those moments, so that everything flows out from that.

This approach may not mean marrying the performance and the space. It may be exciting to establish an implicit dialogue between the architecture and the performance. Foreman explains this approach: "It's the interplay between this place in which you are assembled and the locale to which the play makes allusions that I try to bring to the foreground. To me, it's always something happening in a place." He points out that when the spectator hears "To be or not to be," he or she is experiencing that phrase in Lincoln Center, or the Comédie Française, or wherever. As Foreman states, "The weight of that phrase has a different meaning depending upon what's surrounding it, what it's bouncing off of." Therefore, Foreman prefers to "exploit the ambiance and architecture of the room, so that the set seems to be a superimposition upon what is already given there architecturally, rather than just transporting you artificially to another environment." Respect for the space means that the performance piece should, on one level, be based on the theatre space: "Whatever theatre I am given to work in, that theatre holds the secret of artistic discovery vis-à-vis this particular piece."

According to designer Eldon Elder, in non-traditional spaces, such as those Off Off Broadway,

> the space suggests a design solution. If you're sensitive to it, you will use the idiosyncratic aspects of the space to advantage, rather than trying to hide them, pretend they aren't there, or hope they go away.
> Given a non-traditional theatre space, when any good designer walks in, he or she will have a very strong response to the space. A good designer will take the aspects of the theatre space into consideration. I think it's important to make the design sympathetic with the environment.

## Dominant Architecture Must Be Used

Whether or not one wants to incorporate or echo elements of the space, there are some theatres in which the architecture is so active and dominant that the audience will perceive architectural characteristics during the performance, no matter what the designer and director want. Even if the production does not acknowledge the space around it, some architectural features will not go away. Landesman reports that in many of the renovated spaces in the Joseph Papp Public Theater (New York City), the designer must incorporate and echo the architecture because it is "so dominant." Her approach is to ask, "Okay, what can I do to make this room help me rather than hurt me?" In such a theatre, "You have to start with the space first and then try to design around it. Some theatre spaces are so difficult to deal with that that's the only way you can design for them." Landesman declares,

> Designers make a mistake when they're in spaces that are over-whelming architecturally and their attitude is, 'We'll pretend it's not there, and maybe the audience will pretend it's not there, too.' I don't think that ever happens. It is there; the audience doesn't know that the designers have decided to pretend it's not there. They don't have a background in architecture and design; they don't know that because it's painted black it's supposed to go away—they see these huge black objects there.
>
> If it's there physically, you can't ignore it, you have to use it as best you possibly can.

## SPRAWL OR JEWEL?

One way of considering the production's relationship to the theatre space is to determine whether the performance should reach out to the edges of the room or sit isolated with empty space around it. As Eigsti explains: "Sometimes you want to isolate the set in the space and not relate it in any way. You create a kind of black box within the space that the play sits, like a kind of jewel in a case. Other times you want to sprawl all over and hang on part of the architecture."

Foreman prefers to extend his performance pieces to the far reaches of the space:

> I always think of the limits of the space against which my gestures, my scenery, everything is going to reverberate, as if it were in a musical reverberation box. I always start thinking of how I'm going

to define the edges, and then the center is going to take care of itself, because everything that's done in the center is only done to reverberate on the edges.

It's as if you had a ball and you're going to bounce it off the edges and catch it in the center, but the interesting thing is what it's bouncing on at the periphery. I think of the many aspects of my art as being on a handball court, and things are bouncing off other things.

Lowell Detweiler likes the "jewel" approach in his designs, because of the focus that can be gained: "Just isolate this jewel-like little set in all this vast space. You get more focus on a set by placing it in the middle of a vast space. It's wonderful to get as much 'nothing' around a set as possible."

The issue of reaching to the edges of the theatre space or creating a self-contained set is especially important when performing in a large theatre. While the temptation might be to design up to the proportions of the space, it might be better to keep the set self-contained, creating its own proportions and relating to itself, not to the space. According to Wagner, the set should be a self-contained unit downstage center: it is best to "objectify the set, to keep it in some kind of connection with itself, otherwise you're putting elements all over the place and that doesn't help keep a focus."

But John Gunter has found this design approach unsatisfactory at the large Olivier Theatre in London's Royal National Theatre. He feels that a small, self-contained set is a cop-out and a refusal to exploit and engage what that theatre has to offer:

In the past, as it was conceived, you had a small folly of a set, a 'blob' as it were, sitting in the acoustic center of the stage, and then an actor has got to arrive to that area to deliver a line.

That seems a foolish concept of the way the theatre should be run. The excitement of using an epic space is to use it epicly, use it in all different ways possible.

## INVOLVE OR DISTANCE THE AUDIENCE?

Using or incorporating the architecture will affect the audience's relationship to the performance. The common view is that using the architecture will involve the audience more, whereas ignoring it will allow the audience more aesthetic distance. As Potts explains,

> There are certain plays where as an audience member you really want to feel like you're right there—right in the midst of it. It really helps an audience have a much greater sense of immediacy if where they're sitting somehow just evolves right into the space where the actors are. A very good way of doing that is to take the architecture of the theatre and incorporate it right into the set. It just helps meld the whole thing together.
>
> If you walk into a theatre and see the back wall, the proscenium is somehow nearer. It's a much more organic relationship of the members of the audience with the members of the cast. Even though the spectator may not be aware that the designer has done that, it's much easier for an audience member to feel invited into the whole set.

On the other hand, Potts observes that for other plays one wants the sense of distance gained by not engaging the theatre architecture: "There are those plays where you want a separation, you want to say, 'This is another world, and you're looking into it.' Sometimes you want a clean separation; the curtain goes up, and you're out here and seventeenth-century England is up there."

Using the theatre architecture may be appropriate only when one wants to emphasize that the play is being staged in that actual theatre, such as in *Our Town* or *Six Characters in Search of an Author*. For any other play, using the architecture may destroy the play's fictive realm, as Michael Yeargan, a designer, explains:

> If you're creating an imaginary world, no matter how realistic you're treating that world, to incorporate the architecture shatters that illusion. If you see the actor go over and lean on the column of the theatre, you think, 'Why is he leaning on the column of the theatre when he's supposed to be in the middle of the Sahara Desert?'

Eigsti argues that reminding the spectators of their theatrical surroundings can distance them from the play, drawing them out of an emotional involvement. Eigsti prefers not to use the architecture of the theatre, because he wants the audience to be transported into another world:

The more the audience is confined and confronted with the present reality, the more difficult it is to get them to suspend their belief in that reality, to evoke the larger universe of the play. You want to release the audience from the restriction of the physical world that they have to suspend belief in, in order to evoke the fictional reality of the world in which the play takes place.

Eigsti also makes the interesting point that in a small theatre, even if the architecture is not engaged, it is harder for the audience to suspend their awareness of the theatre space:

If they're sitting right next to the brick wall in Circle Rep, and a character, walking out the door, says, 'I'm going to go to Kansas City,' it's harder to believe it when he goes out and there's a wall in his face and there's a wall right next to you. It's harder to be released from the confines of the present reality to allow that external fictional world to be invoked.

In a larger theatre, the size makes the imaginative transport more possible:

When you're sitting in a Broadway theatre, the space around you recedes into a void. You can focus with enough air around the figure on the stage, and when he says, 'I'm going to Kansas City,' your mind is freer from the restraints of your physical world to imagine and believe that that's what he's going to do. So that fictional world is evoked for you.

•

The theatre artist should decide at what level he or she wants to deal with the architecture: practical, conceptual, or at the many levels in between. But all theatres and performances are different, and the theatre artist should be prepared to take a different approach for each production.

## NOTES

1. As quoted in "The Changing Practice: Theaters," *Progressive Architecture* 46 (1965): 170.

# CHAPTER 3

# USING THE ARCHITECTURE OF THE THEATRE

Once the performance's relationship to the architecture is deter-mined, using the principles described in the previous chapter, the director and designer may choose to actually incorporate or echo elements of the theatre space.

## USE THE UNIQUE ASPECTS OF THE THEATRE SPACE

One way of using the theatre architecture is to find and emphasize what is special about the space. This approach may not be easy, and the theatre's strengths may not be readily apparent; in many cases, the designer or director may first be struck by the theatre's problems. But the director and designer may be able to exploit these unique aspects for the production. For example, Bill Irwin likes to discover the "eccentricities" of any space, and to use them in the creation of his performance pieces. He finds it hard to write in his own room, but when he is actually in the performance space, "ideas start popping in" and the "most specific and useful ideas come up." Ironically, the success of using the architecture can become a burden:

> The problem that it creates is that you do an experiment somewhere in a studio—you really use its eccentricities and it's a wonderful theatre experiment for the eighty to one hundred people. And then people say, 'This is just great. We've got to do this somewhere else.' You have to start all over again, because you can't do there what you did here.

He cites the example of *Largely/New York:*

> We did the show at the City Center, which is a grand theatre with a huge swimming-pool-like orchestra pit between the stage and the

audience. It just begged eventually for a guy to fall in there; he crawled out, became enamored of that, and started diving in and doing acrobatics into it. It was a useful set of ideas, and it made a great building block for the piece.

Now we've been asked to do that show elsewhere and I'm at a loss for how to proceed, because the other theatres don't have that kind of a pit.

## USE THE EXTREMES OF THE ARCHITECTURE

In a space with difficult proportions, one might be tempted to minimize the odd dimensions, to "regularize" the space, but emphasizing those extremes may in fact be more helpful. Heidi Landesman suggests that if the space is extremely horizontal, her tendency is to use all the horizontal space; if it's extremely vertical, to use as much height as possible; or in a deep theatre, to use every inch of depth. Landesman believes that such a design is "more interesting" and "more extreme" than it would be to "compromise the space down into what is perceived to be normal or acceptable proportions."

For example, Bill Stabile designed a production in a theatre that had a low, ten-foot ceiling, and his response was to make the space "even lower by raising the stage and putting in cardboard valances, making it look like brown curtains in a high school auditorium."

Jonathan Miller directed *The Emperor,* by Ryszard Kapuscinki, in a "narrow little corridor of a room," which he made "even more of a corridor. We built artificial doors into it, so that people were looking down a sort of palace corridor through which people emerged."

At Circle in the Square (Uptown) in New York City, the length of the stage has been emphasized for some productions. In several cases, the long stage has been used to underline a feeling of languor and emptiness in the play. Stephen Porter used this effect for his production of *Days in the Trees,* by Marguerite Duras. Porter decided to "stress the strangeness of the place rather than domesticate it." The set had boards running the length of the stage, which, according to Porter, made the stage "seem even longer and

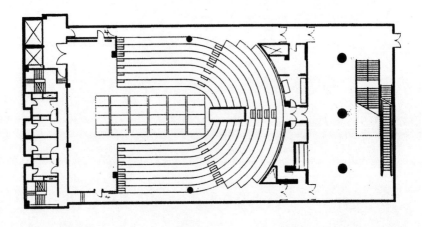

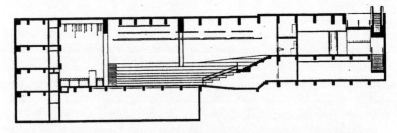

2. Plan and section of Circle in the Square (Uptown), New York City. Architect: Alan Robert Sayles. Reproduced with permission of Alan Robert Sayles.

3. View of Circle in the Square (Uptown), New York City. Reproduced with permission of Circle in the Square.

narrower than it was." His staging tried for the same effect: "I would place the people at odd, remote distances from each other, and accentuate the length of the stage." The effect was to make it look like "a surreal plane," which emphasized "the alienation that all the characters had by placing them in uncomfortable relations to each other." Porter feels that the set helped the production because "it was a play about alienation." The production "worked in the space, precisely because the space was seemingly impossible for it."

## INCORPORATE OR ECHO THE EXISTING THEATRE ARCHITECTURE

The designer can also incorporate actual aspects of the architecture into the set. Sometimes this approach is unavoidable, but in other cases, using attributes of the theatre space is an option for the designer, depending on the nature of the play, design and theatre space. At Circle Rep (New York City), John Lee Beatty generally paints the walls black on either side of the end stage to make them disappear as much as possible, but for a few productions the brick walls have been painted in such a way as to pull them into the dramatic action. If a brick wall is needed, Beatty says the designer can "just paint it to be a brick wall." He notes that "you've got a brick wall for free, and that's a very cheap form of scenery." In this case, "the walls of the theatre become scenery."

For *Swing Shift* (music by Michael Dansicker, lyrics by Sarah Schlesinger), at old Manhattan Theatre Club, Tony Straiges, a designer, took down all the black masking to expose the brick of the existing building and used the actual doors and windows, which made the space look like a factory—the setting of the play.

One of the most notable examples of using the existing architecture was Peter Brook's exploitation of the crumbling Bouffes du Nord (Paris) for the production he directed of Chekhov's *The Cherry Orchard*. While the Ranievskaya estate was not depicted onstage, the decrepit theatre brought a peculiar resonance to the entire experience. The production would not have been the same in a brand new, polished theatre. The point was recognized when the Brooklyn Majestic was "restored" to a crumbling condition for the New York production. As Hugh Hardy, the architect for the restoration, observes,

> The crumbling quality of the theatre contributes to the experience of the production. There's something about the erosion and the layers of time that are present in the architecture of the room that resonate with the production itself. It's more subtle than making the scenery or the stage extend into the theatre.

In addition to using existing aspects of the theatre space, designers sometimes add scenic units that mirror or echo parts of the existing architecture. Designer Eugene Lee likes any "scenic" additions to appear "architectural, so you don't even know it is added." Santo Loquasto, a designer, says that in converted spaces "it is fun to make it look as though you did nothing, so that it really seems, in some instances, environmental."

For example, Beatty replicated the architecture of the Folger Theatre (Washington, D.C.) for his design of *Hamlet,* because "the turning and the detailing of the building is really excellent, and impossible to compete with. Almost any scenery seems to look under-worked next to how beautifully worked the theatre is." For his design, Beatty copied some of the columns and added a balcony and walls: "We literally copied—just took molding gauges and copied as much as we could."

In a theatre with visible brick walls, one can add fake, scenic brick walls that appear to be part of the permanent architecture. Beatty reports that at Circle Rep, "Often we've added a little two-foot piece of wall here and there, put some extra broken-up plaster or pipe on it, and painted it all black to look like the rest of the theatre."

At Second Stage (New York City), almost all the productions have ignored the architecture, as is commonly the case in end-stage and proscenium theatres. But for *Short Eyes,* by Miguel Pinero, which is set in a prison, David Jenkins used the architecture as the setting for the play. Jenkins points out that the space already had "an institutional feeling" from its former use as a gym, and so he decided to "strip it all down and use what's there, not to 'build scenery.'" The major "scenic" element was the permanent glazed brick that surrounds both stage and audience, giving the feeling that everyone in the space was in the same detention cell. The added elements—a new back wall, a low wall around the shower and a column—were "made to look architectural, not like scenery, as if nothing was added."

The set had the desired effect for Frank Rich, who praised the

> wraparound set that envelops the audience in the clammy cinder-block environment of a New York House of Detention. And, after a while, we really do feel that we're in jail. By the time the inmates erupt in an irrational cataclysm of vigilante violence, the audience is squirming uncontrollably, afraid to watch the bloodletting and yet unwilling to look away. When the play ends a while later, a theatergoer may be torn between a desire to applaud and the urge to rush home for a cleansing shower.[1]

## USE THINGS THAT GET IN THE WAY, OR "CUT DOWN THOSE COLUMNS!"

Sometimes using the architecture is not a matter of choice. As Thomas Lynch, a designer, explains, "If there are things that are completely in the way, they're going to need to be incorporated somehow." The most frequent unavoidable architectural element in theatres—the *bête noir* of many designers—is columns.

In general, there are two strategies for dealing with columns: incorporate them into the production, by burying them in the set or decorating them, or simply ignore them. Designer John Falabella takes the first tack, arguing that in a theatre with onstage columns "it's impossible not to incorporate the columns." He says that a designer should deal with columns from the beginning and build the design around them: "If you start with those columns, you begin to hang your architecture on them." In a resident theatre, Falabella suggests that the audience will already be aware of the columns, and will come to the theatre with expectations of their use: "They look to see what you've done with the columns."

There are columns in all the spaces at the Joseph Papp Public Theater, which is a grand landmarked building that was originally the Astor Library. The onstage columns in the Anspacher Theater were stripped down and resheathed in non-decorative sheet metal

to make them more "neutral." Because they sit on either side of
center stage, the columns must somehow be dealt with. Wilford
Leach, who was a resident director at the Public, asserts that "you
have to incorporate them—they're a presence; you can't ignore
them." Lynch says that even though the onstage columns are
stripped, the fact that the other columns in the auditorium are
decorated makes the audience "sense that room as it was." The
effect is implicitly to bring the architecture of the entire ornate
room onto the stage. According to Lynch, the designer therefore
has "to deal with the theatre as much as with the design."

The columns have worked to the benefit of some productions. For
his design of *The Memorandum,* by Vaclav Havel, Douglas Schmidt
feels the columns "worked well." Like Leach, Schmidt believes that
"you have to incorporate the columns; they aren't going to go
away." Schmidt redecorated the onstage columns with the detail
found on the auditorium columns: "We went to great pains to put it
back, to tie it architecturally into the rest of the room, so there was a
little middle-European, bureaucratic look to the room."

In the Public's Martinson Hall, the columns are along the edge
of the stage and auditorium. The onstage columns can be hidden
by placing a wall or curtain in front of them, but the playing area
is then restricted. Instead, designers often opt for incorporating the
columns into the design.

For *Coming of Age in Soho,* by Albert Innaurato, Loren
Sherman used the columns as part of his design. The play is set in
a Soho loft, and in a sense the Public Theater is a Soho loft.
Sherman also felt that the design would "invite the audience in if
they see column, column, column on the set, and then there's a
column next to them in their seat." The effect is essentially a form
of environmental theatre.

In a production of Sophocles' *Antigone,* the designer used the
columns to evoke the Greek setting of the play. The design used
the actual architecture of the theatre, which might have emphasized in the spectator's mind the actual performance space, but
ironically reviewers commented on the illusory effect. Clive
Barnes felt that the designer had "made extraordinary use" of
Martinson Hall:

> It is stunning in its simplicity. It has boldly taken the architectural
> form of the hall itself, complete with its existing Doric columns,

and used it, with walls of painted marble surrounding a raised playing area of simulated stratified rock. The effect is of ancient Greece.[2]

Rosette C. Lamont wrote: "One forgets that the space is Martinson Hall. . . . It is as though a magician had transported us to Epidaurus."[3]

But any attempt to incorporate, decorate or disguise a column may entail too many compromises. One can simply ignore it and let the column exist as a column. If the production makes no reference to it in the scenery or the action, the audience may also ignore it, accepting the column as part of the permanent architecture. According to Jenkins,

> Unless somebody has to run into it and you have a problem with blocking, I don't think it's a visual problem. People take it in, and then they're involved in the play. I don't think they sit there and worry about whether there's a column in the way or not, unless they get bored with the play and start looking around.

Michael Yeargan suggests that the designer should "float" the set in the middle of the stage, separated from the columns, in which case "the columns are there, and they go away." He believes that if the columns are painted black, "they are just treated as the architecture of the theatre." For a production he designed at Long Wharf Theatre, "no one ever touched those columns; no one ever leaned on them. They came down inches away from the set, but the set floated away from them a little bit." He remarks that everyone was "very aware" of the columns in the model, but in the theatre the audience was not.

## USE THE COLOR OF THE THEATRE

Using the color of the theatre space in the design is one way of carrying over the ambiance of the auditorium onto the stage. Beatty says that one of the first questions he asks is whether there is more of the color with which the auditorium was painted. He likes to "paint new pieces of wall to fill in the theatre," or to "actually paint the set the color of the walls." One purpose can be to make "the scenery blend into the theatre." Painting the set the same color as the theatre can also help "the actors come forward," while "the scenery and the theatre blend together upstage of them."

John Jensen, a designer, describes how incorporating the theatre's colors can help break down the audience-performance barrier:

> For a production of Feiffer's *The White House Murder Case* at the old Milwaukee Rep, we upholstered the chairs that surrounded a huge conference table in the same fabric as the audience seats. The hope was that this would blur the line and underscore the fact that the audience was a part of the event—participants as well as onlookers.

*The Real Thing,* by Tom Stoppard, contains a play-within-a-play, and for that scene the designer Tony Walton "tried to incorporate the actual coloring and flavor of the Plymouth Theatre's [Broadway] decoration and rich ornament," so that the scene was visually "related more to the theatre than to the life to follow."

## BASE THE PRODUCTION CONCEPT ON THE SPACE

The most extreme approach is to base the production on the kind of theatre space and what it seems to represent. Irwin developed *The Regard of Flight* for and about the proscenium theatre. According to Irwin, "The basis of the show is a historic rumination on avant-garde theatre of an era gone by." Irwin had worked with Herbert Blau, who "still had a lot of feelings from the '50s and '60s," such as, "Let's do away with the proscenium; the proscenium is what puts things in a little box for us and separates us from the action. Let's start tearing it down—literally and figuratively." The premise of the show, then, was "a satiric reference to this idea of mistrust for the proscenium." Specifically, the former avant-garde's distrust of the proscenium manifested itself as a physical *shtick* for the production: the proscenium arch seemed to tug or suck Irwin, against his will, kicking and fighting, off into the wings. In another scene, Irwin tried to escape the questioning of this interlocutor, and found his way blocked by the proscenium, as Irwin describes: "The proscenium is blocking me—this damn proscenium—I can't get out of here!" The result was a performance piece "about these noble but often silly attempts to do some new theatre, which often had to do with wanting to transform the architecture." Irwin's problem now is the show's success: people want Irwin to perform it in spaces without prosceniums, so he has to build a false arch to frame it.

Richard Foreman reports that the Vivian Beaumont Theater (New York City) had a "profound effect" on his production of Brecht's *The Three-Penny Opera*. He had examined the circumstances of the original production, and then considered his production at Lincoln Center in 1976:

> When *The Three-Penny Opera* was originally done, they wanted to shake up their bourgeois audience, which had affectations of being different from the Berlin low-life. They talked about capitalism, and the image was very raucous, very seedy, very tumbledown—within the context of what looked like a nice state theatre.
>
> Our production tried to have the same kind of dialectic relationship with our audience, in Lincoln Center, which is a big sterile white elephant placed in the middle of this ridiculous culture complex. I tried to make a production that reflected onstage back to the audience the kind of austere, cold image that was indeed the image of Lincoln Center. My idea was to create the same sort of equation between Lincoln Center and the stage as Brecht was trying to create for his particular historical moment.
>
> The theatre had a big influence, because if I had not done it in Lincoln Center, but had done it downtown at the Public Theater, I wouldn't have gone in that direction at all. I was trying to make the building itself, the setting itself, reverberate in terms of the meaning of the text.

Loquasto drew on the blunt lines of the audience rows and the architectural detail of the Newman Theater, at the Joseph Papp Public Theater, for a production of *Miss Margarida's Way*, by Roberto Athayde, a play set in a classroom, with the audience as the pupils. According to Loquasto,

> I tried to recreate my old biology lecture hall. The Newman was perfect, because all you needed were one-armed desks. It really was

like those dreadful science lecture halls, the way it just continues on unrelentingly. You actually felt that it was non-theatrical.

This feeling that the entire space, not just the part onstage, was Miss Margarida's classroom was important "in helping to bring the sense of genuine menace to the performance." Howard Kissel remarked that the set "adds to the wit of the occasion by using materials that imitate those already in the Newman Theater to make the whole thing seem like a modern class room."[4]

For a production of *A Midsummer Night's Dream* in the outdoor Delacourt Theatre (New York City), Landesman found that the setting for the theatre—Central Park—could be incorporated and used to enhance the production. She had heard the "conventional wisdom," which was to create a barrier between the audience and Central Park by designing tall scenery to block the view, in that the Park activities were considered to be distracting. But instead, her approach was to "integrate the landscape beyond the stage into the

4. Opening night of Shakespeare in the Park, Delacourt Theater, Central Park, New York City, June, 1962. Consultant and stage designer: Eldon Elder. Credit: New York City Parks Photo Archive.

landscape on the stage." As Landesman observes, "Instead of fighting the space and the Park, we found a way to make that work for us. It was an honest, genuine response to the space that we were in." She also states that this approach was "conceptually right," in that "the play is about everyone getting lost in the woods and we were creating our own artificial woods in Central Park to get lost in."

In some cases, one may be able to present a play in an actual place that is similar or even identical to the fictive place of the play. Theodore Mann, director and co-founder of Circle in the Square, cites that theatre's production of O'Neill's *The Iceman Cometh* in their original downtown theatre:

> When we did it downtown, we were in a dilapidated nightclub, so it was like Harry Hope's 'Last Chance Cafe.' Everything about us, the lighting fixtures, the walls—part of which were in good shape, part were broken—enriched the space. The whole room was the set; it wasn't just set out on the deck, it was the entire room.

## BASE ON THE "POLITICS" OF THE PLACE

The Living Theatre often bases the production on the implicit politics of the place where they are performing. As Judith Malina, co-founder of the Living Theatre, explains: "Wherever we are, the Living Theater works for what seems to be the burning issue in any given situation. We like to be where there's a possibility of social impact, where we can add our particular partisanship."

For example, a Living Theater performance entitled *Turning the Earth* was about community gardens, and was performed in lots or open spaces in New York City that "could be community gardens, where we are suggesting that a community garden could be planted," according to Malina. Real estate is a highly charged political and economic issue in New York in the 1980s and '90s, and Malina's view is that "the use of land is wrong." One of the purposes of this performance, then, was to show that "community gardens were a little spot of life inside a gruesome situation. The people who create them are very idealistic about them. Very often they just go into a lot and plant, and then deal with the city allowing them to have done that."

The performance began with a procession around the neighborhood of a potential garden site. The performance was not advertised; instead, the audience consisted of whoever gathered during the procession. After a "planting ceremony," the Living Theatre performers left the garden, which might or might not be maintained: "That depends on whether we've inspired them rightly, and if circumstances allow it," says Malina.

Other Living Theatre performances have been about local events, sites, etc. *Six Public Acts* occurred in six places in a city, with a procession between each one. An action was performed that was appropriate to each site, which included a prison, a police station, a school, a residential neighborhood, a bank and a corporation.

•

This chapter outlines but a few of the many approaches that a theatre artist may take in using the theatre architecture. Basing the production on the theatre space, or incorporating, echoing or hinting at the theatre architecture may create effects that would be unachievable in any other way.

## NOTES

1. Frank Rich, "'Short Eyes,' by Pinero, in Revival," *The New York Times* 28 Nov. 1984: 19.
2. Clive Barnes, "An 'Antigone' That Should Be Called 'Creon,' " *New York Post* 30 April 1972, in Performing Arts Library Scrapbook: n. pag.
3. Rosette C. Lamont, "Oriental Antigone," *Other Stages* 6 May 1982, Performing Arts Library Scrapbook: n. pag.
4. Howard Kissel, "Miss Margarida's Way," *Women's Wear Daily* 1 Aug. 1977: 8.

# CHAPTER 4
# INVOLVING THE AUDIENCE

## RITUAL

The idea of involving the audience in the performance is founded on the principle that theatre is based in ritual. This theory has been part of the theatrical vocabulary since the reform movement of the early twentieth century. Reformers, then and now, have been opposed to the illusionistic theatre and its architectural home, the picture-frame proscenium. The aim of the illusionistic theatre is for the audience to believe, with willing suspension of disbelief, that the performance is real, and to diminish the audience's awareness of the theatricality. But the audience-involvers want the spectator to perceive the performance as an artistic—even artificial—theatrical event. Theatrical performance is seen as a ritualistic interaction between two groups of people: spectators and performers. Therefore, performance and architecture should highlight and reinforce this interaction, and the open stage is considered to be the most conducive to this effect.

Tyrone Guthrie was the main exponent of the ritualistic approach in the post-World-War-II period. (It is also no coincidence that Guthrie is generally considered to be the father of the modern thrust stage.) For Guthrie, the aim of the "serious" playwright is "to show a ritual and symbolic re-enactment of certain events, and re-embodiment of certain personages, which they have arranged in an orderly and significant manner: Liturgy, not Illusionary Conjuring.[1] According to Guthrie, this ritualistic basis should affect the nature of the performance: "I believe that the theatre makes its effect not by means of illusion, but by ritual."[2]

Guthrie believes that illusionary theatre is not only poor ritual, but fundamentally self-defeating, because spectators do not fall for the illusion: "They do not believe that the good-humored little

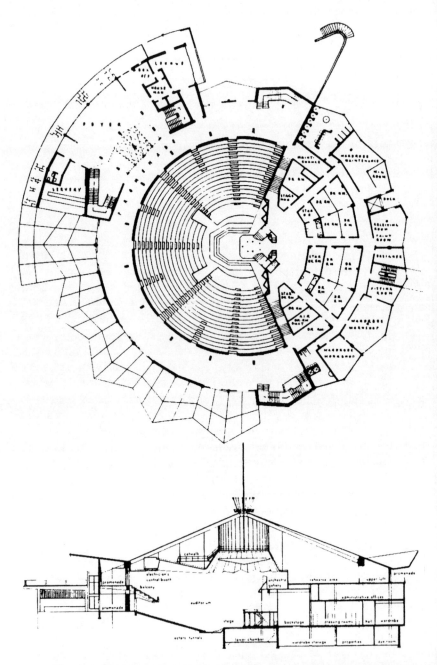

5. Plan and section of the Stratford Festival Theatre Thrust Stage, Stratford, Ont. Architects: Rounthwaite and Fairfield. Consultant: Tyrone Guthrie. Stage Designer: Tanya Moiseiwitsch. Reproduced with permission of Rounthwaite, Dick and Hadley.

6. View of the Stratford Festival Theatre Thrust Stage, Stratford, Ont. Photograph by Jane Edmonds. Reproduced with permission of the Stratford Festival.

lady suspended, in acute discomfort, on an easily visible wire is Peter Pan. They know perfectly well that she is Mary Martin."[3]

## THE TRIANGULAR RELATIONSHIP OF AUDIENCE AND PERFORMANCE

The relationship between audience and performance is commonly viewed as two-way: performance affecting audience, and vice versa. But advocates of ritual-based theatre and the open stage argue that the relationship is three-way, or triangular. James Marston Fitch explains that there is "the actor's impact upon the audience as a whole; the collective response of that audience; and the effect of that response then upon the individual playgoers who make it up."[4]

While many proscenium advocates contend that sightlines, acoustics and comfort make an ideal theatre, Iain Mackintosh, a theatre consultant, maintains, "It is the living actor/audience relationship, rather than perfect sightlines to a scenic *stage à l'Italienne* that determines the design of theatre space." Mackintosh contends that most important "is the three-way relationship among performer and spectator and other members of the audience who by their presence assist both at the actors' performance and at the audience's enjoyment."[5] Hugh Hardy emphasizes this social, even communal, aspect of theatregoing:

> Without question, the idea of going to the theatre is the idea of joining the community of an audience in some way. If it isn't, you might as well stay at home and watch your VCR. It has to be about the communal experience of sharing with other people the discoveries of the performance. The notion that movie theatres are based on—perfect sightlines for a single individual seeing the full screen, which leads to a fan-shaped auditorium—is screwy for theatres. It has to include the audience.

## GATHERING AROUND

The view that theatre is based on a ritualistic, triangular relationship has a corollary in theatre architecture: a configuration with the audience "gathering around" the performer. Jack Garfein, a director, quotes Robert Edmond Jones, who wrote: "The leader goes on. 'Sit around me in a circle—you, and you, and you—right here, where I can reach out and touch you all.' And so with one inclusive gesture he makes—a theatre!"[6] According to Garfein, the audience should therefore partially or wholly encircle the stage—like the gesture of an arm sweeping around the body.

Proponents of the open stage see this configuration as "natural" for a theatrical experience. Richard Southern examines how people tend to gather at a presentation:

> If an individual begins to address a group of people by means of speech, the shape of the crowd that assembles to him is generally a crescent. If the individual, instead of speaking, performs some action such as a dance, then the shape of the crowd is more likely to be circular—it encircles the performer. And if two (or more) persons address a crowd, not by speaking directly to it but by speaking to each other, i.e. by dialogue, then the shape of the audience may possibly be again a circle.[7]

## AUDIENCE SEEING AUDIENCE

Advocates of the open stage use the three-way reciprocal relationship to defend their stage form: in order for an individual spectator to be aware of and influenced by the collective response of the audience, it is best if he or she is able to see a significant portion of that audience, in direct or peripheral vision. This relationship will occur in a thrust or arena theatre, but not in the fan-shaped proscenium auditorium. Guthrie considers seeing other spectators to be a desired affirmation of the theatrical experience:

> Being considerably aware of other members of the audience, as when one is watching an open stage performance, has the positive advantage of reminding one that theatregoing, unlike watching Movies or Television, is a sociable event, and that the audience has a creative, not merely a passive role to play. One's own concentration, participation and enjoyment are intensified by the awareness that they are being shared, that the whole audience is likewise concentrating, participating, and enjoying.[8]

Wilford Leach praises the "warmth of humanity" in a thrust theatre, as opposed to a proscenium, in which "we're all in little rows for some rally." And Jerry Zaks describes the thrust stage as feeling "like a big party."

While spectators may be able to see other spectators, this awareness may not be constant. Director Jacques Levy makes the interesting argument that the audience does not perceive its fellow spectators equally at all times: "The more involved you get in the play, they can go away, but they keep coming back, making an appearance again and then receding again."

## HOW THE PRODUCTION CAN MANIPULATE AUDIENCE INVOLVEMENT

### Verticals

The spectator's awareness of the rest of the audience is not necessarily an absolute in any theatre; rather, the designer and director may be able to enhance or reduce it. Karl Eigsti contends that a simple design technique can minimize the audience's awareness of spectators on the opposite side of the stage:

> You put a vertical in—just one thin vertical—and somehow the eye stops. That vertical is a way of defining the space, so the people you see in the dimness beyond are somehow outside of that world. By breaking the cube, by defining the cube vertically, you are also announcing in a subtle way to the audience, 'This is the world that you want to concentrate on. The people who are sitting on the other side are not part of this imaginary world.' When there is nothing there, they become a part of that world and you have to justify it: 'What are all those people doing in this play?'

According to Eigsti, such a vertical

> becomes a sign post that says, 'This is where it ends.' It seems to identify the world a bit more. It identifies the acting space, and it creates a reference point for the eye. It keeps the eye from wandering, from being distracted by the inevitable view of audience members.

## End Stage

While awareness of fellow spectators is most prominent in thrust or arena theatres, two designers created sets to accomplish this effect in the end-stage Newman Theater. In *A Map of the World,* by David Hare, a backdrop realistically depicted the auditorium of the Newman Theater for a scene presenting a debate in an empty auditorium. The effect was to draw the audience in, to show the relevance of a debate that might seem merely academic. For *Drinks before Dinner,* by E. L. Doctorow, Tony Walton literally mirrored the auditorium: the back wall of the set was made of half-mirrored panels. For the first half of the play the mirroring effect was not apparent, and the audience saw a view of a city through the windows; as the play progressed, the audience increasingly saw itself reflected in the set. Walton was "interested in having the audience become part of the play to the extent that they became more and more visible." Jack Kroll found the device quite effective, calling the set "a dissonant dazzle of glass and chrome in whose narcissistic surfaces the audience sees itself, watching and implicated."[9]

## Where Two Worlds Collide

A key area in the audience's relationship to the performance is where the two worlds meet: the edge of the stage and the first row of the auditorium. Gregory Mosher, former director of the Vivian Beaumont Theater, believes that this vital area must be shaped for each production: "It is up to the designer and the director—not the house manager or ticket seller—to determine the configuration of the seats right around the stage." One of the first decisions Mosher makes is "how that joining up at the front of the stage is going to happen." The designer and director may want "a little spark gap between the front row and the stage," or to have the audience "crammed up against the stage." For *A Comedy of Errors,* Mosher wanted the audience "packed in right there and just a little bit crowded and jostley right up front." On the other hand, Mosher felt that *Anything Goes* (book by Guy Bolton, P.G. Wodehouse, Howard Lindsay, Russel Crouse; lyrics by Cole Porter) "needs a little bit of space there, not a big gap, just four feet or something to the front row."

Richard Foreman also considers this area to be crucial:

> The place I have the most difficulty with is the six to ten feet between the front row of the audience and the beginning of the stage. I go crazy—there's something about that space. I'm always adding things to try and make that transition do something to me and not seem dead. Often I put railings high enough so that everybody can see the edge of the railing.
>
> I can't tell you how many times in the last week or so before the play opens I'm sitting there thinking, 'What can I do about that particular six feet of space?'

Foreman's goal in manipulating this area is "clarity," and he generally finds, "It isn't clear enough, it isn't defined enough." Though this area is a problem in any theatre, Foreman considers it "less problematic in the thrust, because the transition across that barrier is softened or complicated by the fact that it becomes a semicircle."

Foreman frequently extends strings from the stage to the rear of the auditorium to "make it homier." But he also extends strings across the front of the auditorium, between the stage and audience, in order to distance the spectators. Foreman uses such devices, then, both to involve and distance the audience:

I like to play with having decorative elements come out to surround the audience, so the audience is in it, and then, within being embraced, using a lot of distancing and separating techniques—putting up strings. So it's both 'Look, you're embraced,' and 'Wait a minute, don't come too close.' Some of the strings are high up, so that if you're sitting in the back row and you have a string that is just five feet in front of you, somehow the stage comes out that far, so that the actors don't seem so far away. You are not separated by just empty space between you and the play.

## Direct Address

One way of involving the spectators in the performance is to address them directly, such as with soliloquies and asides. Modern actors tend to find direct address more difficult through the proscenium arch and easier when they have spectators around them. Basil Langton has directed *13 Rue de l'Amour,* by Georges Feydeau, on both proscenium and thrust stages, and found,

> It was more difficult on the proscenium than it had been in the round. On a thrust stage I found it worked very well; that kind of open space made it easier for actors to talk to the audience, instead of stepping out of the frame as they had to do in a proscenium theatre.

Stephen Porter explains that asides are clearer for both audience and actor on the thrust or arena stage because the actor "can talk directly to the audience, and they know they're being talked to directly." But behind an arch, the relationship is more ambiguous: "On a proscenium stage, the audience can choose to decide whether the actor is speaking to them or speaking to himself."

Jonathan Miller compares asides to what is called a *Sprecher* in painting: a figure in the painting who looks out at the viewer. Miller points out that the director and actor must be very clear about whether the actor is directly addressing the audience, or is simply thinking aloud:

> In some cases, a soliloquy is not in fact the act of a *Sprecher:* you, the audience, are eavesdropping upon an out-loud meditation, which is not addressed to you at all. And in some cases it is quite clearly the character taking the audience into his confidence, in which case he is a *Sprecher.*
>
> One and the same speech can be treated in either of those ways,

according to what the director or the actor wants. I have done *Hamlet* in which 'Oh what a rogue and peasant slave am I' has been either meditated inwardly, taking the front of the stage as a glass through which you're not meant to hear. And on other occasions I have deliberately made those meditations confidences directed to the audience, in which the character for that moment takes the audience's presence into consideration and confides.

It is a paradox that the *Sprecher* should look at you, because he looks at you from not just simply a different physical, geographical space, he's looking at you from a place which is 'elsewhen.' In many productions I put one in: someone in the middle of a violent action suddenly turns quite silently and unnoticed, and engages the audience, as if to say, 'Look, something very big's going on, elsewhere and elsewhen.'

## Justifying Direct Address

The director can scatter minor characters around the periphery of a thrust or arena stage in order to "realistically" justify what becomes, in effect, direct address to the audience. The actor talks to the "supers" at the edge of the stage, and implicitly addresses the spectators sitting beyond. In this way the production does not actually break the "realistic" frame of the action by directly involving the audience as listeners, but the actor can still address the audience. Michael Cacoyannis used this effect at Circle in the Square (Uptown) for his production of Euripides' *The Bacchae,* for the scene in which Agave exults to Cadmus, her father, over her ritual killing of what she believes to be a lion, which is in fact her son. In this production, the chorus was seated around the edge of the stage, allowing Agave to circumnavigate the stage, thrusting her son's head into the faces of the spectators. According to Cacoyannis: "Agave's walk displaying Pentheus' head to the surrounding Thebans/audience" was intended to "involve the audience in a double identity." For Figaro's long speeches in *Figaro's Marriage,* by Beaumarchais, at the same theatre, Andrei Serban scattered peasants around the stage, justifying the actor's turning to all sections of the audience.

## Involving the Audience in the Argument

Actors placed around the periphery of an open stage can also be used to draw the audience into an onstage argument or debate. The speaking actors can address those situated around the stage, implicitly involving the audience in the discussion. Porter declares that George Bernard Shaw's plays, containing long scenes in which the only action is the clash of ideas during a debate, are particularly effective on a thrust stage. He has directed Shaw's *Major Barbara* in both proscenium and arena, and prefers the latter. In the final scene,

> the family all sit there for forty-five minutes and say, 'Ah, I see,' with enthusiasm. It gets very hard to stay in focus. Meanwhile the two men and occasionally Barbara are having violent and very, very, very long speeches.
> The scene gains enormously in arena. The family becomes part of the actual audience; they blend into the audience. One isn't conscious of the family sitting there like bumps, because the whole audience is doing the same thing. The arguments seem to involve the audience.

John Falabella used the same principle in his design for *The Caine Mutiny Court-Martial,* by Herman Wouk, at Circle in the Square (Uptown): "The audience wrapped completely around and became a part of this courtroom, merely because the witness was center, facing out, flanked by the prosecutor and defense, playing down to the court."

## Sending the Actors into the Auditorium

A controversial method of involving the audience is to send the actors off the stage and into the midst of the audience. When Alvin Epstein directed Ibsen's *The Pretenders* at the Guthrie Theatre (Minneapolis, Minn.), he staged the opening scene, a big public event, with a grand processional from the back of the auditorium and down the aisle: "The more I could set up right from the start the feeling that the audience in the theatre was the populace of the city, that they were part of the action, the more the play would have its effect, to make a single unity out of what was happening." Epstein feels that this choice was "perfect" for a thrust stage like the Guthrie: "The whole space was included, the house lights did not come down, the audience was there, as part of the scene, and gradually we focused on the action on stage. But the impression at the beginning was of a mass meeting."

One of the most famous and effective examples of the actors invading the auditorium is the Royal Shakespeare Company's production of *The Life and Adventures of Nicholas Nickleby*. John Caird, one of the directors, explains that the purpose was to emphasize the idea of witnessing the performance: "We thought it was important for the actors to be the witnesses of their own storytelling. By seeing that the actors were the witnesses, the audience would feel closer to the idea of being witnesses themselves."

To Caird, the issue is not whether to involve the audience, and the issue is not whether some plays are more involving than others. Rather, Caird believes that sending the actors into the audience's domain implies, as in *Nicholas Nickleby*, that the events of the play are mutable and unpredictable, and partly to be defined by the act of witnessing:

> The result was to give the audience a feeling that anything could happen on that day, because the actors didn't know what was going to happen. They hadn't seen the story before, and there was an actor seated near them, watching it, who maybe hadn't seen it exactly as it had happened before. The feeling derives from that. This story could go anywhere. It could end sad, it could end happy.

Caird explains that in other plays the outcome is inevitable, in which case sending the actors into the auditorium is inappropriate:

> There is a necessary distance between actors and audience in many shows, though it doesn't mean it is less involving. You can't have a production of, say, *King Lear* or *Hamlet* that has as a hallmark a terrific amount of audience participation. Audiences in plays like that are witnesses to a dramatic unfolding that is, by its tragic nature, inevitable. Therefore there must not be anything they can do to intervene, and there should be a certain coolness in the relationship between actor and audience.

But sending the actors into the audience is a dangerous enterprise. Caird, despite his work with *Nicholas Nickleby*, cautions,

> One has to be careful not to do anything that's going to make a cliché out of audience contact. All audiences are different, but they're not stupid; they know when they've been contacted. They

know when they're watching a real sense of coming together and when they're watching a show—a sham of that. One has to be very careful that one doesn't present a group of actors just pretending to be very close to the audience.

Others dislike deploying the actors into the auditorium under any circumstances. Mark Lamos, director of the Hartford Stage Company, has "never" found it to be effective; he worries that the actor will fall or that something unpredictable will occur. Ron Lagomarsino, a director, "hates" to send the actors into the auditorium, considering it to be a "leftover from the '60s." Far from involving the audience, to Lagomarsino, it makes the spectators "self-conscious and nervous," with a resulting "loss of focus."

John Tillinger, a director, is even more adamant; he declares: "Hate it. Would never do it, ever. Hate it. Hate being in the audience, hate doing it as an actor. I hate it. I just think it's bullshit."

## Using the Intermission

One can also exploit the period of intermission to involve the audience. Richard Schechner feels that intermissions are "very, very important," and are usually "thrown away." Schechner points out that intermission has great potential for enhancing the sense of community inherent in the theatrical event: "Freedom of movement encourages the formation of groups. At intermission there is socializing, patterns of friends speaking with each other, and even chances for strangers to meet each other and strike up relationships."[10] Schechner suggests including the intermission as part of the performance, for instance, having a discussion or providing entertainment of a different kind. But in any case, "You don't want to throw away that social moment, and just have them forget about the performance."

For *Road*, by Jim Cartwright, the first act ended with the characters dancing, and the audience was implicitly invited to join in during intermission. According to Simon Curtis, who directed the production, the actors and spectators are

> all dancing together. There's no difference between a real disco and that. The audience who don't want to dance are panicking, like they

would if they were in a real dance hall. Extroverts are dancing, like they would in a real dance hall. Characters and actors are *tête à tête* in a Northern town hall, blending together in a perfect moment. I loved that.

Involving the audience is not the domain of one approach to theatre, and is not to be achieved by only one technique. Theatre artists differ widely on how audience involvement is to be achieved: what some consider involving, others consider distancing. One should decide, however, to what extent one wants the audience involved in the production, and then how to manipulate the theatrical variables to achieve the desired effect.

## NOTES

1. Tyrone Guthrie, "Argument for the Open Stage," *World Theatre* 13 (1964): 81–82.
2. Tyrone Guthrie, *A Life in the Theatre* (New York: McGraw-Hill, 1959) 349.
3. Tyrone Guthrie, *In Various Directions* (New York: Macmillan, 1965) 69–70.
4. James Marston Fitch, "For the Theatrical Experience, an Architecture of Truth," *Theatre Design and Technology* 16 (1969): 17.
5. Iain Mackintosh, "Old and New: The Rejection of the Fan-Shaped Auditorium and the Reinstatement of the Courtyard Form," *Theatre Design and Technology* 14 (1978): 15, 24.
6. Robert Edmond Jones, *The Dramatic Imagination* (New York: Theatre Arts Books, 1941) 46.
7. Richard Southern, "Unusual Forms of Stage," *Actor and Architect*, ed. Stephen Joseph (Manchester, Eng.: Manchester UP, 1964) 48.
8. Guthrie, "Argument" 82.
9. Jack Kroll, "Cocktail Party," *Newsday* 4 Dec. 1978: 131.
10. Richard Schechner, "On Environmental Design," *Educational Theatre Journal* 23 (1971): 390.

# CHAPTER 5

# THE PROSCENIUM ARCH'S
# EFFECT ON PERFORMANCE

The size and shape of any theatre greatly affects the production, but a particular proscenium theatre has less effect than a particular open stage. There are generic effects of a proscenium theatre, but the proscenium frame can be manipulated to suit the particular production, minimizing the effect of the individual theatre's architecture.

The audience in a proscenium theatre views the stage essentially from one direction. The proscenium frame and the masking control the view of the stage, so that the audience sees only the portion chosen by the designer. The production therefore does not have to relate to the architectural features of the stage, such as the side and back walls, or to the auditorium. The production can lead an existence relatively autonomous from the space it inhabits. The effects of a particular proscenium may include only tinkering for proper sightlines and masking, and creating methods for shifting the scenery in the given amount of space. As Marjorie Bradley Kellogg, a designer, observes, "In a proscenium, you've got a frame around the set, and the frame is what you are dealing with. Anything that goes on behind the frame is so flexible that one is the same as the other. All you really need to know is the size of it." According to designer Hugh Landwehr, the proscenium is "more neutral, so in a way one has to worry about it less. It's a frame, and even if it's loaded down with gilt, it's not going to intrude in the same way that a thrust will."

## UNIFORMITY OF PROSCENIUM THEATRES

The advantage of proscenium-arch theatres for directors and designers is that they tend to be more uniform than thrusts. The model proscenium theatre for many years and across the United States has been the Broadway theatre. Though the design of Broadway theatres was strongly influenced by the high real estate prices of Times Square, far-flung cities and towns adopted the form, in part so that the theatre could readily house touring productions "direct from Broadway." Robin Wagner points out that the Shubert theatres, "built over a long time span and with many architects," have similar stage dimensions: 35′ from the curtain line to the back wall; a 40′-wide and 24′-high proscenium, and 20′ of wing space on each side. As Wagner explains: "That's a box, and in that box has gone the American theatre in our memory." Though many proscenium theatres vary from these dimensions, the proportions and sizes are extremely common.

This relative uniformity can be very helpful to the designer and director. In many cases, they may not know which theatre a production will be performed in, or a production may transfer from one to another. The designer can create the set with the standard proscenium in mind, and then adapt it to the specifics of the particular theatre. John Lee Beatty asserts that he "could design a show and it could fit into some ten different proscenium theatres without much visible difference." If a production is moved from one proscenium theatre to another similar theatre, the designer can often simply adjust the masking to the new proscenium dimensions.

## THE PROSCENIUM AS A FLEXIBLE THEATRE

Some directors and designers maintain that the most flexible theatre form—the one able to present the greatest variety of plays and styles of production—is the proscenium. David Potts believes that the proscenium is the most flexible "because it allows you stylistically to go any way you want," i.e., staying within the picture frame or breaking it, and using minimal or elaborate scenery. This flexibility in performance style means that the proscenium "will accommodate more variety of plays than any other form."

The proscenium frame may also be best for the creation of illusion and magic. The frame hides the "magician's strings," so the audience does not see how the "tricks" are created. Robert Kalfin, a director, comments, "Someone can appear or disappear through the floor or come down from the flies, or in from the sides. There are places to magically transform people and objects. To make magic, you need all of the support of space around you, under you, and over you."

In that a curtain can be opened to reveal an unexpected sight, the proscenium is also best for a surprise effect. David Mitchell sees the framing of the proscenium as helpful to his work as a designer because "behind that proscenium arch anything can happen. You can be totally surprised each time the curtain goes up, even though it is an illusion. Its capacity for surprise is infinite."


## USE OF AN APRON

Some theatre artists believe that the proscenium stage is the most physically adaptable form, in that most of the advantages of the thrust stage can be gained by adding a forestage or apron in front of the proscenium arch. Peter Moro, for instance, says that an apron

> permits the action to intrude into the audience or retract from it into the stage space, partially or wholly. The possibility of an actor crossing from one space into the other, from the world of the stage into the world of the audience, is still theatrically one of the most powerful devices.[1]

Others argue that an apron in front of a proscenium gives the worst of both forms, in that the action may still need to occur amidst the environment of the scenery, and therefore upstage of the apron. In this case, the apron becomes a barrier that distances the audience from the actors. Richard Southern explains that the apron

> is a deceiver—promising much to the trusting when the plans were made, but fulfilling nothing—save that all full stage scenes forever afterwards must be played on an area from which the audience is divorced four (or more) feet farther away than it otherwise need be.

No wonder it has got about that a forestage is an obstacle to actor-audience intimacy, rather than a promoter of it! [2]

In addition, an apron does not change the architecture of the theatre—the essential audience-actor relationship. While an apron may offer some features of a thrust, the relationship is still fundamentally that of a proscenium. As Tyrone Guthrie maintains, an apron

fails to solve the main problem because behind this dignified forestage there remains a proscenium arch; and inside that arch—here's the rub—is a perfectly conventional stage, framed by the arch which the whole audience faces, inside which they have been conditioned to expect 'a picture.' So long as that picture frame remains, some kind of a picture has to be put inside it.[3]

## TOTAL UNIFORM EFFECT

Proponents of the proscenium arch promote this form as the most conducive to what Harold Burris-Meyer and Edward C. Cole call "total uniform effect":

Maximum appreciation and enjoyment of, and in a very real sense participation in, the theatre experience by each individual member of the audience depends upon maximum enjoyment of it by the entire audience. Group reaction to a single performance stimulus is something less than total unless the stimulus be perceived *at the same time, in the same measure, and with the same significance by the entire group.*

. . . The best efforts of theatre artists stand the best chance of appreciative reception by audiences if the audience-performance relationship fosters total uniform stimulus and reaction, hereinafter called *total uniform effect.*

Following from this premise is the conclusion that the proscenium theatre "is the form most conducive to the production of total uniform effect." In the open stage theatre, "it is unavoidable that viewpoints will be maximally different and it becomes impossible for directors and actors to compose the performance so as to produce total uniform effect."[4]

## FOCUS

One advantage frequently claimed for the proscenium stage is that the director and designer can control the focus better than on any other theatre form. In the open stage, the spectators view the performance from many different angles, making it impossible for the director and designer to present the same image to the entire audience. The varied angles of the open stage make focusing the production more difficult: what is foreground to one spectator may be background to another, and vice versa. But on the proscenium stage, the viewing angles are greatly narrowed, so the director can compose a picture with the confidence that a greater portion of the audience will perceive it as intended. As Stephen Porter explains, "In the proscenium, when there are six people on the stage, it's wonderful to be able to control exactly what the audience sees, so they all see the same thing at that same moment. It controls—to be frank about it—the laughs." Porter notes, for instance, that a simple turn of the head can be perceived by everyone and provoke a reaction. On the proscenium stage the director can use "visual composition," "tell your story by composition, as Giotto does," and "control primary focus on somebody and secondary focus on somebody else" by placement of the actors. The director can achieve these effects "only if the people are seeing roughly the same thing."

Arvin Brown, artistic director of Long Wharf Theatre, observes that on a proscenium stage "every movement is heightened by this power of focus—and I mean every movement, every gesture." According to director Tony Tanner, this powerful focus derives from the "four arrows" in a proscenium arch, one in each corner, "saying, 'Look! This is where you look!'"

For example, Jerry Zaks says that when *The House of Blue Leaves,* by John Guare, transferred from the Vivian Beaumont thrust to the Plymouth proscenium,

> it was much easier to control the focus. There was the satisfaction of knowing that at the moment I wanted the audience to be looking at Bunny, then Artie, then Bananas, and then back to Bunny, I knew it was happening. In the Beaumont, it took more work. It demanded greater discipline from the actors. The slightest tick at the wrong moment could destroy the story of a non-verbal moment.

Farce benefits particularly from this intense focus. In this very physical form of comedy, many jokes depend upon the audience seeing a very specific event. According to Ron Lagomarsino,

> Ideally in farce, everybody sees everything at the same time. That's why I think proscenium is best for farce, because the audience is such a key participant in the comic machine. Something makes an audience laugh, and you get that pistol-fire response, and you move on. Often in three-quarter, people will be seeing things at a different time and therefore the response is unpredictable.

Jonathan Miller argues that farce needs the flatness and artificiality of a proscenium stage:

> Farce is a mechanical device that depends on a sort of ledge-like format. It is as mechanical as those processions that pass on a shallow stage in those clockwork devices in sixteenth-century south German towns. Therefore there has to be an extremely sharp edge to make that device work. Farce is totally mechanical anyway, and therefore you need something that sharply delineates the margin of what is mechanical and then what is not.

## PROBLEMATIC PROSCENIUMS

While these general characteristics apply to most standard, Broadway-type theatres, not all prosceniums are alike. In fact there are wide variations from the standard type, and the designer and director must carefully note these deviations. It may be a trap to assume that any given proscenium is like any other, and that the architecture can be ignored. While this uniformity may often be the case, there are specific variations to watch out for.

### Sightlines from the Side Seats

Use of the upstage area in a proscenium theatre is restricted by the sightlines from the extreme side seats. While the stage may be rectangular, the upstage left and right corners may be of limited usefulness. The area fully visible to the audience may in fact be a triangle. Jo Mielziner, while designing the Vivian Beaumont

Theater, studied "hundreds" of Broadway productions in order to
"make a study of where the most dominant action has been located
on the stage." He found that there was "a distinct triangle. The
triangle started a few feet in from each side of the Proscenium and
ran straight across the apron; its apex was located almost center
stage, and not over ten feet back of the setting line."[5]

Mielziner's triangle is commonly used by most directors and
designers on Broadway-type proscenium stages. Melvin
Bernhardt, a director, is "shameless" about keeping action within
the triangle, and will "stage the important things downstage center
whenever possible." He uses other areas of the stage for "variety,"
but for key moments, "I want them down center."

The Asolo Theatre (Sarasota, Fla.) and the Goodspeed Opera
House (New Haddam, Conn.) have horseshoe-shaped auditoriums, with poor sightlines from the side balconies. When he first
directed at the Goodspeed, Thomas Gruenewald's reaction to the
side seats was, "The hell with them if they can't see. I can't
accommodate the production to this silly space." In the course of
seven shows he discovered the Mielziner triangle: "There's a
golden space about 10′ across the front of the proscenium, maybe
8′ deep; a triangle where you can be sure that everybody is going
to see everything." Though parts of the set were outside the
triangle, Gruenewald squeezed all important action within that
zone. For instance, he had the actors "cheat in the zinger exit line
three or four feet" from an upstage door or the edge of the stage,
"so most of the people have a chance at it." He recounts the story
of an actress who always got applause on her exit, but after
Gruenewald had been away for a few weeks, she reported that she
had lost the applause: "I watched it and it was very clear. She was
already 'offstage'; she was dealing with the space as if it were a
normal theatre, which put her essentially offstage. I said to her,
'Travel, stop, say the line, then go.' And the hand returned."

In some cases, seats may have been added to the sides, making
the auditorium wider than originally intended. Beatty points out
that these seats may force the designer to make a box set, for
instance, much wider than it should be in order to open up the
stage to those seated on the extreme sides:

> The room has to be a certain width just to accommodate the
> sightlines, and sometimes it's very hard to find a reason for a small

apartment living room to be 36′ wide. We know from personal experience that they are all about 26′ wide. You then have to have about 10 extra feet that have to be made to look less big.

To make the room look smaller, he suggests breaking up the wall or adding a foyer, even if it is not called for in the script.

Others maintain that one should not sacrifice the overall success of the production for a few bad seats. In this view, the director should gain the optimal effect for the large majority, and then forget the rest. Few admit publicly to this position, but John Tillinger calls the extreme side seats with poor sightlines the "fuck you seats." According to Tillinger, "You just cannot please everybody. They are just people who should have booked earlier." He asks, "What can you do? Suddenly you're directing the whole play for these poor people who are sitting with the wall in front of them." Zaks also feels that one shouldn't compromise what is important in a scene in order to make it available to every single person:

> The people in the seats furthest to the sides are just not going to see exactly the same show as the people in the seats more centrally located. They just won't. I hope they will see enough of it to have that ecstatic experience, whatever that is. But if I try to stage democratically and try to give everyone an equally good show, I end up not serving the play in an attempt to accommodate the less than ideal seats.

## Wide Stage

A theatre in which the proscenium arch is oddly proportioned can also cause problems for the director and designer. Thomas Lynch observes that when the proscenium has a wide opening, the stage "seems to go on and on and on at the sides," resulting in "a placid, disconnected feeling." Designers offer several suggestions to cope with a wide proscenium. One obvious solution is somehow to narrow the opening. David Jenkins recommends using a second portal inside the proscenium: "Design a portal that gives your production its own frame that looks like it belongs to your production and segues from the permanent stage frame to yours."

The designer can also cut down the size of the opening with black masking, but this may result in vast expanses of black on either side of the stage. Instead, Beatty suggests reducing the width of the stage with scenic units. He cautions, however, that these pieces may have to be so large that they become "overwhelming." To avoid this problem, Beatty designs these units to "look like they are just part of the theatre" rather than the scenery, "so that they won't be an overwhelmingly monumental scenic effect."

Landwehr finds it helpful to "iris in" the opening, in order to get "the audience's focus tightened in on an area that's more ideal for the scale of the actors." He offers several ways that this tightened focus may be accomplished: "repeated walls," "a series of carpets," "changes in elevation in plan," or changes in color, i.e., "the color at the center is brighter or more intense than the edge."

A wide stage can be helpful, however, if that shape can enhance the production. Lynch notes that with a wide proscenium, "you can get nice big, broad beautiful pictures." Heidi Landesman suggests the designer may choose to emphasize the width of the frame "to make the horizontal quality of the stage work for the production." According to Landesman, "It's really interesting, because people are not used to a long, low horizontal, so it comes as something of a shock."

## MOMENTS UNIQUE TO THE PROSCENIUM

Like any theatre, the proscenium can produce theatrical moments that are unique. For example, Austin Pendleton describes his production of *Little Foxes,* by Lillian Hellman:

> There was a moment that the whole production was organized around, that you could only make work in a proscenium theatre. When Horace, Regina's husband, comes home from the hospital, all of the people are in having breakfast behind the sliding doors. He went down and stood right in the middle of the stage, all the way downstage, with his back to the audience. Addie and all the other characters come out of the sliding doors, running directly toward the audience and directly toward him—because he was with his back to the audience—to envelop him, to welcome him. They come running out of there, screaming and yelling, right toward us and right to him. You saw these greedy people descending on him, coming right at you and so you had the same experience that he did.

There's no other place but a proscenium theatre that you could have done that. Had we wanted to adapt it, say, to the Long Wharf or Circle in the Square [both thrust stages], we would have had to totally reconceive that, and we would probably have had to lose it.

Gregory Mosher directed Wilder's *Our Town* at the proscenium Lyceum Theatre on Broadway, and says he would find it difficult to direct the play in any other form: "The Stage Manager is leaning against the proscenium arch," which is necessary because one would want "the narrator in an intimate, downstage position." But in a thrust theatre, "there's no proscenium arch." According to Mosher, "There certainly needs to be that bridge between the actors and the audience, physically as well as in every other way." In a thrust, one could place the Stage Manager leaning against the upstage portal frame, but "that is upstage of the action"; one could place him in an aisle, which would gain the effects of intimacy and relating to the permanent architecture of the theatre, but Mosher considers that "a little affected."

## PROSCENIUM CONVENTIONS

Many people criticize the thrust stage for requiring staging conventions, but the proscenium theatre has its own set of conventions. Perhaps because most theatre artists are still more accustomed to the proscenium stage, these conventions seem "natural," as opposed to the "imposing" conventions of the open stage. But Beatty explains that there are "very stringent require-ments" in a proscenium theatre, which he calls "limiting." For instance, there are strict furniture conventions for a realistic play: there will generally be a couch in the middle of the room, facing downstage, with a coffee table in front of it, a table behind it and end tables on either side. Beatty also describes the sightlines necessary for a realistic play in a Broadway theatre, in which first few rows are below the level of the stage:

All the furniture gets taller as you go upstage. You start with a stool or a coffee table downstage, and then the next thing upstage is a desk or a high table, and then the next thing up is the dresser or the bureau, and then the next thing up is the armoire and the bookcase.

Karl Eigsti recounts an "old saying" of Broadway:

> As a rule of thumb when doing a box set on a Broadway theatre, you
> had to have the coffee table kiss the curtain, meaning that when you
> started out with your groundplan, your coffee table was right at the
> curtain line, with the sofa and the chair and everything else fairly
> close behind it.

## USING THE CURTAIN

Another convention of the proscenium arch theatre is the curtain
rising and falling at the beginning and end of each act. According
to Pendleton, the act curtain is "part of a proscenium experience,"
in that it separates the audience from the stage until the moment
that the performance begins:

> The whole point is that it is removed from you. At one end of the
> place that you are in is a magic world that is detached from you, set
> off from you, and the curtain helps to emphasize that. It creates the
> magic of it. If we are going to do it in a proscenium house, let's
> remind the audience that that's what it is.

Pendleton holds that a production in a proscenium theatre should
take the theatre architecture into account as much as in an open
stage. While the audience-performance interaction is not as overt
in a proscenium theatre as in an open stage, it still exists: "It's a
very particular kind of interaction, but it has to be honored, and it
can be honored."

•

The proscenium remains the most common theatre form in
America and Europe today, the one that audiences and theatre
artists are most accustomed to, and the one most taken for granted.
While the individual aspects of the "standard" proscenium have
less impact on production than those of the open stage, clearly the
proscenium, like any theatre form, affects production. It is a
misconception that the proscenium is "neutral" while other forms
"impose" themselves on production. In addition, some proscenium theatres do have particular characteristics that must be
accounted for. The influence of the proscenium must be under-

stood, respected and incorporated into the production—as with any theatre. By recognizing the effects of this common form, and how the proscenium theatre can be exploited for production, theatre artists can more readily see how each and every theatre can be used creatively.

## NOTES

1. Peter Moro, "A. D. Briefing: Theatres," *Architectural Design* 43 (1973): 167.
2. Richard Southern, *The Open Stage and the Modern Theatre in Research and Practice* (London: Faber and Faber, 1953) 67.
3. Guthrie, *Life* 206–7.
4. Harold Burris-Meyer and Edward C. Cole, *Theatres and Auditoriums,* 2nd ed. (New York: Reinhold, 1964) 128, 130.
5. Jo Mielziner, *The Shapes of Our Theatre* (New York: Clarkson N. Potter, 1970) 132–4.

# CHAPTER 6

# COMPARING PERFORMANCE ON
# OPEN AND PROSCENIUM STAGES

Should the style of the production derive from the theatre space or from the play? To some extent, the answer must be both: the production should be appropriate to the play and harmonious with the theatre. But individual theatre artists tend to give more weight to one or the other. Some argue that the form of the theatre space dictates a specific style; the production should therefore follow that style, while still taking into account the nature of the play. Specifically, this position has it that a proscenium theatre results in an illusionistic production, while an open stage results in one that is presentational. Others maintain that the production should be based almost entirely on the play, and that any style can be made to work in any space.

Definitions of theatrical styles are tricky and slippery; in fact, some argue that one cannot define styles of performance. With that caveat in mind, I offer working definitions that can and will be undermined. "Illusionism" is applied to a production in which the spectators are meant to imagine, with a willing suspension of disbelief, that what they are seeing onstage is an illusion of reality. The production is "realistic" insofar as what the spectators see onstage matches their mental image of observable reality, or at least how theatre represents that reality. A "presentational" style, on the other hand, refers to a production that emphasizes the theatricality of the performance, in which the spectators are deliberately made aware that what they are seeing is an artificial, artistic creation.

## OPEN STAGE: PRESENTATIONAL
## PROSCENIUM: ILLUSIONISTIC

In a proscenium theatre, the audience and the performance are in two different rooms, with the audience looking through an opening into the other space; in an open stage theatre, the audience and performance share one space and are under one roof. According to Ming Cho Lee, a designer, this architectural distinction determines the nature and reception of the production. On the open stage,

> it is not illusionistic theatre. It's a platform and you come on and do the play. The fact that you are in the same room, under the same ceiling, makes the representational or illusionistic approach to the work almost impossible. The architecture is going to fight against it.

Theatre artists who believe that different stage forms require different production styles use various terms to express this distinction. Ming believes that on the open stage "you have to *present* reality, you have to present the real thing." Ming calls this style "real," not "realistic." The designer can pull off illusionistic design stunts on the proscenium stage, using materials to represent something else, but on an open stage Ming would "think three times before using styrofoam to look like gravel."

Michael Yeargan describes his technique for a "presentational" production on an open stage: "It is as if you take a platter; on that you put these objects and you present it to someone, and usually you tip it a little bit. You have a raked floor with objects on it that say, 'I'm a real fireplace. I'm a real stove.' It is as real as you can make it."

John Jensen expresses the difference between designing for the proscenium and the open stage in terms of "illusion" and "allusion":

> Traditional proscenium design leans to illusion, whereas on the open stage, you can select and suggest, because the convention exists and is accepted that all of the walls are removed—not just the fourth wall. Those people sitting right and left are looking at the rest of the audience. A whole bay window onstage is replaced by a simpler gesture to suggest the window. It can be an allusion to a window. A window seat may really count for a whole room, even a very elaborate room if you carefully design it to describe the room's character and allow the actor to approach and use the unit appropriately.

Even starting down the path of illusionism on the open stage may be dangerous, in that this course opens questions that are best not addressed. According to Karl Eigsti,

One of the worst things you can do is to define too carefully, in terms of conventional architecture, where everything is. You want to know that if the actors are going down 'vom one,' they are going to the kitchen, or the bathroom, or the bedroom, or outside. Obviously you have to define that to a certain extent. But when you put up a door frame and they have to go through it to get to that place, then you are creating a barrier. You are creating a wall to the audience through which they see the play. Then it becomes increasingly difficult for the audience to participate.

Illusionism may simply fail to be effective on the thrust or arena stage, making the presentational approach preferable. Ming points out that the visible technical apparatus of the open stage makes illusionism unattainable, in that the audience can see the means by which the illusion is created: "When you are sitting in the same room, all the mechanics—the functional things that create the show—are all in view. You cannot mask those things off."

In addition, sightline problems may doom illusionistic techniques on an open stage. In a proscenium theatre, the designer can successfully employ illusionistic devices to represent reality because of the relatively controlled viewpoint. But in an open stage theatre, the spectators view the stage from many directions, so illusionistic effects may fall apart. Perspective effects may not work for spectators on the sides of a thrust stage, and parts of the scenery may be entirely invisible to them. Some designers have tried using illusionistic devices, particularly forced perspective, on the thrust stage of the Guthrie Theatre: Jensen observes that "they worked for two-thirds of the audience, but there was one-third for whom the technique did not work. The illusion became distortion."

Another practical problem is the proximity of the audience to the stage: the audience as a whole in an open-stage theatre is closer to the stage than in a proscenium theatre. On the open stage, therefore, the designer does not have the distance to pull off certain tricks. According to Michel Saint-Denis, "Verisimilitude as well as magic needs distance. Both depend upon a physical separation between the public and the stage."[1] John Gassner believes that a distinct separation between audience and performance is necessary:

Only an actual gulf between the stage and the auditorium can sustain the illusion of a distinctive environment. Only a spectator who is physically separated from the stage can function as a detached observer and can partake of the illusion that the stage is an environment. And only the actor who can ignore the audience can consistently treat his stage as an environment rather than a platform on which to play to the audience.[2]

Seeing the audience on the other side of the stage may also undermine efforts toward an illusionistic effect. Ming states, "In the arena stage, illusionistic production is impossible because you are looking at other people, and so the picture is not there; it isn't really a picture."

As for the proscenium theatre, many maintain that this stage form is uniquely suited to illusionism. George Izenour, a theatre consultant, declares, "The proscenium theatre is an illusionistic theatre, and I think it is wrong to think that it was ever intended to be anything else." Santo Loquasto suggests that the proscenium theatre is the most practical stage for achieving an illusionistic effect: "If you want to create pure illusion, choose the proscenium stage. You can achieve effects more successfully because the audience is viewing essentially from one vantage point with all the machinery contained within the floor and ceiling."

Some directors and designers feel that the proscenium arch not only encourages a pictorial approach, it is in fact a frame that demands filling. According to Tyrone Guthrie,

> In a 'picture-frame' theatre it is impossible not to put a picture in the frame. The whole intention of the building's design is to isolate and emphasize a visual impression. Even if the picture is of the simplest, least representational character, the actors are seen against this particular background; it cannot be excluded from the audience's attention; it has perforce to be an important element of the performance.[3]

The illusionistic tendency of the proscenium is so strong that some designers maintain that any attempt at a presentational approach is difficult at best; the result may even end up being illusionistic. According to Ming, in a proscenium theatre, "When you are looking through an opening you almost have to fight the pictorial, illusionistic approach in order to create a presentational production." Thomas Lynch states that in a proscenium theatre, a presentational design often collapses into an illusionistic effect. If you are trying to do something really pulled apart and bare-bones and Brechtian, you always get stuck with this problem of an illusion, no matter what you are doing, and you keep feeling that it is not what you wanted.

## NO DIFFERENCE IN STYLES

To other directors and designers, there is no inherent, stylistic difference between the proscenium and the open stage. Illusionism is possible on the open stage and presentationalism is possible on the proscenium. The designer/director should choose a style and a theatre, independent of each other, based on what will best serve the play. Robin Wagner maintains that either approach can work in either theatre: the designer can create a "picture" and use fourth-wall techniques on an open stage, in which actors and audience both pretend it is an illusion of reality—"a pact, in which both participate."

Jacques Levy cites an example of using the proscenium in a deliberately presentational way for his production of *Oh, Calcutta!* (devised by Kenneth Tynan), in which the opening number involved a brightly lit "satiric strip tease":

> Up there, on the stage, distant from you, framed, beautifully lit, these ten people came out on the stage. It was *presented* to you, as opposed to part of your environment. It was for you to look *at* and experience in that way: 'This is not an informal act. This is a formal act. This is a declaration that says something.' It all takes place within the frame, and in that sense the actors become bigger than life, and more extraordinary than life, not just life.

In addition, it may be possible to achieve illusionistic effects on the open stage, in fact better and more thoroughly than behind a proscenium. When performing a realistic production on an open stage, actors can employ softer voices and smaller gestures, which may be perceived as more "natural." Furthermore, the need for actors to "face front" in a proscenium theatre, considered artificial by some, is obviated in thrust or arena theatres. While the blocking techniques of open stages are also rigorous and artificial, the fact that actors can face various sides, rather than play predominantly in one direction, has often been perceived as more "natural."

Stephen Joseph writes that one can achieve "an intensity of truth . . . between the actors, whose movements and relationships can be real."[4] Joseph also claims that actors can still use "fourth-wall" techniques and create a sense of reality on an arena stage:

> If the actors play to each other (and not to the audience), if they move and speak with concentration on the relationship between them and with no apparent regard for the audience, then this small vision of reality has an absorbing and tremendous appeal.[5]

This illusion of reality may be achievable on the open stage because audiences are now used to the conventions of that theatre form; they are willing and able to use their imaginations to fill in what is missing. If the theatre artists invite the spectators to engage their imaginations, not only is less scenery required, but the audience will enjoy this active participation in the creation of the production's "environment." Tony Tanner directed *The Mousetrap,* by Agatha Christie, for an arena theatre, a situation he calls "a real bugger." The murder mystery seems to require "the whole sense of being enclosed, with shadowy paneled sets and doors that go bang." He feels, though, that the production was successful because people are accustomed to the alternative conventions of the open stage:

> They're used to making advances. They're used to using their imaginations, coming half way to meet everybody, and they usually have a wonderful time. What you depend on in those situations is the good will of the audience, the fact that they're prepared to make these leaps in the dark on your behalf.

Other psychological reactions of the audience may also create an illusionistic effect. According to Arvin Brown, the difference between the stage forms is in the audience's ability to willingly suspend its disbelief:

> Realism in the three-quarter demands a powerful suspension of disbelief that the proscenium, after the first moment or two, does not demand. We are much more likely to accept a picture that is at some distance from us as having a reality that is complete, once we get past that initial stage.

This initial disbelief can be overcome in any theatre form, albeit in different ways:

> When the curtain goes up on a proscenium stage, gradually there is the suspension of disbelief and the spectators are inside the picture frame, to a certain extent—whatever extent the play is successful.
> When the lights go up on a three-quarter stage, there is the sudden distancing of the bright lights and the people in much closer proximity to them than they would be in a proscenium. Then, once that suspension of disbelief is bridged, the involvement can sometimes be extraordinarily powerful.

Brown believes that the key to spurring this suspension of disbelief on the open stage is to maintain a separation from the audience:

> When there is a kind of scrupulous distance that is maintained from the audience to the actor once the stage lights have gone up, then the sense of surround, the sense of closeness, the sense of camera-like detail in acting terms, takes on a new reality, a reality of its own. When one is lost in that reality, there is an experience that can have about it a tremendous power, almost a voyeuristic sensation.

Judicious use of realistic scenic elements may also create an illusionistic effect. Lowell Detweiler uses the "duck test" for determining whether the setting is illusionistic or not: "If the floor is real and the furniture is real and the juxtaposition of them all is real, you've got real. You don't need a surround."

In order to pass the duck test, however, the scenic elements may need to be more detailed than on a proscenium, requiring greater precision to make the props and scenery plausibly real at close range. John Lee Beatty says that the "tactile quality of thrust scenery has to be greater. It has to be touchable by the actors. And, since people are sitting around it, it has to be finished on all four sides, and it ends up having to be much more dimensional."

Eldon Elder points out that sets on the open stage tend to use more "real materials" than those on the proscenium in order to achieve an illusionistic effect:

> If you are going to make an appropriate environment, if it isn't honest, truthful and real, the audience can sense it immediately

because they can be as close as three or four feet away. You can paint something on canvas for the proscenium stage that on the thrust [stage] you have to build with real wood and brick, or good simulation brick.

The degree to which the scenography imitates observable reality need not be constant for all aspects of the production, however. At the Guthrie Theatre, according to Detweiler, the approach is to make those elements that the performers interact with the most realistic; the production then becomes more abstract as it works away from the actor. Most important, he says, is the actor's head, therefore making wigs and makeup important; next is the actor's body, so costumes are second; next important is what the actor touches, putting props third; what the actor walks on—the floor—is fourth, and last is the set. Detweiler explains the rationale for this approach:

A four-million-dollar set, a fabulous production design can be ruined by a bad wig. A bad wig makes it all look like high school. But a bad wig on a proscenium stage is very different than a bad wig on a thrust stage: A couple of steps away from the audience and you can get away with a lot more.

Hugh Landwehr observes that while detailed realism may seem necessary because of the close proximity of the audience, this approach may remove some of the mystery from a play: "If you load down a play like *The Glass Menagerie* with the minutiae of their apartment, haven't you put something in the way of the poetry of the play?" Landwehr advises that the close proximity of the audience should be taken into account in the precision of the design, but it does not dictate a style: "I don't think it means that you can't use other styles besides hyper-realism. Detail in some way may really need to be present, but maybe it is just detail of texture and painting, as opposed to objects." Landwehr points out the irony that the thrust stage, which started out in the twentieth century as an avant-garde form related to ritual and mystery, has become "the ultimate bourgeois theatre, because you can count all those things on stage, and you can see the materials; you know what it all costs."

## PROSCENIUM: PLANES
## OPEN STAGE: THREE-DIMENSIONAL

Illusion versus presentation is not the only way of looking at the differences between the proscenium and open stages. The audience's orientation to the proscenium stage may make the production take on a two-dimensional, planar quality, while a production on the open stage may appear more sculptural. Because the audience views a proscenium production from one direction and through a frame, Eigsti suggests that the audience sees the stage as a picture: "In the proscenium space what you're looking at is a series of overlapping planes, and essentially you design that way. You see through one thing to another, through that one to another, through that one to another."

It is difficult for an audience to gauge the actual depth of the stage behind a proscenium arch, which is why overlapping planes can manipulate depth perception. This difficulty also means, however, that simply using the actual stage depth with actors or scenery moving up- or downstage will not give the spectator a strong sense of movement. Beatty explains that in a proscenium theatre,

> your perception of up- and downstage distance is very warped; you can't really tell. You can measure left to right very easily, but up- and downstage the difference between four and six feet is hardly noticeable. That is why scenery in a proscenium theatre that is moving downstage towards the audience isn't normally as exciting as scenery that is moving from the sides, because you can't really see how far it is moving.

Using overlapping planes can be especially helpful for giving the illusion of depth on a shallow stage. Circle Rep has a very shallow end stage, and often produces realistic plays needing an impression of vast space. Beatty, who has designed there countless times, tries to "give the illusion of layers of depth on the up- and downstage axis" by "breaking the stage into areas." He explains, "It gives different planes to relate to, and therefore you get a sense of more depth."

Beatty has found that he can employ the scenic devices of the proscenium stage at Circle Rep to give the illusion of depth, even though the audience is close and in the same space as the stage:

I didn't see why I couldn't do forced perspective, with slanted walls and slanted floors and slanted ceilings, which would not be your normal choice in that space. The audience is conscious that the technique of forced perspective has been used, but still, even though they are conscious of it, their eyes cannot divorce the information that they have been given. You can say, 'Yes, it is forced perspective, and it looks artificial,' but it still makes it look bigger, nonetheless.

Directors also tend to view their work more sculpturally on the open stage and more pictorially on the proscenium. Joseph maintains that on the open stage, "the actor can be seen to be a three-dimensional being, belonging to a three-dimensional world," whereas "behind a frame, on an enclosed stage, even the best of actors is flattened."[6] According to Mark Lamos, the thrust stage "requires a much more sculptural sense of stage picture, whereas the proscenium is like dealing with a canvas; it's flatter."

One reason the open stage may have a more "sculptural" effect is that the audience perceives the space as more three-dimensional. The spectators share the same space with the performance and they may surround the stage, to a greater or lesser degree. Being close to the action and seeing spectators on the other side may increase this perception of three-dimensionality. Eigsti says that the open stage is more sculptural "because everybody has a different point of view. The perspective of the seer is constantly at a different angle, so you are not viewing it frontally any more. You are viewing it from a surround."

•

The differences in approach between the open stage and the proscenium come down to the taste of the theatre artists involved and the practical necessities of the architectural form. The proscenium does frame a picture, does provide greater focus and does entail greater distance from the audience as compared to the open stage. In an open stage theater the audience is closer and wraps around the stage more than in a proscenium. In addition, sightline problems limit the height, size and placement of scenic elements. These differences in the nature of the space will entail certain practical production choices that result in different styles. The proscenium production will tend to be more focused and more pictorial in its effect. The open-stage production will tend to be more environmental, intimate and seen in greater detail. But to label these practical results as "presentational" or "illusionistic" seems to limit the theatre artists' aesthetic choices and imply an architectural dictatorship that does not exist.

The theatre artist should be aware of the practical requirements that result from the architecture, and shape the production accordingly. The Guthrie approach, for instance, seems a sensible response to the architecture: deal with the fact that the actor will be seen close up, but avoid any gesture toward creating an illusionistic set that the open stage cannot achieve.


## NOTES

1. Michel Saint-Denis, *The Rediscovery of Style* (New York: n.p., 1960) 58.
2. John Gassner, *Form and Idea in the Modern Theatre* (New York: Dryden Press) 55–56.
3. Tyrone Guthrie, "Shakespearean Production," *The Year's Work in the Theatre 1949–50* (London: Longmans, Green: [1951?]) 38.
4. Stephen Joseph, "Arenas and All That," *Twentieth Century* 169 (1961): 114.
5. Joseph, *Round* 155.
6. Stephen Joseph, *New Theatre Forms* (New York: Theatre Arts Books, 1968) 65.

# CHAPTER 7

# DESIGNING FOR THE OPEN STAGE: PROBLEMS AND SOLUTIONS

While the characteristics of an individual "standard" proscenium will not have a significant impact on performance (see Chapter 5), the effects of the individual open stage are enormous. First, there is no "standard" size or shape to the open stage. And because the stage is partially or wholly encircled by the audience, that entire size and shape is visible and must be accounted for. Second, the degree of the audience's encirclement varies greatly, from semi-thrust, to three-quarter thrust, to arena. Third, because the stage is in the middle of the room, the entire space—not just the stage—must be taken into account for the production. There are generic effects of the open stage on performance, but, because each open stage theatre is unique, the individual effects of the particular theatre are far more important.

The effects of the open stage on design are often viewed as limitations, especially by detractors of the form. No doubt, the open stage does impose limitations when compared to the proscenium theatre. But these limitations do not mean that the designer cannot exploit the open stage for scenic effects.

## REALISM

### Requirements of Realism

A play that requires, or seems to require, a realistic approach or scenic effects poses the greatest challenge on the open stage. As Santo Loquasto explains,

> The trick is that you have to design a lot of plays where people sit and talk in a living room or around a card table. We all want to think

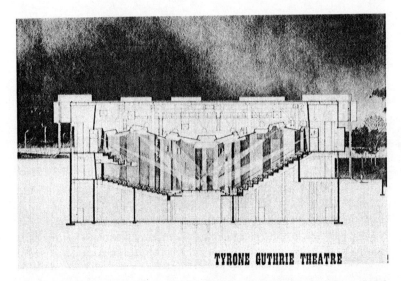

TYRONE GUTHRIE THEATRE

7. Plan and section of the Guthrie Theater, Minneapolis. Architect: Ralph Rapson. Consultants: Tyrone Guthrie, Tanya Moiseiwitsch, Jean Rosenthal, Robert F. Lambert. From Tyrone Guthrie, *A New Theatre* (1964), McGraw-Hill. Reproduced with permission of McGraw-Hill.

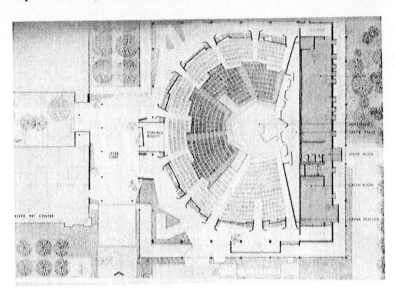

8. View of the Guthrie Theater, Minneapolis. Reproduced with permission of the Guthrie Theater.

of a thrust design as an exquisite rake with two attenuated trees upstage. Well, every few years you get to do one of those plays, if you're lucky. Usually you are dealing with people talking while they unwrap Chinese takeout, and you have to find as much importance in that as you would two people discussing Galileo's thoughts. It's much harder, and it's even harder to make it interesting.

For instance, designer Zack Brown states that *The Man Who Came to Dinner*, by Moss Hart and George S. Kaufman, "demands verisimilitude of detail and many entrances, but there are only so many places to put the details and entrances" on a thrust stage.

One of the greatest problems on an open stage is attempting to create illusions relying on perspective or *trompe l'oeil* (see Chapter 6 for a full discussion of the problems of illusionism on the open stage). Lowell Detweiler points out, however, that this problem applies primarily to "vista" plays:

When you need a vista, when it is important that you see something
on the stage that needs illusion, then you have got problems. For an
Agatha Christie play—where you may have to see something
outside a window for the play to work—you've got real problems
in-the-round. It's arrogant to ignore the demands of the play. If the
play's demands are real, then it has got to be real.

Creating a realistic atmosphere or environment for the play may
also present a scenic challenge for the open stage. Martin
Gottfried writes,

> Chekhov is devoted to absolute realism. It is *about* realism. It
> demands a stage look faithful to life's—the daylight streaming
> through the windows must look real as real; leaves must flutter in
> the breeze; a parlor must look, in every detail, like a parlor. Such
> stage design is impossible on a thrust stage, which severely limits
> furniture, flats and props. . . . This can be ruinous for Chekhov.[1]

On the open stage, one also may lose the claustrophobic,
enclosed feeling that can be achieved in a proscenium theatre.
Jack Gelber, a director, believes that Williams' *A Streetcar
Named Desire* "depends on a kind of hot, steamy, insular,
claustrophobic humanity piled on humanity. To open it up and
direct it out is to destroy one of the things the play is trying to do."

When considering the proper theatre space for a play, one tends
to think of the onstage space, but John Lee Beatty points out that
many plays written for the proscenium arch also depend on readily
accessible, ample offstage space:

> We forget in arena staging how much a play is serviced from
> offstage in a proscenium theatre. If you have ever designed *A
> Streetcar Named Desire*, you know that the whole show basically
> feeds out of the bathroom. There are an enormous number of
> costume and prop changes, and the bathroom door, oddly enough,
> usually becomes the place from which people come out during the
> blackouts.
>   You get into an arena and all of a sudden people are traveling
> twenty feet further to get onto the stage to do these changes, and
> there is not a hidden place where you can stack up all the tons of
> props that these plays really take—even though they give the
> illusion of being very simple.

## Expense

Illusionism, relying more on substance and less on imagination, may be achievable on the open stage, but at a substantial cost. In the early days of modern thrusts and arenas, proponents claimed that production costs would be greatly reduced because the open stage would require less scenery. But Beatty, well-known for his realistic, elaborate sets on both open and proscenium stages, explains the flaws in this argument, and why the promise of economy hasn't always panned out:

> Often the open stage makes the scenery more expensive, partly because you can't fake anything. Everything has to be finished on four sides because it's seen on four sides. The chair has to be seen from all four sides, so you can't put a brace away from the audience. You have to upholster the back of the sofa and you can't hide things behind it.
>
> Often in a 'sofa play' on a proscenium stage, you can put some old orange crates behind the sofa for a table, and nobody knows because nobody can see it. But you go into a thrust and every piece of furniture has to be acceptable, visible from all sides and self-supporting. You can't cheat nearly as much, and that can be very expensive.
>
> Also people are closer to a lot on things. In a thrust or round, I usually find that the upholstery has to be better; you can't cut corners as much.

## Doors and Windows

Such a simple requirement as doors and windows may be especially problematic on an open stage. On a thrust, doors and windows may all have to be on the back wall, which may pull too much of the action upstage. Actors can mime the action of opening and closing doors or windows, but this conceit may be jarring if other actions are not mimed. John Jensen found that at the Guthrie Theatre,

> if a play is wed to doors and windows, then I think you have a real problem as to how to do it, because on the three-quarter stage it means you have to put all those upstage—by necessity. That means that some of the major magnets for the activity, ones that draw the

actors out into the space, are where you least want them to be. They are pulling the actors away from the audience and back into the setting, rather than pulling them forward and releasing them out into the space.

Doors and windows are frequently required in farce, which may pose significant problems on the open stage. Even though farce is a highly artificial, contrived form, it needs a solid underpinning of belief and reality. Tony Tanner states that English sex farces need

> walls and doors that don't shake and have a solid, bourgeois, Victorian realism, because that's the society that we're trapped in. It's the pressure in farce that makes it funny. It's the risk of discovery at any point. What makes it funny is the pressure of trying to conceal something in a big armoire, behind a door, or behind a bed.

Basil Langton underlines the importance of solid doors in a story about a production of *13 Rue de l'Amour*, by Georges Feydeau, at Circle in the Square (Uptown), with Louis Jourdan:

> We built a false door down at one end. Of course, the doors are the essential thing. I begged the technical director to build it as strong as he could, and he didn't. We came to the first preview, and the door completely collapsed and fell on stage, and we didn't have a door. Of course, Louis Jourdan was absolutely wonderful. When the door fell in and was totally useless, Louis just turned to the audience, still very much in character, and said, 'You will have to imagine a door, and when I go, "Click, click," that means I've locked it.' And he did, and it worked wonderfully.

While these problems cannot be solved, the issues must be addressed. On an arena, or the downstage side of a thrust, entrances and exits may be through the voms. Placing doors there, however, may cause sightlines problems. A simple door frame may be used, but a door frame just standing in space may look odd. In addition, the partial realism of a door frame may be inconsistent with the overall style of the production. Beatty calls door frames "a big cheat," because they "indicate things that really would be there if the audience didn't have to see through it." Beatty also points out that simply reducing or eliminating some scenery because of sightlines problems can cause stylistic inconsistencies: "You can't blend a non-door with a door. You can't have three real doors and then fake the fourth door, either by mime or just having people go offstage." Another problem with a door frame is that the audience may see "behind" the door, ruining the elements of surprise and concealment.

Another choice on an open stage is simply to do without doors in any form: real, partial or imagined. John Falabella recommends that the designer can "make the space such that a door would be there; a door would make sense, just by the movement that you create."

An arena stage may have one advantage over the thrust in the door department. The audience in an arena theatre implicitly knows that architectural realism is unattainable, and therefore does not expect it; but in a thrust theatre, the existence of a scenic back wall leads the audience to expect a complete scenic environment. According to Falabella,

> The audience in a full round goes with you a little. They will say, 'Okay, I know there's really a door there. I know that this play should have doors,' and they will accept it. An audience is very willing to suspend their disbelief in something like that, if the stage works.

## Selective Realism

Rather than create a complete scenic environment, such as might be designed for a proscenium stage, the designer can pare down to the absolute essentials for the play, a style known as "selective realism." This approach need not be looked at as a limitation, but can be a stylistic choice. The designer may be able to focus the production on the essentials—the very essence—of the play, and dispense with what might be considered clutter. The set consists simply of a few, well-chosen pieces that are necessary for the action, as well as to convey the style and tone of the production. Tony Walton suggests that when designing for the open stage, one should look for the "basic necessities that the performer must have in order to achieve the requirements" of the play.

The nature of the "realism" in many late-nineteenth-century plays may not be taxing for the open stage, in that the text may

refer only to furniture, not to a vista or a realistic environment.
Beatty points out,

> *Ghosts* doesn't have an enormous number of requirements, and the
> requirements are not like kitchen cabinets. He certainly always has
> some symbolic items in his sets, but they are not items that the
> actors have to touch, and that makes a difference: those are usually
> things that you can transform into another conceptual idea.
>     Nineteenth-century realism doesn't end up getting terribly in-
> volved with the scenery as much as we have in our age of movies
> and hard-built realism. They tend to use furniture more than they
> used the walls. But it is a little easier to divorce them from all that
> than some twentieth-century realism.

Falabella contends that the designer should create a "visual
image" for an open-stage production of Chekhov's *The Three
Sisters*, but all the play really needs are a few pieces of furniture.
    Minimalism may even be more important for an arena theatre.
At Arena Stage (Washington, D.C.) the only ways of getting
scenery on and off are through the voms or from the grid.
According to Robin Wagner,

> The best productions were those that had the least amount of stuff.
> It was very minimalist. The floor became like the slide in a
> microscope, and whatever you placed there was very intense. The
> props became like lines of dialogue: If there was no need for
> them—they didn't have their moment, they weren't uttered, they
> weren't used—get rid of them.

## Reconceive for the Open Stage

Rather than create attenuated versions of proscenium sets, the
designer can cut the tie to the proscenium altogether and take a
design approach that is unique to the open stage. Instead of paring
down a realistic set, the designer can eschew realism completely
and take a more symbolic approach.
    One way of conceiving the play for the open stage is to use pre-
sentational techniques in which there is no pretense that an illusion
of reality is being represented onstage. This approach avoids the
illusionism of the proscenium altogether. Tyrone Guthrie describes
the Stratford Festival Theatre Thrust Stage (Stratford, Ont.):

The stage is so planned that no illusionary scenery is possible. Yet with its gallery, its pillars, its various levels and entrances, the necessary facilities are provided for grouping the actors and arranging the scenes in a logical and expressive way.

. . . The stage is planned upon the theory that illusion is not the aim of performance. The shape of the auditorium, in which the spectators are constantly and inevitably aware of the presence of other spectators, is a constant reminder that the performance is what it is: a ritual in which actors and spectators are alike taking part. This idea appeals, I think, because it happens to be true; whereas the idea of illusion demands self-deception, demands that you believe that to be 'really' happening which is clearly fictitious.[2]

The designer should also look at the given stage in a positive light, thinking of what can be achieved rather than what cannot. John Conklin, a designer, advises,

If you are doing a drawing room comedy in an arena, the secret is not to do it in the same way that you would in a proscenium. You try to think of ways of making the space work for you, not trying to jam the idea of a proscenium production into a thrust or arena, even if it was written as a proscenium piece. That's where I think you get into trouble. Then it is difficult, and you are fighting the space, fighting the medium. If you use the space to liberate yourself from preconceptions about what a piece should be, then the space will act as a positive, liberating force.

The open stage may also have benefits for realistic drama, in that the symbolic aspects of the play can be emphasized over the realism. John Gassner cites Ibsen's *Ghosts*, hoping that an arena production would "capture Ibsen's ironic and nightmarish 'Fall of the House of Usher' poetry along with his incisive meaning, by contrast with the one-dimensional view of that drama which has resulted in flat productions that have made it look as dated as a furbelow."[3] According to Guthrie, in his thrust stage production of *The Three Sisters*, "The delicate interior life of the play unfolds on an open stage where a profusion of props sufficiently defines the scene."[4]

Ulu Grosbard, a director, believes that Miller's *A View from a Bridge* is better performed on the open stage than on a proscenium, because the latter stage seems to encourage "big, literal sets," and the designer tends to "create the whole neighborhood." On the other hand, on the open stage, "it all becomes unnecessary.

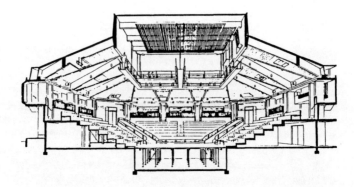

9. Drawing of Arena Stage, Washington, D.C. Architect: Harry Weese and Associates. Consultants: Bolt, Beranek and Newman. Reproduced with permission of Arena Stage.

You're simply dealing with the space. It's all created by the playwright and the actors." Grosbard finds that solution "purer," because it "leaves more to the imagination."

Carey Perloff, artistic director of American Conservatory Theatre, was concerned about directing *The Birthday Party* on the thrust stage of CSC Rep (New York City), but she came to the conclusion that the proscenium is not always useful to Pinter's dramaturgy:

> The reason Pinter is so terribly done is that people insist on making it so naturalistic that the language falls into the furniture and dies. I wanted it to just be a platform—just a playing platform. When people stepped out on it, you didn't know where they had come from. You had no idea if that door led to a beach or a no-man's-land, or what; but you knew that when you stepped onto that platform, certain rules prevailed.

## STAGE SHAPE

### Oddly Shaped Stages

The size and shape of the stage is a critical factor on the open stage, in that the stage extends into the audience and cannot simply be "masked off," as on a proscenium stage. Some stages

10. View of Arena Stage, Washington, D.C. Reproduced with permission of Arena Stage.

have such an eccentric shape that the designer is forced into dealing with that shape, like it or not.

In order to design successfully for thrust or arena, the shape of the stage must become part of the designer's thinking about the production from the outset. Marjorie Bradley Kellogg states that when designing for Circle in the Square (Uptown), "The only way to design in it successfully is to think about the space from the very, very beginning." She says it would be impossible "to even conceive vaguely of a set without taking the theatre into account." This approach is different from that for proscenium theatres, in which the designer "can think about the set and then think about the space." In a thrust theatre, according to Beatty, "you have to keep that particular situation in mind, and the production basically won't fit into any other theatre."

For instance, the Guthrie Theatre's stage is roughly rectangular, but the downstage corners are cut off and the whole shape is askew and asymmetrical. The asymmetry and odd angles are reflected throughout the auditorium. As Jensen declares, "The entire auditorium, the seats, the clouds, the accordions, the shape of the stage all make visual statements, none of them are neutral. They must be contended with. They must be treated as part of the setting."[5] Ed Call, former associate artistic director, says that the architecture imposes design techniques: "It's like Tanya and Guthrie are just standing at your elbow and saying, 'You can't do that, shithead, because there's a tunnel on this side . . . and the stage is this deep, and it's this wide.'"[6]

James Dale Wallace studied ten years of set design at the Guthrie, and concludes: "The shape of the stage floor is the single element which most affected the work of the designers." He reports,

> All designers agreed that it was almost automatic to make platforms, benches, window seats, and large abstract shapes reflect the asymmetry of the stage. Almost without exception, for example, every platform that Tanya Moiseiwitsch designed . . . was an irregular shape which appeared to be an adumbrated version of the stage.[7]

Hartford Stage is generally considered to have one of the trickiest stage shapes. It comes to a blunt wedge downstage, faced by the two front-most seats, which Hugh Landwehr says are like the "two front seats of a car." He recalls that when the theatre first opened, "We wanted to put a steering wheel next to the left-hand seat." According to Mark Lamos, the artistic director, the downstage wedge is "a very weak space for actors. It's completely useless as a playing space." Ron Lagomarsino points out that in a well-designed thrust theatre the actor "should be able to stand downstage and turn upstage and feel fairly powerful," but at Hartford Stage the actor needs "to stay fairly far upstage in order to feel most powerful. The downstage area felt like dead space. Often this area was simply not used."

Designers agree that this area of Hartford Stage's thrust is in most cases unusable, and that it is best to find a creative way to ignore it. Landwehr remarks that "it is very difficult to put anything there. You can't really put furniture, because the sightlines cross from too many directions." Michael Yeargan suggests that the designer can ignore this area by painting it black or "lifting a platform above it."

## Design the Stage Shape

The designer can create a playing area that is the size and shape best for the given production. As Loquasto explains, "You want to present a space and place specific to that play." Kellogg argues that on the open stage the designer should control and define the stage space: "Controlling it rigidly is about trying to manhandle it into an interesting configuration."

On an arena stage, the need to control space becomes even more intense, because of the limited design palette. Simply put, controlling space is one of the few, and perhaps the most effective, design opportunities on an arena stage. According to Kellogg,

> You don't have the help provided by the fourth wall. You have nothing but the floor to deal with; that means you really have to work hard at it, because that's all the information you can give people. It's the only way. What else do you have? You can't put walls up. You can paint the floor, but that's a kind of augmentation rather than a strong way to manipulate space. If all you can have is a flat floor, then a painted design on the floor will lead to some sense of spatial manipulation.

There are two basic methods for changing the shape of the stage. The first is to add platforms to the existing stage, or remove platforms if the stage is flexible. But one can also implicitly change the playing area by adding or removing seats. In some theatres, it may be possible to fill in the downstage or side areas with seats. In other cases, the designer may be able to remove seats in order to extend the stage.

If it is not possible to make the stage as a whole larger or smaller, the designer can control the stage space by defining shapes within it that are appropriate to the production. Instead of using the entire stage platform as is, the designer breaks it into several discrete spaces, or defines one area with a different shape from the permanent stage. The designer can use platforms, floor coverings or furniture to define these shapes.

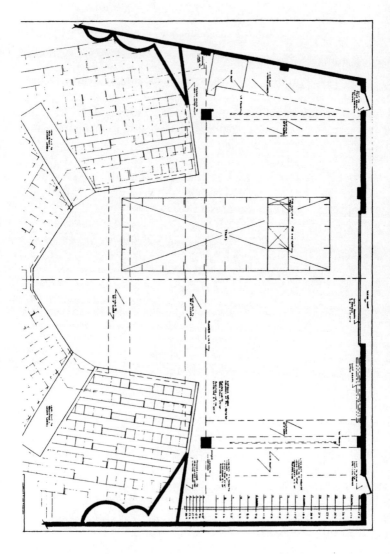

11. Plan and section of the Hartford Stage, Hartford, Conn. Drawings by James J. Keller from original designs by the architect, Robert Venturi, Venturi and Rauch, Philadelphia. Reproduced with permission of the Hartford Stage.

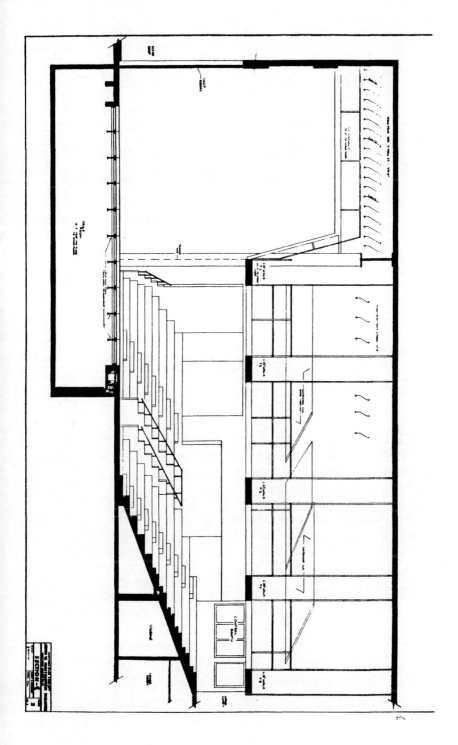

12. View of the Hartford Stage, Hartford, Conn. Photograph by Nick Lacy. Reproduced with permission of the Hartford Stage.

## EMPHASIS ON THE FLOOR

From the shallow-raked auditorium of a "standard" proscenium theatre, with the audience looking slightly up or straight on, the audience sees the actors against the background of the scenic walls, drops, etc. But in a open-stage theatre, which commonly has a steeply raked auditorium, with the audience looking down (see Chapter 11), most of the audience sees the actors against the background of the floor, which in effect must be considered as the scenic backdrop. Therefore, because of vertical sightlines and the need to convey information somewhere in the performance area, the floor is prominent in most open-stage theatres.

Landwehr says that when designing at Long Wharf Theatre, with its steeply raked auditorium, "I usually think of the floor before I think of anything else." Robyn Goodman, co-founder and former artistic director of Second Stage, observes that even though that theatre is an end stage, the steep rake means that "the play becomes about the floor."

The audience's encirclement of the stage in groundplan also

causes this emphasis on the floor. In a thrust or arena, the sightlines are such that the designer cannot employ a box set or other scenery that enfolds the performer. In addition, any wall, drop or vista on a thrust stage is to one side of the actor for much of the audience. And in an arena theatre there can be no large-scale vertical scenery at all. The diminished visual importance of vertical scenery means that the designer must find other means to convey the place, period, mood, etc. The steeply raked auditorium in a thrust or arena makes the floor the obvious candidate. David Potts submits that when designing for arena, the floor is "the beginning, middle and end" of the design: "No matter what the script is, you know that you are going to have to pare it down to just that, because you really have no other alternative."

Circle in the Square (Uptown) has such a strong emphasis on the floor that it can serve as an example for other open stages. The auditorium does not have an especially steep rake for a thrust, but because the stage is so long (40'), the floor is particularly prominent. Thomas Skelton, a lighting designer, contends that this is the "most extreme theatre in this regard. The backdrop is the floor—not whatever design backdrop the designer has come up with."

Productions have frequently featured the floor as the principal design element. Many have had very realistic, detailed floor treatments, and the floor is often used as the chief element in gaining period, place and atmospheric effects. For *Design for Living*, by Noel Coward, Thomas Lynch created a different floor for each of the three acts: tiles for Act I, worn rugs for Act II, and "miles of shiny parquet, marble and glass brick" for Act III.

The floor can also be used for spectacular effects. For *Once in a Lifetime*, by Moss Hart and George S. Kaufman, Karl Eigsti designed a floor that was "a multicolored light-box in an Art Deco design." For scene changes, the entire floor was lit from below and a tracery of lights chased around the stage. Beni Montresor's design for *Figaro's Marriage* also had chaser lights around the perimeter of the stage and the entire floor was mirrored.

The floor can also be trapped, not just for entrances through the stage, but as a significant design feature. Walter Kerr described how this effect was used as a visual symbol for Euripides' *Medea:*

> The stage floor . . . [is] a perfect summing up—and summoning up—of all the dark forces that Euripides saw underlying love, lust,

the power of procreation. At the core of the mottled blue surface that might just be volcanic ash a vast wound opens up, a red-tinged crater ringed with steps descending into the netherworld of womb or tomb. . . . It is exactly the savage rent in the earth from which the sorceress-mother Medea . . . might appear.[8]

Michael Cacoyannis also had a pit for his production of *The Bacchae*, and he attributes this feature specifically to the nature of the theatre space: "Limitations, as you know, often give birth to invention. The idea of having Dionysus appear—or spring out of the center . . . was inspired by that particular stage space totally surrounded by eyes."

## USE OF LEVELS

Breaking up the stage space into levels is particularly effective in an open-stage theatre, because of the inherent emphasis on the floor, the relative lack of other scenic options and the need to control the stage space. Levels can provide a visually interesting floor and manipulate the space, horizontally and vertically. Level changes serve several functions: conveying localization, aiding composition, defining space and providing an interesting floor.

Level changes can be quite small, however, and still provide definition to the stage area. Lynch comments that when designing at Arena Stage, "You always think that you're going to need a lot of change of level in order to make any difference. It turns out that you can really get the effect from only three inches. The eye is very perceptive to small increments." For a set at Circle in the Square (Uptown), Lynch used a "warped terrain" with rakes and platforms "to give the feeling of definition."

In the case of a wide thrust, a single platform that redefines the playing area can help regularize the stage dimensions. Some designs may try to span the entire stage, but the result can be a playing area that is unmanageably wide. At the Juilliard Drama Theatre (New York City), Douglas Schmidt used platforms to "force the action into the center," so that "you don't have to deal with all that space." The idea is to "localize the action on the center platform and deliver performers to that platform." Schmidt calls this platform a "crumpet": an octagonal platform on a $3/4''$ rake, $18'$ deep, $20'$ across in slightly forced perspective.

Much higher levels—balconies, bridges, etc.—are also very effective on the open stage. High platforms fill the sometimes yawning volume over the stage so that it does not seem empty and looming, and allow for additional acting areas. Designer Kenneth Foy points out that the volume over the thrust stage both allows for and necessitates the use of upper levels:

> Upper levels become almost obligatory in a thrust theatre. In a proscenium theatre the upper levels become a problem for sightlines from the balcony. But in a thrust, it's an absolute advantage because it varies your acting patterns. What you can't have in the illusion of a proscenium, you can make up in the activity of the thrust.

At the Vivian Beaumont Theater, Schmidt sometimes added upper levels because of the height: "There's no reason for there to be an upper level in [Brecht's] *Good Woman of Setzuan*, but frankly, what are you going to do with all that space?" Hugh Hardy observes that this theater "only works really with a two-story set. If you use the full height of the Beaumont, you're home free."

While upper levels can be used in an arena theatre, the sightline problems can become a nightmare. But Heidi Landesman did find a way to successfully employ a second level for a production of *A Midsummer Night's Dream* at Arena Stage. As with most designs for an arena theatre, she designed a very detailed floor, "which then grew out into trees on the four corners that created a canopy overhead, a second level that was transparent and unified to the level below it. It gave a lightness that arena doesn't normally have."

Levels can also be helpful to the actor and director, aiding in composition and movement. Paul Weidner likes to have the designer provide him with levels for composition: "I love levels—levels just make everything easier. You put people on two different levels and you've got a picture. You put the people on the floor, and you've got people on the floor."

Platforms may be most effective when placed on a slight diagonal to the main up- and downstage axis of the theatre.

According to Lynch, "If you're wanting to pull out of the space and create a slightly separate world for the characters, canting things one way or another from the room architecture can help dislodge it a little bit, unmoor it a little from the existing architecture." In addition, these diagonally placed platforms will help the director employ diagonal crosses in the blocking (see Chapter 9).

The difficulty with using platforms, as Perloff points out, is that they generally cannot be mocked up for rehearsals. Therefore, Perloff declares, "you have to have enough experience to know what it's going to look like spatially even though you're not going to see it until you get in there."

## BREAK UP THE STAGE INTO AREAS

One way of defining the stage area, especially for realistic plays requiring several locales, is to divide the stage into separate areas. In this case, all of the locales are simultaneously and permanently onstage; scene changes are effected with light and placement of the actors. Eigsti observes that the designer's challenge in this case is to create the illusion of a "stage-wide effect," where in fact only a portion is being used: "When the area is highlighted, it is present and the actors can be believed in that area. And when you want to highlight something else, it will fade away and not intrude upon the illusion of what you're trying to create."

Foy tried to control the unwieldy stage length at Circle in the Square (Uptown) by breaking it cleanly in half for a production of Shaw's *Candida*. Though Shaw sets the play in one room, Foy knew that the stage was too long for a single room. In response to the stage shape, he created an indoors upstage and an outdoors downstage: "I was then working with two well-proportioned spaces that were linked. The room was the size of a room—a very human space."

Dividing up the stage, however, may create other staging problems. A scene that occurs in one imagined locale must always be placed on that area of the stage, whether or not that is theatrically effective. This enforced placement may impose a rigidity on the blocking. Arvin Brown states:

It is the one way to make three-quarter staging seem truly static. You are usually asking your actors to work in a very confined area to begin with, and a very defined area that often is somewhere at a part of the stage that is not really where you want it to be. That is a terrible, terrible trap in three-quarter staging—but it is the most immediately available. It's the mistake you easily make.

Instead, Brown suggests that the director and designer should "find a way to shape the stage afresh each time."

## FLATTEN OUT THE THRUST

If the theatre is a semi-thrust, with a shallow thrust and most of the audience in the center, it may be possible to approximate the proscenium form by flattening out the stage. When John Tillinger directed two Joe Orton farces at the Mark Taper Forum (Los Angeles), he was "very very nervous" about them, but he and Beatty were able to "cut the whole apron off, so it became virtually a proscenium arch play." Beatty refers to this method as "cheating," and explains, "We just cut eight feet off the front of the thrust and put seats down there. We did as much as we could to put a large apron on a proscenium production. It had to be basically a proscenium production, even though it was in Mark Taper Forum."

But this approach may be considered an attempt to deny the very nature of the theatre that one is performing in. Weidner argues that the director and designer should

> accept the fact that you are doing it in a thrust. You should not decide, 'Well, farce needs a flatter space, so move it all upstage.' That's a mistake, because then you are neither one thing nor another. You are pretending to be something that you really aren't.

•

The problems of the open stage do not negate its value and power, nor are they insurmountable. In fact, every stage form has its problems and conventions. The responsibility of the theatre artist is to face and acknowledge them; or, perhaps, to see them as attributes to be exploited for the gain of the production, rather than as obstacles to be battled and overcome.

13. View of the Mark Taper Forum, Los Angeles. Photograph by Jay Thompson. Reproduced with permission of the Mark Taper Forum.

The strategies posed in this chapter underline the importance of the designer approaching each production and space afresh. There are no rules, or even guidelines, and this chapter is not an attempt to offer any. Instead, the aim is to show how accomplished designers have confronted specific problems. Their strategies may be helpful to other designers faced with similar situations. On the other hand, their solutions may help to inspire others not to imitate these approaches, but to be as creative as these designers have been.

## NOTES

1. Martin Gottfried, *The Theatre Divided: The Post-War American Stage* (Boston: Little, Brown, 1969) 127.
2. Guthrie, *Life* 336.
3. Gassner, *Times* 520.
4. Tyrone Guthrie, *A New Theatre* (New York: McGraw-Hill, 1964) 130.
5. As quoted in Donald Dewey Fogelberg, "The Impact of the Architecture of the Tyrone Guthrie Theatre on the Process of Play Production," diss., U of Minnesota, 1979, 44.
6. As quoted in James Dale Wallace, "Set Design at the Guthrie Theatre in Its First Ten Years," diss., U of Minnesota, 1975, 17.
7. As quoted in Wallace 175, 189.
8. Walter Kerr, "This Medea Is More Hausfrau Than Horror," *The New York Times* 28 Jan. 1973: 1.

# CHAPTER 8

# USING THE PORTAL ON A THRUST STAGE

One of the most common forms of the open stage is a thrust with a portal—a quasi-proscenium—upstage. In effect, this form is a hybrid of thrust and proscenium. The advantage is that the downstage platform provides the intimacy of the thrust and the upstage frame allows for a scenic area, often complete with trap and fly systems, that can accommodate major scenic units. The portal, however, architecturally divides the space, which may entail a host of problems and pitfalls.

For instance, staging any action upstage of the portal line removes the very *raison d'être* of the thrust stage: the actors and audience sharing the same architectural volume. When the actors move upstage of the portal, they are in "another" space, which is connected to the audience's space only by the hole (portal) in the wall separating the two spaces.

Marjorie Bradley Kellogg refers to the portal area as "way the hell and gone out in God's country." Thomas Lynch describes the portal as a "big volume with scenery" that is "miles from the audience," and the thrust in front as "a flat area with acting."

The frame at the rear of the stage may also seduce the designer into creating a proscenium-like picture there, because it is often deep and well-equipped for scenery. The two-dimensional nature of this pictorial approach runs counter to the three-dimensional, sculptural quality of the thrust (see Chapter 6). John Jensen asserts that filling the portal at the Guthrie with a picture "was a constant apology that we weren't a proscenium stage and that the umbilical cord had never really been cut.[1] According to Jensen,

> There are moments when you tend to wander back into the illusion of the proscenium stage: 'There's a space back there. Let's do something back there at that hole.' I felt that we had begun to retreat off the thrust and were suddenly making elaborate back walls—big, built drops through which the actors came. You are sucked into that.

Proscenium heritage, I guess, makes that space back there demand to be ornamented in some way. It's very easy to spend your energy making a statement back there and then you realize that you have neglected a lot of audience who aren't getting the message.

You have to keep saying to yourself, 'No cyc, no stars, no vistas, no panorama in the traditional sense.' You must make it a space where the actors can work. You do this by making it necessary for them to move out onto the thrust to complete their intentions.

A practical problem when using the portal area for scenery is that the sightlines to the upstage area are often quite bad from the side seats. Even though the upstage area may be a large rectangle, the sightlines usually converge to a very shallow version of Mielziner's triangle (see Chapter 5), with the flat side along the portal and the point upstage. Lowell Detweiler reports that Alabama Shakespeare Festival (Birmingham, Ala.) has a wonderful backstage, but a third of the audience can't see it: "What all of that allows you to do is a fluid and wonderful backdrop, but the people on the sides don't see it." He refers to such theatres as "deceptive," in that the portal area may not be as useful as it seems at first glance:

There's a fabulous backstage space. They've got an extraordinary fly loft and all of this electrical stuff and a great number of line sets, and great wing storage space. Then you're in the theatre and you realize you can't use any of it because people on the sides can't see it.

In addition, for much of the audience, whatever scenery is placed in the portal will *not* be the actors' background. Renderings of the set might depict the actors against a background of scenery in the portal, and this might be the view from the center of the auditorium. But for those seated on the sides of a three-quarter thrust, the scenery will be "over there," off to one side and separate from the action of the play. According to Karl Eigsti,

If you just design the scenery and leave it upstage, it will be forgotten. It really won't have any impact on the play, because most of the audience is really looking across at each other. Only one-third of the audience is really looking at the show from a frontal point of view.

Even a deep three-quarter thrust with a portal at the rear can cause problems. Though a stage surrounded on three sides would seem like a committed thrust, a portal can keep a strong link to the proscenium. Mark Lamos feels that Hartford Stage is a "sloppy thrust," because of the large portal at the rear: "You can kind of do a proscenium staging on it, and you can kind of do thrust staging on it, but you don't have the power of either as distinctly as you would on a true thrust stage such as Stratford's," which has a back wall with no portal.

Too much scenic emphasis in the portal may also cause problems by pulling the focus and action upstage, away from the downstage thrust. In most cases, the designer in a thrust theatre wants to help the director pull the action downstage (see Chapter 10). Heidi Landesman maintains that in most thrusts "the scenery becomes something that happens upstage of the proscenium, which is frequently way upstage of the action, and it becomes rather an adjunct to the action rather than a part of it." The director may be tempted to stage action behind the portal, in that there may be scenery there and the actors may be easily seen by the entire audience. But the portal area may in fact be quite "weak" for the actors, in that it is far from the audience, and the sightlines and acoustics may be poor.

Despite these problems, the portal cannot be ignored; it is a major architectural feature and it will not simply go away. Michael Kahn, a director, says the portal in the Juilliard Drama Theater is "problematic," but comments, "you must deal with it. You can't pretend it's not there. It's a strongly defined area."

## PORTAL-PORTAL-VOM-VOM

There are usually four strong architectural points in a thrust theatre that the set must somehow relate to: the two sides of the portal and the two downstage voms. Ted Ohl, former Juilliard production manager, sums up the effect of the voms and portal at the Juilliard Drama Theatre on set design: "The voms and the portal define the space. They define 90% of the set. It's vom-vom-portal-portal: These points set the design. The space determines the aesthetic."

John Falabella believes that those "four points" and the "shopping list" (the most important physical elements of the play) are where the design process begins. He also likes to use diagonals on a thrust stage, so he combines all these factors in configuring the design: "I pick the most important pieces of my shopping list and establish them, probably on two opposite points, and then start filling in."

## THE RELATIONSHIP OF THE PORTAL
## AND THE PLATFORM

One of the most important determinations the designer and director must make is about how the production should nest within the theatre space. In the case of a thrust-and-portal combination, the designer and director need to gauge the relative strength of the downstage platform versus the portal frame, and weight the production accordingly.

Loren Sherman views this relationship of thrust and portal as paramount in designing for the thrust stage:

> If you have a theatre that is a little bit of each—a proscenium and a thrust stage—you should ask, 'Am I designing this volume to feel like a picture in a frame, or am I designing it to feel like something's being presented on a platter to the audience?' It's important to be clear about which way you're going about it, instead of doing it half and half.

In order to determine this relationship, Sherman suggests that the designer ask, "How many audience members see that proscenium arch as part of the total picture of what they're looking at?" As the designer looks from the side seats, he or she should ask, "For how many spectators is the proscenium involved in their peripheral vision when they're looking at an actor out on the open stage?"

## OPEN THE PORTAL WIDE

In order to minimize the importance and effect of the portal, the designer can either open the portal wide or wall it off with scenery. In the first case, the strategy is to open up the space as much as possible and give the sense of the space extending far back. This approach may be possible if the theatre has movable panels on the sides and top that can be used to adjust the size of the portal opening. While it would seem logical to make the thrust platform larger than the portal in order to give emphasis to the thrust, many designers feel that opening the portal wide actually emphasizes the thrust more. Opening up the portal gives the frame less visual importance, in that it is more removed from the scenery and action of the play.

Lamos explains that at Hartford Stage when the portal is closed in, "it actually becomes more distancing" because the audience senses that "there are too many parts of the house that feel left out." He believes that opening up the portal as wide as possible makes this large thrust theatre more intimate: "We have a better chance at intimacy than if we try to pull in the proscenium, pull down the back wall and bring it way downstage. If you can sense the set going off beyond you, you feel closer to the actors."

Lamos believes that the wide open space can help focus the production. He describes an "immense" production of *Hamlet* with a "vast" set, for which the portal panels were pulled out very wide and the set extended out of sight on the sides. While the large volume might have seemed looming and empty, and might have diminished the effectiveness of a lone actor, in fact he found the set "great for soliloquies," which were played well downstage. Lamos explains, "I thought it would take the eye away from the single actor, but it did exactly the opposite—it focused the eye. If there's one tree in a barren landscape, that's what you'll look at, and the landscape will go on forever *around* you."

## WALL OFF THE PORTAL

The other major strategy for dealing with a portal is to simply block off the rear stage with a wall of some sort. In this way, the wall unifies the space by cutting off the portal volume, and there is no temptation to stage action up there. Douglas Schmidt refers to this approach as the "bookend": "a back wall and a plate to act on." Lynch often walls off the portal area, and tries to make the relationship between that back wall and the floor of the thrust platform a strong one, "so that your strong image has to do with that floor and wall." John Lee Beatty's common technique is to

> continue the theatre wall around behind the actors to the other side, in fact, just closing off the proscenium. When I'm doing ground-plans for that type of theatre, I almost always just informally draw a little line, as if there weren't any proscenium at all, so that the actors would actually be in front of a hard wall. Sometimes the scenery comes very close to just completing the wall across. That's a very nice effect, reminding the audience that the actor is out in front of them, instead of being sucked upstage into something. It completes the room, so the actor is literally in the room with the audience, rather than having a large escape hatch upstage of him.

Walling off the portal may also help to enhance the feeling of intimacy so important to the open stage, restoring the sense of "one room" that the portal may undermine. As Michael Yeargan explains,

> It focuses the space more. When you block it off, people look across the stage to their fellow audience members as if they're in the same room, and the actors have just thrust through it. When you leave the portal open, you're seeing the actors against that background, and so it disperses the eye, or makes it feel more open. But somehow when you block it in, you really feel concentrated; all the energies are right here.

Walling off the portal may also be helpful to reduce the size of the playing area and to provide the sense of compression valuable for realistic drama. Ulu Grosbard cites the example of his Vivian Beaumont production of *The Floating Light Bulb,* by Woody Allen: "Given that it was a small, intimate play, we had to find a way to cut off all that space in the back." Grosbard points out that "directors get seduced by all that space and try to use it for realistic plays," with the result that the space "kills" the play and the actors get "lost." For a small, realistic play, Grosbard says the best approach is "to bring the set as far forward as possible and to literally box it in, to have a small playing area—very restricted, way downstage, and not to use the upstage area."

A variant of the wall technique is to put a scenic structure in the portal area that projects forward, similar to the structure at the

Stratford Festival Theatre Thrust Stage. Michael Langham, a director, believes that the angled front should create two diagonals across the stage, each projecting forward from one side of the rear facade. Langham maintains these diagonals aid both the director and the audience: spectators in thrust theatres often do not like to sit at the sides, because directors tend to direct for the center section; with these diagonals, the action is pushed left and right, not directly downstage.

## KEEP THE ACTION DOWNSTAGE AND USE THE PORTAL FOR DECORATION

In most cases, the action of the play should be downstage and the portal area should be used only for decorative purposes, such as scenery, secondary actors or overall composition. The portal area is usable, according to Kellogg, primarily as an "entrance area" or a "view out a window," but not, she emphatically declares, as an acting area: "It's so far away from the other end that it would be a horrible thing to stage a scene forty feet" from the audience. Kellogg says the upstage area is "essentially dressing. People can come in and out of there; they can pass through it; it can be for atmosphere and shape," but not for acting. Bernard Gersten, managing director of the Lincoln Center Company, states that at the Vivian Beaumont Theater the proscenium is "just a gateway to the back. The life of that stage is the thrust."

When one compares the two primary forms of open stage—arena and thrust—the benefit of the portal becomes clear: it is the one area that can be exploited for large, vertical scenic units. As Sherman points out, "You're usually pretty happy to have some kind of vertical surface that you can decorate to give information about where you are." He suggests that the portal area can be helpful for solving script requirements "in a pictorial way."

The tremendously deep stage of the Vivian Beaumont (originally designed for repertory storage) can be used for decorative effect, but the designer and director need to recognize that the spectators seated on the sides will miss a great deal. When executed well, the portal area can provide spectacular effects unattainable on any other thrust; when done badly, the problems cited above can swallow a play. Robert Symonds, former associate director of the Beaumont, recalls that the first production, *Danton's Death*, by Georg Buechner, used the depth of the stage "for some striking visual effects." He comments, however: "That's just about all it could be used for. You have a strikingly vivid scene of a crowd running on, but sooner or later you have to get down to the business of acting, and then they have to come downstage."

For the Beaumont production of *Trelawny of the 'Wells'*, by Arthur Wing Pinero, David Mitchell used the upstage areas for entrances of the sets, rather than actors. A decorative, nineteenth-century proscenium arch was placed inside the theatre's permanent portal, with a view beyond to the backstage of a Victorian theatre. Each of the four elaborate and realistic sets emerged from the far reaches of the stage, rolling on platforms into position inside the decorative proscenium frame. Mitchell describes the effect:

> We could make a kind of poetic dissolve. If you were in the first few rows, you would see the set sixty feet away, and very slowly coming close to you, and by the time it came into place, you could reach out and touch it. The scenes would just recede and the lights would go down.

Jack Kroll admired the "magical device, the equivalent of a zoom lens."[2]

Tony Walton has been praised for exploiting the portal area of the Beaumont stage without letting the scenery dominate the play. Walton uses the upstage area to create a massive setting that establishes the context of the play, but is not actually required for the action. In this way, the portal is used and not ignored, but there is no temptation to pull the action upstage, in that the scenery there is purely evocative. For *The Front Page*, by Ben Hecht and Charles MacArthur, Walton designed a massive view of the exterior and lobby of the Criminal Courts Building, which, he admits, "is not required by the play." It was, however,

> an attempt to use contrast by having this huge, daunting, cold marble exterior of the building and the interior of the lobby, playing off against this small, warm sort of alcohol-colored rats' nest.
> Our instinct was that if you just put the rats' nest there, it might

not have taken command of the daunting space of the Beaumont, in
a way that the warring combination of the two things did.

Similarly, for *The House of Blue Leaves* Walton designed a view
of Queens around the apartment "to fill the proscenium frame, so
that you had no impulse as an audience to think, 'I wonder why
they're not using that.' Something was filling the space, and it was
forcing the playing area to be out in front of it."

But whatever scenery is placed upstage should be designed in
such a way that the action of the play is forced onto the thrust
platform. Jensen stresses that "the designer's statement must be
made on the thrust," and then, "incidentally, something must be
designed" for the portal, because "it is too big a space to leave
open."[3] Beatty recommends that the designer shouldn't always
think of using the back wall of the thrust stage for entrances; if the
actors enter from the voms, the action will be kept downstage:

> You don't always have to use the upstage entrances in a thrust
> theatre; you can do the entire show coming from the voms. You can
> usually use the two voms and two side entrances, and never use an
> upstage entrance, which forces the thrust to be a thrust and keeps the
> actors out of those proscenium effects. It keeps them from posing in
> silhouette.

Kellogg even suggests that the best way of keeping the action
on the thrust is to fill the portal area with seating, making the
theatre in fact an arena: "When you use it as an arena, there's no
temptation to drift upstage, and that helps bring the focus back
into the center."

## UNIFY UP- & DOWNSTAGE

Using the portal area for vertical scenery and the floor for
horizontal scenery, the designer may face the problem of unifying
these two areas, so they don't look like two distinct planes.

Unifying the stage may be an especially difficult problem for
plays that require realistic scenery, in that the only place to put it
may be upstage. According to Kellogg,

> The real problem on a thrust is relating the downstage space to the upstage space. You have to figure out that relationship carefully so that you don't have all the scenery in the background and strand the actor downstage in the middle of an empty space. It's really about integrating that whole experience in one. And the deeper the thrust, the harder that is.

For a realistic production, this goal can be achieved by placing the large, highly detailed scenic elements upstage, where more scenery is possible, and then tapering off both the size and degree of detail as the set progresses downstage. Upstage, Kellogg explains, the set is "at its greatest height in detail," and downstage, the set "fans out to get out of the way of the audience," while retaining the feeling of the detail upstage.

The audience will then perceive the space as unified and equally realistic, as John Conklin maintains: "If your set has some sort of naturalistic richness upstage where you can do it, the richness of detail upstage will carry the eye completely into the space." The result is that the spectators "read the whole space as a naturalistic space."

Another way of unifying the space is to incorporate the back wall into the action of the play. John Tillinger uses "a step or something on that back wall that is organic to the action, so that something will have to take place there. And once one thing takes place there, a couple of other things begin to take place there." Jensen also stresses that upstage scenery should be utilitarian, not pictorial: "If it's something where the action can happen, that's fine. But if it's just something to illustrate how beautiful Venice is, that won't work. It's too enticing for the eye."

The upstage and downstage areas can also be linked by projecting scenery out from the portal into the thrust. Again, most of the scenery will be upstage, behind the portal, but by carrying a portion of it downstage the two spaces can be united. Paul Weidner, former artistic director of Hartford Stage Company, says designers at that theatre would project "structural, architectural elements" downstage of the portal: "If it's an architectural part of the upstage set it makes you feel like that portal line is broken."

At the opposite extreme, it can be effective to emphasize the architectural boundary implicit in the portal, in effect creating two worlds. For the production he directed of *Spring's Awakening,* by

Franz Wedekind, Liviu Ciulei divided the Juilliard Drama Theatre stage at the portal with an 18′-high chain-link fence. According to Ciulei:

> Behind this mesh was the world of the parents, a very antiseptic world, a very proper world. In front of the mesh was nature, which was indicated only by fallen leaves. The effort of the young people was to break the mesh, to crawl under it or climb over it and enter into the world of nature, of instincts. The structure of the space was metaphorical.

This production used, with little adornment, the architectural features of the theatre to convey symbolically a separation of space appropriate to the play: the upstage, architecturally enclosed area as the "confined" area, and the open, accessible-to-the-audience area as the "natural, free" area.

•

When asked about the portal area of a thrust stage, designers roll their eyes and exclaim that this indeed is the trickiest architectural feature and the one that most often trips up designs— and even entire productions. The danger posed does not mean, however, that the portal need be damaging to a production. It does mean that the designer and director should be aware of the pitfalls and open to the possibilities.

## NOTES

1. As quoted in Wallace 204.
2. Jack Kroll, "The Stage IS the World," *Newsweek* 27 Oct. 1975: 52.
3. As quoted in Fogelberg 78.

# CHAPTER 9
# THE OPEN STAGE'S EFFECT ON STAGING

The staging conventions of the thrust and arena theatre are neither more nor less exacting and artificial than those of the proscenium, but the conventions are different. One stage form may seem to allow "freedom" of movement and staging, another may seem "restricting" and "confining." No doubt, individuals may be more comfortable with one audience-performance configuration or another, but every stage exacts certain requirements, as well as allowing other opportunities. This chapter examines the perceived requirements of the open stage and explores some of the opportunities.

## THE NEED FOR MOVEMENT ON THE OPEN STAGE

On thrust and arena stages the actors must keep moving so that all the encircling spectators can see the actors' faces. The need for movement can be seen either as an obstacle to be overcome or as an exciting mode of staging. Tyrone Guthrie emphasizes the "advantage" of "greater flexibility of movement and grouping,"[1] and Brian Murray, an actor and director, likes to "tell the story through movement" on the open stage.

Keeping the actors moving does not mean that everyone sees everything, but rather that no section of the auditorium is ignored. Everyone needs to get a share of the action, and significant moments can be "sprayed" throughout the auditorium. Stephen Porter suggests that the actor can deliver part of the line "in one direction, turn and say some of it in the other direction." Far from being a detriment, Porter says that in some instances, this technique "adds a little extra fillip." Theodore Mann explains that when blocking on the Circle in the Square stage,

It's like a geometric design. There are three areas (center, upstage and downstage) of the theatre. The director must try to find theatrical logic for the action to move from area to area so that the action is equally distributed, taking into account the play's dramatic necessities. The whole audience must feel that they are a part of the play and not isolated from it.

The director should not become too obsessed with a formula of time and space for sightlines; the audience will be satisfied if the production keeps moving. Arvin Brown emphasizes that if the scene is played with sensitivity and power, the audience will accept the actors' backs longer than many directors think:

People can watch an incredibly packed, moving scene seeing only the back of the head of one of the performers for a remarkable length of time and not be locked outside the emotional experience. Human beings do send such signals in terms of body language and everything else.

If the need to keep the actors moving is not handled well, the blocking can seem artificial, busy and formulaic. Some find thrust-stage productions to be too predictable because they feel that the stage form dictates certain repeating patterns. Alvin Epstein cautions that at the Guthrie Theatre,

I had to be careful of thrust mannerisms, which seemed to place actors on imaginary individual revolves that kept turning. Some of the long-time company actors would constantly swivel. On occasion it really annoyed me. I would say, 'Stop displaying yourself— act the scene.' But they were instinctively obeying the unwritten law of perpetual motion.

Drama that inherently requires a great deal of movement fits comfortably with the staging patterns of the open stage. In Shakespeare's plays, for example, lines are specifically included to cover the actors' movement around the large thrust stage. A play with many scenes may also implicitly require a great deal of movement. Gregory Mosher cites the example of *Woyzeck,* by Georg Buechner: "There are twenty or thirty scenes, and so there is going to be movement. Even if the actors are cold still in one scene, three minutes later that scene is over and another scene begins."

But the movement required by the open stage works at cross-purposes with plays that do not have a great deal of inherent movement. Mark Lamos points out that in some plays, "so much of the power of the dramaturgy of the play depends on stillness." According to Ulu Grosbard,

> The play may dictate the relationship that the characters have to each other, depending on what's happening in the scene. You have to violate those relationships in order to accommodate sightlines. You then have to move them arbitrarily—not because he should move, but simply because he can't be seen. You're screwing up the play, you're screwing up the moment. You add those up, and you can't put your finger on it, but something is off—a cumulative number of moments where the organic relationship between the actors has been violated. A lot of plays have suffered from having to be done on those stages.

For example, Tony Walton believes that the Vivian Beaumont's thrust is not "beneficial" to a play such as Beckett's *Endgame,* "something that depends for a great deal of its strength on its stillness and simplicity." (But Mosher contends that *Waiting for Godot* "has enough agitation" to work on the thrust: "The whole sense of movement versus 'They do not move' is the very theme of the play.")

Porter cites his production of Wilde's *The Importance of Being Earnest* at Circle in the Square (Uptown). Porter is "absolutely sure that the way Wilde visualized it was that the actors were lined up so nobody upstaged anybody, and each one froze while the other one got his laugh." Instead, Porter "had to put in a lot of movement so that the people could be seen from all sides— movement that was not organic to the script."

But Brown argues that movement on the thrust is no more or less artificial than on the proscenium stage:

> Why in the world would one consider living in a picture frame a more natural state of being than in a three-dimensional space?
>
>     There is a set of rules in proscenium, having to do with upstaging, that are matters of high artifice, and its just that people have grown used to them. Those who are more used to them are more comfortable working on a proscenium stage, and suddenly they feel that they have a requirement now of the audience on three

sides, or perhaps four sides, that there must be some very artificial trick to allowing those sections of the audience their full weight. If you are not used to it, it can feel very artificial. It can feel like you are constantly moving people for no good reason. You are breaking a contact to feature this side of the house or that side of the house. But I think it has to do with not being comfortable in the form.

Paradoxically, seeing the actors' backs may be less of a problem in arena than in thrust. According to Porter, in a thrust with a back-wall set, "the audience feels entitled to see every face all the time, which is impossible." But in a four-sided arena, the spectators "look across and they see somebody on the far side, and they feel much less cheated visually when that person turns to face the other side." Porter therefore feels that movement patterns are much easier to manage in arena, "because you are freer to turn your back on members of the audience."

## SEEING REACTIONS

One way for a spectator to be involved in the action, even if the speaker's back is toward him or her, is to see the reactions of the person the actor is talking to. Stephen Joseph observes:

> Few plays demand that an actor should be onstage alone, speaking, for very long; in most plays there is at least one other person to help egg on the drama. Thus the audience may usually expect to get at least one face. At times the reactions of one character will illuminate the intentions of another. . . . It even gives a special responsibility to those confidants, usually considered such dreary parts, in French classical tragedy.[2]

Epstein explains this staging can be accomplished:

> In a two-character scene, for instance, stage the actors so the audience sees one face and one back, then reverse them so the audience never loses sight of either actor's face for too long. But the 'expressive' back of one actor can hold the spectator for quite a while if the spectator simultaneously sees the other actor's face.

This technique can be especially valuable for a scene with little inherent movement, in which the director wants to keep the actors relatively stationary.

## COMPOSITION AND FOCUS

As described in Chapter 5, proscenium advocates contend that only on the proscenium stage can the director and designer compose a picture that most of the audience will perceive in the same way. On the open stage, these critics argue, such controlled composition is impossible. But proponents of thrust and arena stages maintain that composition is possible, even though the techniques and results are different. Porter says the director should not simply "forget composition"; instead, "you can compose for a large percentage of your audience, with the realization that some of the others are not going to see so well." For instance, the director can arrange the actors into triangles, so that for each section of the audience "there's always something to see."

Another frequent criticism of the open stage is that the director cannot control focus as well as he or she can on the proscenium stage. But Carey Perloff maintains that the director

> can control focus on the thrust. You just have to know how to do it. You can do beautiful visuals on a thrust, if you learn to work on a diagonal and to create pictures that move rather than flat tableaux. It's much more plastic. When you see someone die over a tomb, and you can see it from all sides, you're seeing a very living thing, which is very different from seeing a remote picture of it.

John Jensen points out that the different focal qualities of the thrust stage place an "enormous demand" upon actors, including, or especially, those with small parts. The actor has to

> stay alive, because very often people are not seeing the main speaker in a scene. They are seeing these six or eight court ladies huddled down on a step and the main speaker is over there. They are watching the main actor through this vignette of characters. The actors have got to be with it, even if they are spear carriers, as much as the actor who is doing the speech, because if they aren't they will

destroy the moment of the scene. It takes veracity on everybody's part. The design must stay alive too, not attempting to be the same for all, but providing evocative objects for all.

## DIAGONALS AND CURVES

The diagonal is an important staging technique, frequently employed on the open stage. Take the example of a thrust stage with the audience seated on three sides and with two voms located at the downstage corners. The sightlines are such that the best way for two actors to be seen by the entire audience is to line them up on a diagonal. In this way, the actor nearest the vom, facing diagonally upstage, has only the vom directly behind him, and the other actor, facing downstage, has no one at her back. Wilford Leach says that at the Anspacher Theater, "the only safe position on the stage is lining the actors up with the voms." In addition, Brown points out that the actor who is facing upstage is in a very powerful position, "but it's a very hard sell to make the actors realize that it's a strong position to be in. Actors' training works against that—it makes them feel that they are upstaging themselves."

Columns are a common feature of thrust stages in renovated buildings, and they can further restrict sightlines. According to Leach, the columns and voms all but dictate the blocking at the Anspacher Theater:

> The columns block all but a small triangle of the stage. If I put anybody outside this triangle, they're just decoration for the people who can see them, and the people who can't see them think they're missing something. So you have to keep everybody in this small triangle, then manipulate people around the rest of the stage so it doesn't look like you have an empty stage.

Leach cites the example of staging Puccini's *La Bohème* on the Anspacher stage:

> Mimi has to die, so once you've got old Mimi in the bed, there are only two spaces—the two corridors lined up with the voms—in which you can move anybody. If you move anybody out of that, somebody can't see Mimi and they don't appreciate her suffering

and dying as an artist. There are these long arias with five people onstage, and you have two two-foot corridors in which you can put actors without constantly moving them.

So you have a choice: either you constantly move them, which is distracting and sort of arbitrary, or you put them in those corridors. What you do is some combination of that: try to move those people and think three-dimensionally. You have to think, 'What does it look like over here and what does it look like over there?'

There are other important reasons for using diagonals in the blocking. One is that a diagonal movement is inherently powerful on the thrust stage. Because the audience perceives the thrust as a three-dimensional, cubic volume, as opposed to the flatter, more two-dimensional proscenium stage (see Chapter 6), the diagonal cross forcefully pierces the stage volume. In addition, such a move engages the entire stage platform—left and right, up and down.

Paul Weidner observes that the diagonal is a "very strong line visually from a lot of different points in the house, much more so than two balanced actors flat upstage." One way of setting up the diagonal, according to Weidner, is to have an upstage right entrance, for instance, and a scenic anchor down left to draw the actor in that direction.

Diagonal blocking also makes the performance more accessible to those seated on the sides of the auditorium. In a proscenium theatre, the director will often establish a "front" in the blocking and the set, which corresponds roughly to the plaster line. By and large, the set, furniture and blocking will reinforce this front, which is perpendicular to the audience's line of sight. In a thrust or arena theatre where the audience is on more than one side of the stage, there is no need to establish this single front; in fact, it is best to avoid any single, frontal orientation. One way of breaking any front (the section most likely to be favored in a thrust theatre is in the center) is to work on a diagonal. Using this method, the staging does not seem to "face" or favor any section of the audience. Leach describes his method:

What I try to do in the Anspacher is keep it informal as in life or in a room—never defining a front, always contradicting a front, shifting a front. If you think of it being any front, the front is the voms; then you do it twice: once for each angle, never for the front angle.

In addition, diagonal sets and blocking will help break up the sometimes rectilinear lines of the stage and the theatre.

The curve is the other related blocking movement common to thrust stages. Director José Quintero is often credited with popularizing this approach in thrust staging, as Gerald M. Berkowitz reports:

> Quintero was the first to sense that arena staging was not just a matter of audience placement but required a wholly new kind of blocking and movement, that the straight crossings and diagonals of the proscenium stage must be replaced by wide arcs and more circular motions, to reflect the audience's sense of the room they were in.[3]

The curve, like the diagonal, is now part of the vernacular of thrust staging. John Tillinger states that on a deep thrust stage,

> You don't make many direct moves. You tend to do half-circle moves, and if an actor has never worked in that particular theatre, they think you've gone stark raving mad. They say, 'Well, why would I walk to this person this way?' But it's an attempt to open up the stage and give everybody a look at people's faces.

At Repertorio Español (New York City), Rene Buch uses "round" and "rhomboid" movements, and refers to the blocking as a "minuet."

## JUSTIFYING MOVEMENT

Directing for the open stage should not be a matter of winding up dervishes and letting them whirl. It is the director's responsibility to find ways to justify the technical staging requirements of the open stage. The blocking must not appear arbitrary and imposed by the stage, but rather integral to the nature of the play. The director must meet certain requirements of entrances, exits and sightlines, while at the same time creating the mode of performance appropriate to the play. The need to make the play available to the audience is vital, but must not become an end in itself. John Gassner, writing in the early days of open staging, stressed:

Nothing can do more harm to the art of staging plays than to turn a stage director into a new kind of traffic cop whose prime function is to be that of directing actors' movements in a centrally located area. I fear that there has been too much talk about developing an arena style of production as if it were unnecessary for the director to achieve a highly individual style for each particular work he undertakes to stage.[4]

Jerry Zaks suggests that the director's and actors' lives will all be easier if the actors understand "the technical requirements of the stage form and don't interpret that kind of directing as restricting their freedom."

For certain plays, the strong, broad movement can actually benefit the performance. Porter comments that thrust staging is more easy to accomplish in plays with a "grandiose sweep like [Molière's] *The Misanthrope,* where people can make very, very, very long entrances and it's fine."

But in "fourth-wall" drama, it is still possible to move in a way that contributes to the overall production, without appearing like a convention imposed by the stage form. In Austin Pendleton's production of Ibsen's *John Gabriel Borkman* at Circle in the Square (Uptown), for the scene in which Mrs. Borkman (played by Rosemary Murphy) attacks Borkman and Ella (played by E. G. Marshall and Irene Worth), Pendleton staged it "so that Irene and E. G. were right in the middle of the space and Rosemary moved all the way around the edges of it." Pendleton remarks,

There's no way you could have achieved that in any other space, and it really released the actress. She was able to circle them—circle them in spirit too. It had a kind of power that it wouldn't have ever had in a proscenium; in fact the idea probably wouldn't have occurred to us in a proscenium space.

For another moment in the same production,

E. G. Marshall and Irene Worth embraced in the middle of a long argument, and then in the course of the embrace she had a long speech. As they were embracing, they turned slowly in a full circle.

   Now I suppose that idea occurred to me out of necessity, because it was pretty much in-the-round. You never would have thought of that in a proscenium stage; it might even have looked funny in a proscenium space. But it didn't look funny in-the-round, and it gave a quite emotional coloration to a moment that you wouldn't have had any other way.

## USING VOMS

Voms are important on a thrust to provide downstage entrances and exits. Without voms, as Hardy points out, productions get "sucked to the back." Voms can keep the action centered on the stage platform, helping to avoid the gravitational pull upstage on a thrust.

Voms can provide sudden surprises in the staging, as Lamos observes: "You can make a whole company of twenty-five people suddenly drop out of sight and have one person alone onstage," or "suddenly there's somebody coming out of the voms, bounding onto the stage." According to Lamos, voms are effective because they "rearrange the whole energy of the space."

In some thrust theatres, there is only one vom directly downstage center, as at the old Milwaukee Rep. Jensen explains why a single central vom is ineffective: "The actor has to come in, walk several steps, and turn around before he is master of the audience." In addition, a single down-center vom makes the diagonal cross, so powerful on the thrust, more difficult.

Using voms also implies a theatricality that many consider compatible with thrust performance: the actor comes through or from under the audience, implicitly including the auditorium in the performance. But some directors don't like this theatricality. Richard Hamburger didn't use the voms for his production of *Treats,* by Christopher Hampton, at Juilliard Drama Theater, for these stylistic reasons:

> Because we were trying to create the illusion of another world, it made little sense to come from the audience. With a tightly focused play like *Treats,* we were trying to create something that's almost behind glass—another world. But if you're doing an expansive Shakespeare, it can be quite delightful to use the voms.

## MOAT

A common form of the thrust stage, one which many directors find useful, is a raised platform surrounded by steps. These surrounding steps form a "moat" around the central stage. Guthrie, who used this stage form at Stratford, Ontario, and in Minneapolis, explained how the stage and moat can be used for *Henry V:* "[The king] stands on the top level and the troops are all around him, lower down, so that Henry can be seen addressing them. The throne is set anywhere near the centre and the courtiers are on a lower level."[5] A director can use this moat to move crowds "offstage" from the major characters, but still within reach and sight. Using the moat, crowds can in effect disappear, but be quickly back onstage when needed. In this case, the moat allows the stage to operate, in effect, like a zoom lens: the stage picture can be very wide and large, with many actors on the stage and surrounding steps, and then zoom in to a tight focus on a single actor, as the others descend the steps and exit through the voms.

•

Proponents of the open stage argue that the proscenium requires confining, arbitrary and artificial staging conventions because of the need to have actors face front, while they see the open stage as liberating and free of staging conventions because the actor can face in any direction. On the other hand, proponents of the proscenium stage feel that the open stage dictates heinous staging conventions: the need to turn to all sections of the audience, etc. The proscenium is seen as simpler in that almost all of the audience perceives the performance in the same way at the same time.

But both prosceniums and open stages require staging conventions that are, in their own ways, confining, arbitrary and artificial. There is not one kind of theatre that affects productions and another that does not; rather, each theatre form, and each individual theatre, affects production in its own way. For a play that does not suit the given theatre, or that is not conceived in such a way as to suit that theatre, these effects will be destructive to the nature of that play. But if the production is suited to the theatre—of whatever form—it will seem natural and free of constraints.

The blocking conventions of the open or proscenium stage

should not be viewed as rules to be followed for a successful formula, but as techniques to be mastered and incorporated into the production. The stage should not dictate the production. Rather, the director should attempt to marry what is required by the play and what is required by the theatre. They should intertwine seamlessly and support one another.

## NOTES

1. Guthrie, "Argument" 82.
2. Joseph, *New* 37.
3. Gerald M. Berkowitz, *New Broadways* (Totowa, N.J.: Rowman and Littlefield, 1982) 29.
4. Gassner, *Times* 518.
5. Tyrone Guthrie, "Theatre at Minneapolis," *Actor and Architect,* ed. Stephen Joseph (Manchester, Eng.: Manchester UP, 1964) 41–42.

# CHAPTER 10

# DIRECTOR-DESIGNER COLLABORATION ON THE OPEN STAGE

The designer and director need to collaborate on the open stage to create a kind of machine for acting. That is, the designer needs to be conscious of the staging conventions and "requirements" of the open stage, and to help the director make these movements seem natural and integral to the production. The designer and director need to cooperate to create a space that makes these movements possible, and even easy.

## TRAFFIC PATTERNS

The set establishes movement patterns for a production. It allows—even encourages—some actions, and discourages—even prohibits—others. The director, in conjunction with the actors, usually determines the blocking for the production, but it is the designer who creates the ground for these figures. Eldon Elder observes, "The designer as much as the director sets the general movement pattern of the play." He goes on to note that the designer's influence on the actor's movement is "particulary evident in the thrust stage; that the shape of the platforms, the placement of furniture, entrances and exits are determined by the designer. He has to help the director have the right kind of dynamics."

In order for this collaboration to be productive, however, good communication must exist between director and designer. The director and designer should agree on the overall staging, as Karl Eigsti explains:

> The patterns that you create in terms of entrances, exits and platforms definitely show up in the blocking. I don't try to block the

play myself, but I do try to think of the moments in the play that are important and isolate those with the director, so that we can have certain moments in which there will be a certain physical picture on the stage. Then I try to link up those moments with interesting ways of getting there and getting out of there, rather than trying to create an infinite variety of labyrinthine paths for the actors to move. It's really more a case of taking these moments and then connecting them together in a sculptural way that allows for the action to flow.

Arranging the traffic patterns does not necessarily mean that the designer should make it easy for the actors to move every which way. Paul Weidner prefers for the designer to give him a groundplan "that is sort of messy, so that you have circuitous ways to get to places. If you have to go through or over an obstacle, it's a visually interesting trip for the actor to make."

## AIDING BLOCKING FUNDAMENTALS

There are certain fundamentals of blocking on the open stage the designer must keep in mind, as described in Chapter 9. Elder points out that the designer needs to support these blocking conventions in the set:

It is very important to set up the space and the islands of furniture in such a way that they will establish the right kinds of dynamics for the director to create diagonal movements, making it possible for him to have the actors address each other in confrontations that give every member of the audience some face to look at, even if they can't see all of the faces.

The designer can help the director by establishing diagonals in the set. John Lee Beatty explains that if a set on a thrust stage has doors on the back wall, the designer should "try to get the doors to open so that the actors are propelled onstage on a strong diagonal, so that they will be shot into the room at an angle, which will force them into the center of the action, which is downstage of the scenery."

The director also wants to make the actors available to all sections of the audience that encircle the stage. In order to aid this blocking technique, David Jenkins tries to make it "difficult for the director to play everything on one side of the stage." On a thrust or arena stage, Jenkins will "spread the groundplan around a little bit more generously," and not be "locked in to naturalistic ideas about where a fireplace should be in relation to the wall or sofa."

## ENTRANCES AND EXITS

On a deep thrust stage with access only at either end, the length of the stage can create difficulties for entrances, exits and crosses in modern realistic drama. The problem does not exist in drama crafted for the thrust stage, such as Shakespeare's: lines are written to cover the actors' crosses to and from upstage doors. But most modern realistic drama is written for the more tightly contained proscenium stage, in which the actor can cross from the doors to the playing area in a few steps. If the designer and director fail to collaborate closely on the location of entrances and exits, the staging can suffer immeasurably.

Well-timed entrances and exits can be especially important for farce. In an almost "Laugh In" style, the actors need, literally or in effect, to be able to poke their heads in, say a line, and exit. Exit lines are a strict convention in farce, requiring the actor to deliver the line at the door, which is fully visible, and then leave immediately, with the door slam punctuating the line. The sightlines to the doors, therefore, need to be good and the proximity between the doors and the primary playing area needs to be close.

Comic exit lines are almost impossible to deliver according to the proscenium convention on a thrust stage. The sightlines to the upstage wall may be poor, so entrance and exit points may be in weak or even largely invisible areas of the stage. In addition, the distance from the upstage wall to the downstage playing area may be great, so the actor must remain farther from the actual exit while speaking, and then cross a longer distance to the exit. Or conversely, an entering actor may need to walk a longer distance to the place where he or she can be seen by the entire audience. Director and producer Robert Whitehead states, "If it requires fast appearances and disappearances and almost a Mack Sennett use of doors and ins and outs, then I think you almost can't do it on an open stage." Dana Ivey describes her frustrations as a comic actress on the Circle in the Square (Uptown) stage:

> First of all, you frequently don't have doors to begin with, and doors are very useful for that kind of punctuation. And even when you do have a door, for example in *Present Laughter* [by Noel Coward], it was so far off on the ramp, up in the aisle, that you had to say the line and still walk several steps before you could get to the door. This is not the way to do a clean exit line.
>
> A lot of plays that have a wonderful built-in rhythm and a built-in indication—'Do this thing at this moment, technically,'—which will help to create the impact that you want. All those indications have to be overlooked and you have to find some other way of doing it. It takes a certain *élan* out of the style.

Bill Stabile points out that on the open stage the actor is often seen "for a half mile going on a ramp, or tripping over programs in the aisles."

The Vivian Beaumont Theater's large stage has frequently caused problems with staging: long crosses may interrupt the action and may be difficult to sustain. According to Julius Novick, "entrances and exits go on for miles, the actors are isolated and hung up . . . their high spirits and their pathos both are dissipated in the emptiness around them."[1] Robin Wagner recalls that a running joke at the Beaumont was that the entrances up the voms were so long "that you had to pack a lunch to make it to stage center."

Ulu Grosbard directed *The Floating Light Bulb* at the Beaumont, and remarks,

> I wanted quick entrances; I didn't want an actor to wander in. I had seen *Macbeth* on that stage, and for an actor to make it from the open wings to the front of the stage would take six, seven, eight seconds. It's interminable to just get there. You add it up in the course of a production and you've distended the play, you've killed the play, and there's nothing you can do about it. Once you're in it, it's too late. Once you've committed yourself to a set, particularly a groundplan, and have staged it accordingly, you can't throw it out and change your mind.
>
> It's very subtle, and it doesn't reveal itself very obviously, but there's an inertness about the production that does come from a

cumulative effect of all those dead beats that occur in the course of people coming and going.

Alan Ayckbourn is well known for his farces, which he writes expressly for an arena stage. He was therefore able to solve the problem of door-slamming on an arena stage for one of his own plays, *Taking Steps,* as Frank Rich recounts:

> The dramatist and director wanted to concoct a low farce of the door-slamming school . . . but as always, Mr. Ayckbourn needed to tailor his grand plan to fit his home company in Scarborough, England, the Stephen Joseph Theater in the Round. How do you send actors popping in and out of rapidly slamming doors when they are always in full view of the spectators ringing an arena stage?
> Mr. Ayckbourn's ingenious solution was to substitute floors for doors. In 'Taking Steps,' the sitting room, master bedroom and attic of a creaky English mansion are all placed side by side at ground level, with the 'steps' between each of the three floors represented by flat carpeted paths on which the frantic characters mime their mad dashes up and down stairs.

For the New York production at Circle in the Square (Uptown), Rich commented, "For once, a problematic New York playhouse can house a script expressly conceived for its unorthodox topography."[2]

## CONTROLLING THE PACE

The pace of a production is very important on the open stage, especially because of the blocking difficulties described above. Thomas Lynch suggests that the designer needs to create the design in such a way as to control the pace and speed of the movement:

> I often think in terms of speeds more than shapes. The speed of approach and how long it's going to take someone to get on and off stage, or in and out of a certain playing area, are crucially important, because a designer dictates that. If the actor has to walk twenty feet across a no-man's-land to get to a playing area, that's going to be a certain number of seconds, and we better like seeing that later on, or otherwise we're in trouble.

Expressing the same idea, Robert Kalfin calls the design "the physical music of the play."

## THE GRAVITATIONAL PULL UPSTAGE

There is usually only one area of a thrust stage where the actor's face can be seen by all three sides of the audience without the actor turning significantly: upstage center. When an actor is down center and facing downstage (the "strongest" area of a proscenium theatre), his or her face is lost to the side sections; when the actor works the periphery of the stage, his or her face is visible only to the section the actor is facing. Only when the actor is up center and facing downstage can the entire audience see his or her face.

Philip Bosco recalls that during rehearsals for Shaw's *Heartbreak House,* in which he was acting, the director attempted to block Rex Harrison, the star of the production, into the downstage area of the Circle in the Square (Uptown) thrust, but

> Rex was always upstage, never downstage. Maybe he'd make an entrance or walk through the downstage area, but eventually he'd always end up upstage. He'd be blocked downstage and he'd say, 'This simply won't do. People can't see me. This is no good.' So when you're like that, it doesn't matter what the staging is; you find the best spot and you stay there. And that's what he did.

Remaining upstage, however, creates the problem that the actor can be quite far from most of the audience, with a vast expanse of stage from the actor to the first row. This distance makes it difficult to establish a rapport and robs the theatre of its greatest asset—intimacy. Martin Gottfried refers to a production at Circle in the Square (Uptown) in which the director "staged the first act at the far end, an effect something like watching a tea party at the distant end of a race track."[3]

Grosbard describes this dilemma for the director on the thrust stage:

> If you stage anything downstage in order to have good sightlines for the third of the house in the center, all the people to the sides can't see. But you do want to stage there, because you want to have a

certain intimacy. If you stage it upstage, you've created ten to fifteen feet between the actor and your first row in the center. You've created an enormous dead space—dead air—which makes it very hard for the actor to reach across. This distances what is happening onstage, and really makes it remote. Every foot of space counts. The closer you move it to be more intimate in relation to the audience, the more people you lose on the sides.

On an especially deep thrust, this problem becomes acute because of the length of the stage. At Circle in the Square (Uptown), for instance, when the actor is upstage at the portal line (and he or she could be even slightly further upstage), it is 40′ to the closest seats in the center section. The elongated "U" shape of the auditorium also puts the actor in a poor position vis-à-vis the spectators on the sides: they must look almost directly sideways to the upstage area.

Another reason for the gravitational pull is that in a thrust theatre, upstage may be the only place to put large scenic units; anywhere else may block sightlines. For realistic productions that require significant scenic elements, placing scenery upstage will further pull the action in that direction.

Despite this gravitational pull, it is imperative to force the action downstage. Gregory Mosher says that at the Vivian Beaumont and Mitzi Newhouse, where he was artistic director, "I've just learned to be bolder about pulling things down into the circle implied by the thrust." Mosher observes that directors at the Beaumont learn that "you can't chicken out, you can't slide upstage in order to 'improve sightlines.' The sightlines are improved, but the experience of seeing the play is hurt."

Mark Lamos suggests that the actors can engage the downstage area by moving through it and returning upstage, especially if a canny director has given him or her a motivation: "As soon as you get downstage, with most of the audience behind you, you need to find a motivation to clear back up. You've always got to remember to leave a character back up there for him to talk to as he turns around."

## PLACES TO BE

The designer can also use furniture or other scenic units to create what Marjorie Bradley Kellogg calls "places to be." Santo

Loquasto points out that if the designer does not modulate the stage space, "the actors are just out there floating around." The designer is then "asked to chase after them with odd bits of furniture—strewing the space with objects." Kellogg maintains that the designer must understand the actors' and director's requirements on the open stage, and try to aid and support their work: "I control the stage space rigidly, not letting people flop all over the place, but focusing the stage in a way that gives the actors discrete 'places to be,' so that it's not like being in the middle of a great void." According to Loren Sherman,

> The most helpful thing is to give the director some place to be taking the actors to. You want to avoid it looking like a fashion show, where people are spinning meaninglessly in order to simply make sure the people on the west bank of seats can see them some of the time. The designer can provide some less phony motivation for people turning around than just to display themselves to a part of the audience that they've neglected.

Sherman suggests providing "something that an actor could interact with, get a prop from, or rest on." Tony Walton creates "magnets to try to draw the movements in certain directions."

For instance, Zack Brown's design for Williams' *The Night of the Iguana* at Circle in the Square (Uptown) broke up the space into many areas—terrain, sand, terrace—with an anchor in each area so that there was "always a reason for movement."

## ARRANGING FURNITURE

Creating traffic patterns for a realistic production often means arranging furniture in order to achieve effective blocking, rather than a realistic environment. Thomas Gruenewald observes that "the temptation for the actors is to lock eyes with their partners and not let the audience in at all, because there's such a greater expanse of fourth wall for the actor to deal with." He contends that "it's up to the director to help," by placing furniture or scenic units around the edge of the stage in order to open the actors up to all sides of the auditorium. In order to create furniture arrangements that keep the actors open and available, Eigsti has "made a joke to directors of putting the furniture in a circle—a circle of sofas."

While Eigsti is not entirely serious here, furniture does need to be arranged according to the conventions of the open stage, not necessarily the conventions of actual rooms. As Gruenewald explains,

> You have to force those curves. You can't have the couch and the two chairs and the coffee table, because you are creating an enormous obstacle. The key to arranging furniture is to force curves on people, so that you can justify those three-quarter turns that seem so artificial in the rehearsal hall, but once you are in the theatre you can justify them because more people can see.

As to specific furniture choices, Tony Tanner says that "the most important decision" for the director and designer in a realistic play is "the sofa decision," in that it is "the biggest piece of furniture and it's got the longest back," potentially causing sightline problems. But since furniture on the open stage has to be low so that the audience can see over it, designers frequently use backless, open furniture, which can also be helpful to the director. Beatty points out that a chaise, for instance, which doesn't have a long back and "is going to allow people to face two directions" may be better than a sofa. Similarly, stools are better than chairs, in that one can sit on a stool in any direction.

For these same reasons window seats are frequently used on the open stage. Gruenewald refers to the window seat as a "much overused cliche," but notes that it can be "very helpful" for a realistic play on an open stage, in that it "doesn't have a back, as a chair would, it's a place where two people would sit, and the actor can open up from there by playing the fourth wall window from the window seat."


## DOWNSTAGE ROCK

One of the most important pieces of furniture on the thrust stage is what many designers and directors call the "downstage rock," a scenic unit that can help incorporate the extreme downstage area into the action. Simply put, the designer needs to give the actors an excuse to walk all the way downstage. Kenneth Foy defines the downstage rock as "an anchor, a focus of the downstage area." According to Michael Yeargan, "You're always trying to find something to put right downstage, because you've got all this scenery—the walls or whatever—upstage, and the sofa is in the middle." Downstage rocks come in all shapes, sizes, and forms: ottoman, pouf, stool, milk crate, tree stump, bench, etc.

Directors agree that a downstage rock is helpful to their work. John Tillinger suggests that the downstage rock should be "something without a back," so that an actor can sit facing in any direction. The actor seated on the downstage rock can face upstage with his or her back to part of the audience, but this problem can be minimized by placing the downstage rock in front of a vom or aisle. This arrangement can also set up a diagonal: the seated actor faces diagonally upstage to the audience on one side, and the standing actor faces diagonally downstage to the spectators in the center.

The downstage rock helps actors counteract the gravitational pull upstage. At Hartford Stage, Weidner likes to have a

> constant reason for the actors to come down, because if they're not used to that kind of thrust stage, they tend to want to stay upstage where they can be seen by the whole house. But if you can convince them that the downstage rock is the strongest position on the stage, they'll all gravitate to it.

Weidner points out that a downstage rock creates vigorous "coming and going" and "allows for a lot of good tension between the two poles": the downstage rock and the upstage entrances.

These techniques are not necessary for all drama on thrust stages, or for all approaches to production. By and large, these principles apply only to realistic productions on the open stage, in which a character needs external motivations from his or her environment to move about the stage. According to David Mitchell, "It's only when you have realistic dimensions of a room or several rooms, or in general where you have imaginary walls" that these techniques apply. The downstage rock may not be needed for drama originally written for the thrust stage, such as Shakespeare, as Stephen Porter explains, "The upstage throne or the upstage bench will work, because people can always come downstage and talk to the audience and lie on the floor and kick their legs on the edge of the stage and they don't really need it." In other words, for presentational drama that acknowledges the existence of the audience, the actor is freer to range about the stage for theatrical, rather than realistic, reasons.

The downstage rock may also be unnecessary if a more presentational approach is taken in production, whatever the mode of drama. Alvin Epstein maintains that the need for a downstage rock "depends on whether or not you're attempting the illusion of naturalism. If you're not going to be illusionistic, you don't need anything there at all—just stage your actors in the best possible positions to play the scene."

## TREATS ALL AROUND

Because the spectators are viewing the stage from more than one direction, they will be seeing different stage "pictures." These multiple viewpoints bother some directors and designers, who want to "control" what the audience sees, and who want the audience to see the same thing at the same time. Others argue, though, that it is all right if spectators see different pictures, so long as no one feels cheated. John Jensen refers to this technique as "treats all around": "Everybody gets, not the same thing, but the flavor of the same thing." Jensen tries to "find things to show people at the right and left that people in the center couldn't see."[4]

These "treats all around" also help the director to keep the action moving, in that the actors are drawn to the objects around the stage. The director can also provide treats all around, mirroring the action left and right, so that those seated on one side see one of the activities, though not necessarily both or the same one as those seated on the other side. Walton comments that for *The Front Page* at the Vivian Beaumont,

> whenever a group of people were running to find the mayor, Zaks [the director] duplicated the stage action, so even though one section of the audience isn't seeing what the other section of the audience is seeing, they're actually seeing a sort of mirror image of it.

Walton explains that this technique was in part a reaction to the
auditorium:

> Because the configuration was three-quarters of a wheel, we were
> conscious that anybody who had gone through the up-center door
> could only be seen by a certain number of people. So it was used
> very selectively and never for crucial dialogue.
>
> We consciously try to find ways of using what has been thought
> of as dead space in non-crucial, 'grace note' ways, rather than
> something that is going to disrupt the action if somebody misses it.
>
> We have generally used it as a way of adding another accent,
> somehow getting more excitement or more pleasure, out of a
> moment that would perhaps have only just been holding the stage if
> it had only been using the conventional forestage area.

Creating a production that is harmonious with the open stage is
not the job of the director or designer alone. Each must understand
the nature of the other's work, and find ways of creating a
production in which the movement flows easily and the entire
production, including actors and scenery, is available to all of the
audience.

## NOTES

1. Julius Novick, "A Giant Step from Ho to Hum," *Village Voice* 16
   March 1972: 56.
2. Frank Rich, "Slamming-Door Farce Sans Doors," *The New York
   Times* 21 Feb. 1991: B3.
3. Martin Gottfried, "Ibsen's 'Sea' a Washout," *New York Post* 19
   March 1976: 24.
4. As quoted in Wallace 205.

# CHAPTER 11

# STAGE UP OR STAGE DOWN?
# THE VERTICAL RELATIONSHIP OF AUDIENCE
# AND PERFORMANCE

A vital element in the creative use of theatre space is the vertical relationship of audience and performance, affecting design, directing and audience perception of the theatrical event. Looking straight on at a performance is not the same as looking up or looking down. The relationship of audience and performance in plan—i.e., to what degree the audience encircles the stage (proscenium, thrust or arena)—has been much studied. Much less examined is this relationship in section. Is the performance on the same level as most of the audience, on a pedestal above the audience, or in a pit below the audience? How does that relationship affect the audience's perception of the theatrical event? How does it affect the work of the designer, director and actor?

Two factors determine the vertical relationship of audience and performance: the rake of the auditorium and the height of the stage. In a standard proscenium theatre, such as on Broadway, the audience in the gently raked orchestra looks slightly up or straight on at the actors on the raised stage. The auditorium in an open-stage theatre, whether thrust, arena or end stage, tends to be steeply raked, with most of the spectators looking down at the stage.

## AUDITORIUM RAKE

Almost all open stages have a steeply raked auditorium in order for spectators to see over the heads of the row in front and to see the floor of the stage, an important design feature of the open stage. Raking the audience steeply means that the last rows of the theatre are brought closer to the stage, whereas a shallower rake stretches out this horizontal distance. A steeper rake can therefore provide a greater intimacy by bringing more of the audience closer to the action.

A steeper rake can also provide a more energized theatre. The audience and actor are brought closer together, and the actor, faced with a wall of spectators, can more readily play off their reactions. The spectators tend to be more aware of each other, in that the stage may be encircled by the audience. They see a "wall" of people that fills the space vertically, as opposed to a shallow-raked auditorium, in which the audience fills only a narrow angle of the height.

The steep rake also pitches the spectator into the action of the performance: he or she will tend to sit more upright or forward in order to see the action below, whereas with a shallow rake and raised stage, the audience can lean back, more comfortably and relaxed, and may therefore be less involved in the action. Mark Lamos wishes the auditorium rake at Hartford Stage were steeper in order that the audience would feel "more in the lap of the action." With the present rake, "you can sit back and relax, and there's a sense of distance." Lamos suggests that the designer can compensate for the languid feeling "by thrusting the design into the space a bit more."

## STAGE HEIGHT

The second major factor in determining the vertical relationship of audience and performance is the height of the stage. In a proscenium theatre, the stage is usually a raised platform, with most of the spectators looking slightly up or straight on at the actors. In thrusts or arenas, there are three common relationships: 1) The stage is a platform raised above the first few rows; 2) The stage is on the same level with the first row, with no architecturally defined stage; 3) The stage is a sunken pit below the entire audience.

### Raised Stage

A raised stage can provide a clearly defined performance area. In addition, a raised stage helps counteract the disadvantage that actors can have in an open-stage theatre: in a steeply raked auditorium, the spectators look down on the actors—literally and metaphorically. A raised stage provides a rostrum that lends the actor more importance and significance, even though most of the audience still looks down.

Raising the stage above the first few rows, however, can cause sightline problems from those seats. In a thrust or arena, it is helpful to use "downstage rocks," furniture or low scenic units near the outer edge of the stage (see Chapter 10). The problem is that if people are seated below stage level, even a low downstage rock will block their view to actors who are upstage. In fact, even actors who are downstage may block the view upstage.

The stage of the Vivian Beaumont Theatre is raised above the first few rows, and many designers have complained about the resulting problems. Douglas Schmidt explains that unless there is furniture downstage, "the actors can't come out there, they can't bring their ashtray and put it down out there." Without downstage rocks, the stage is problematic for presenting plays needing a realistic environment: "It makes it very difficult to justify using that space as a big empty platform, unless it's something like *Antigone*." David Mitchell observes that directors often try usual thrust staging techniques at the Beaumont, until they encounter the actual sight-lines: "Directors come in and have great resolution about a piece of furniture downstage, but when they get in there they find that the piece of furniture begins moving back," because of the sightlines.

## No Defined Stage

In some theatres, there is no defined stage at all; it is neither a raised platform nor a sunken pit. The stage is the floor, on the same level as the first row of seats. This relationship is most common in undefined "black-box" theatres, in which audience bleachers can be moved about on a flat floor to form the various audience-performance configurations, and the performance takes place on the floor. The lack of a raised or lowered stage means that the stage is not vertically defined, or set apart, from the rest of the theatre space. The floor level is continuous across the entire space; the actors perform and the audience walks on a level that continues unimpeded to the walls of the space. The areas of the theatre—stage and non-stage—are not clearly differentiated.

This vertical relationship adds an extra ingredient to the production process. The designer and director need to determine what space the performance is occurring in: the area created by the seating, i.e., the negative area in front of the seats, or the whole space of the room. If the stage is not defined somehow, the entire theatre space can implicitly be the performing area. If an undefined stage is a deliberate choice, it can involve the audience in the performance; if not, it can muddy the audience-performance relationship and rob the production of clear definition.

If one wants to define a stage area in such a theatre, a raised platform or a groundcloth can be added. At CSC Rep, Carey Perloff set *The Birthday Party* on a raised, white platform floating in the otherwise all-black space. For Racine's *Phaedra,* Perloff wanted a "very claustrophobic" and "isolated" world, with "a sense that you couldn't get out." In this case, the borders were "very specific," defined by rattan mats and benches around the periphery.

## Sunken Stage

In some open stages, the entire audience is above the stage; the performing area is, in effect, a sunken pit. This vertical relationship has been compared with a bullfighting arena and an operating theatre—favorably and unfavorably. The fact that the spectators look down at the actors has been criticized for diminishing and distancing the performance, and praised for being exciting and theatrical.

The steeply tiered auditorium at the Mitzi Newhouse Theater has been referred to as a bullring, and this effect has been part of the very concept for at least two productions. Schmidt accentuated the "bullring" effect by adding a low wall around the entire stage for a production of *Play Strindberg,* by Friedrich Duerrenmatt. He describes the circular playing area as "a cockfight, a bullpen. It was like looking into a pit." Jack Gelber "needed a tiered bullring feeling" for *Kool Aid,* by Merle Molofsky, which he directed there. At the climax of the play the actors "met at the center of the stage in a wrestling contest, both verbal and actual. The whole feeling of the fight was emphasized by the aura of the auditorium."

The Juilliard Drama Theatre has one of the most extreme sunken stages, and has been referred to as a "moated bearpit."[1]

The thrust stage is so low that an actor standing onstage is roughly at eye level with a spectator seated in the first row; the rest of the auditorium is raked steeply up from there. Gerald Freedman and Michael Kahn, who both directed there, comment that the sunken stage makes them acutely aware as directors of blocking patterns. Freedman finds actors "moving in space" to be "exciting—more interesting than a picture frame." Kahn prefers looking down at the actors rather than "through them," and comments that this relationship caused his shows to be "more choreographic, more so than they would be on a proscenium. The actors move in circles, figure-8s, serpentines. On a proscenium they would move more linearly. Here they move in space. It's freeing for the director."

Looking sharply down at the actors can also cause problems of scale: the actors' bodies are foreshortened against the background of the stage. According to Kenneth Foy, a steep auditorium rake "confuses the scale. You don't realize how tall someone is." In *A Midsummer Night's Dream,* several jokes rely on Helena being

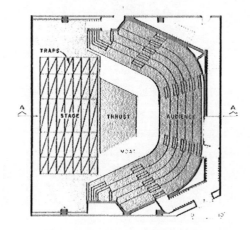

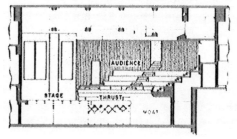

14. Plan and section of the Juilliard Drama Theatre, New York City. Architects: Pietro Belluschi, Helge Westermann, Eduardo Catalano. Reproduced with permission of Helge Westermann.

15. View of the Juilliard Drama Theatre. Reproduced with permission of the Juilliard School.

taller than Hermia. Though Helena was in fact quite a bit taller in the Juilliard production, it was not apparent from the elevated audience; Helena had to be placed on a 12″ platform during the lines about the disparity in height.

A sunken stage need not remain at that level, though: the stage "pit" can be filled in so that the stage is level with the first audience row. This change provides a more "undefined" stage, reducing the differentiation of the stage from the rest of the theatre space. Andrew Jackness raised the stage at the Anspacher Theatre up to the level of the first row and covered the entire floor with sand in his design for *Salonika,* by Louise Page. He felt that the sunken stage was the wrong relationship for this play:

> I didn't like the pit feeling. I wanted the first row of audience to feel that they could walk out onto the stage. We wanted an endless sensation to that beach. If you set it in a pit, you give more of a sense of the architecture of the theatre than I wanted. You give it away—exactly how this theatre is constructed, and if you just let the

sand flow off into the seating area, you're not sure where it starts and stops.

## POWER RELATIONSHIPS

The vertical relationship of audience and performance raises complex psychological issues of dominance and intimacy. Dominance is usually viewed as who is on top: the most common view is that a sunken stage makes the audience dominant, while a raised stage provides the actor a greater sense of presence and power. Richard Leacroft, for instance, writes: "The raised stage . . . permits the actor to dominate the audience."[2] But with a steeply raked auditorium, such as the Vivian Beaumont, Robin Wagner observes, "It's hard for an actor to intimidate an audience when he's not above them."

Looking down at the actors, with an implication of judgment or superiority, may enhance aspects of some plays. Bill Hart, a director at the Public Theater, feels that looking down at the actors, especially in the "basketball court" arrangement of LuEsther Hall at the Joseph Papp Public Theater, was effective for *The Normal Heart,* by Larry Kramer, a play about AIDS: "The actors felt very naked. We were looking down, watching these people struggle for their lives, and they were caught."

The Royal Shakespeare Company has several theatres in Great Britain, and John Caird points out that each vertical relationship creates a different power relationship. The Other Space in Stratford-upon-Avon and the Pit in London's Barbican Centre are small studio theatres that usually have raised stages, and Caird considers each to be "actor spaces. You go in there as a member of the audience and you feel you are in some sense a voyeur of what is happening on stage, but it belongs to the actors. It's not your space; you're just lucky to be there watching them." On the other hand, in the main theatres in Stratford or at the Barbican, with much of the audience looking down from high galleries, "it's the audience's space, and they are sitting in judgment waiting for the actors to be good, and they'd better be good, because we paid a lot of money, we haven't come here for nothing. So the actors have to work for the audience." At the Swan Theatre in Stratford, with roughly half the audience on the gently raked floor looking up at the stage and the rest perched in high galleries, "there is an absolute feeling of equality and balance between actor and audience."

Bill Stabile is intrigued by the effect of a high stage, especially in proscenium theatres. He likes to elevate the actor: "Being up high is a much stronger position. If the actor is up in the air, a good part of the child comes out in the spectator—you are looking up, like a kid." Because of this effect, Stabile often builds high stages into flexible theatres.

Jonathan Miller, on the other hand, maintains that there is no inherent dominance in the vertical configuration, and that the nature of the relationship is entirely dependent on the behavior of the actor. In other words, the actor can manipulate the configuration to whatever end he or she wants. According to Miller, "People are very, very naive about space as being automatically, self-sufficiently an expression of dominance." Instead, Miller argues,

> It depends on how the gaze penetrates the space. If they gaze arrogantly down from their height to the audience, in other words acknowledge the audience's lowliness, then it becomes dominant. It depends on what the people are doing at that height, and what they are doing at that depth.
>
> The authority is invested in the role of the person and the relationship that he has by virtue of the authority invested in his glance, not by his spatial relationship to the audience.

## INVOLVING OR DISTANCING?

The second major psychological issue is whether one vertical relationship is more intimate or distant than another. The most common view is that a slightly raised stage, with the audience looking slightly up or straight on at the actors, can make the action more intimate, while a sunken stage can be more distant. Though the Anspacher Theatre is small, Wilford Leach feels that the sunken stage deprives the space of intimacy: "There is a feeling of remoteness from the actors being down in a hole. You might as well have a proscenium." Many have commented on the distancing effect of the "moated bearpit" of the Juilliard Drama Theatre. Director Gene Lesser, for instance, says,

> Even though it's a small theatre, it has the effect of being a large theatre. It didn't lend itself to intimate moments. It was like doctors watching an operation. It's very detached. It's very clinical. It detached the audience emotionally; you're an observer. You can't get emotional.

The distancing effect can be overcome somewhat with a raised platform. Schmidt has found at the Juilliard Drama Theatre that a platform can compensate for the "distancing effect" of the sunken stage: "Push it forward, get it closer, get it higher, get it into the audience's lap." At Hartford Stage, Lamos uses raised platforms frequently:

> I decided that one of the answers to making the theatre more intimate was to play everything on three or four foot platforms, to build a stage on top of the stage, which actually made faces of actors closer to your face in the audience. You weren't looking down on them so much.

On the other hand, the distancing effect of a sunken stage may be appropriate for some plays or approaches to production. Freedman likes "looking down as a theatrical relationship," because "it puts the audience in the power position." In a proscenium theatre, "the production is in the commanding position." In the Juilliard Drama Theatre, "you feel as if you're in an examining room, which makes it more ritualistic," and therefore good for classical drama. While many criticize the distancing effect, Freedman "likes the play being removed, examined, distanced."

Stephen Joseph compares the vertical relationship in the theatre to the relationship inherent in the play:

> [The raised stage] puts the actors *above* the audience; it gives them an authority, and puts the audience in an *inferior* position. The actors *look down* on the audience, which *looks up* at the actors. This literal description of the situation is loaded with deeper meaning. The raised stage is ideal for Kings and Heroes, exalted characters,

the protagonists of classical and romantic drama. But modern
drama has very different protagonists. I suggest that they are
usually *on the same level* as the audience which may properly look
down on them. . . . It seems to me that this relationship between
actor and audience reflects very accurately what so many of today's
playwrights are striving to achieve. Further, it is a relationship that
puts old plays into a new focus. What happens when Hamlet or
King Lear forsakes the commanding platform and comes down to
our level? We judge them as though they were men like ourselves,
we sympathise with them, despise them, love them: surely not
entirely against their creator's wishes?[3]

## VARYING THE VERTICAL RELATIONSHIP

The effects of the vertical relationship on audience and performance have led some theatre artists to modulate the configuration
for each production. Depending on the nature of the piece, the
actor is placed above the audience, or vice versa. Varying the
horizontal audience-performance relationship is commonly considered in flexible theatres, but variations in the vertical relationship are rarely discussed.

The Wooster Group uses the Performing Garage (New York
City) exclusively in an end-stage arrangement, but varies the
height of the stage and audience for each performance piece. The
vertical relationship is adjusted in order to determine the atti-
tude—physically and mentally—that the spectator is to have
toward the performance: to look down analytically or to gaze up in
awe.

For *Nayatt School* the audience was perched on steeply raked
bleachers eight feet up, in the position of the students in an
operating theatre, scientifically examining the operation below
them. For this piece, which dealt with the nature of madness,
James Leverett describes the

> literal descent into the mental hospital—literal because performers
> have been seated precariously along an eight-foot-high ledge facing
> the high risers on which the audience is situated. The actors' climb
> down to the stage floor is, of course, metaphorical—a fall into
> madness, chaos, death.[4]

16. *Nayatt School,* Performing Garage, New York City. Photograph by Nancy Campbell.

*L.S.D. (. . . Just the High Points . . .)* reversed the vertical configuration of *Nayatt School.* The audience was now on the floor, looking up at a high, long platform. This "conventional" vertical relationship of audience and stage—looking up—was exaggerated to accentuate the effect. The result, according to David Savran, was that "there was something heroic about the figures in the play, larger than life, with a spatial delineation of the hero—who and what gets oppressed in the course of the hero's heroism."

Richard Schechner, who started the Performing Garage, also used the vertical relationship as a correlation for the nature of the performance. For Seneca's *Oedipus,* the spectators were seated in a full circle, a version of the Roman circus, with the seats tilted forward, making them feel that they were "going to be thrown into a pit," and that the performance was "a judgment being passed on a person's life, an investigation into past life. The audience sits in judgment, as judges, looking down at this operation."

For *The Tooth of Crime,* by Sam Shepard, at the LaMama Annex, Stabile provided George Ferencz, the director, with a stage raised high above the floor and very steeply raked. The high stage achieved the vertical relationship of a rock concert, with the rock star as a demi-god placed high on a pedestal and the adoring devotees dancing below, gazing and reaching. This vertical relationship of audience and performance supports an aspect of *The Tooth of Crime:* the nature and consequences of stardom. Ferencz explains that the high stage

> changed the dynamic of how the audience communicated with the show. You're viewing it much more like you're viewing a rock-and-roll concert. For *The Tooth of Crime* it definitely worked much more effectively, because they're gods, it's bigger than life, elevated.

•

Looking up at a performance, as in most proscenium theatres, is not the same as looking down, as in most open stages. Looking down at the stage drastically affects the work of designers and directors. Designers must design the floor as background for the actors and juggle the sightlines in relation to the downstage scenery and the few spectators seated below stage level. Directors tend to pay more attention to the "choreography" of their blocking, since the audience looks down at the patterns of movement. The rake of the auditorium and the height of the stage greatly affect the audience's perception of and involvement in the performance. Is the play to be on a pedestal—up there? Is the play to be in our midst—with as little differentiation between audience and performance as possible? Or are we to look down—to examine the play, scientifically and judgmentally? Should the actors and the play be in the "power position," or should the audience? Or should it be as equal as possible?

In some theatres this relationship may be fixed and inflexible because of sightlines and permanent architecture. In this case, it is the director, designer and actor's responsibility to understand the theatre and respond to it appropriately. In other theatres, the vertical relationship is flexible, in which case the theatre artists should consider it as vital and important as the horizontal relationship.

## NOTES

1. "A Drama School's Moated Bearpit," *Progressive Architecture* 51 (1970): 55.

2. Richard Leacroft, "Actor and Audience, Part Two: A Study of Experimental Theatres in the United States and Canada," *Royal Institute of British Architects Journal,* 3rd series 70 (1963): 203–4.
3. Joseph, *Round* 121.
4. James Leverett, "The Wooster Group's 'Mean Theatre' Sparks a Hot Debate," *Theatre Communications,* in Wooster Group Scrapbook, n. date: n. pag.

# CHAPTER 12

# ENGAGING THE STAGE VOLUME

## WHY VOLUME IS IMPORTANT

An essential aspect of producing plays in an open-stage theatre is to engage the volume, i.e., the space, over the stage. A thrust or arena theatre tends to have a much more steeply raked auditorium than a proscenium theatre, and therefore has a great deal of height over the stage that is available for exploitation. Dealing with this volume is one of the most critical concerns that differentiates the open and proscenium stages. In fact, some theatres have such height available that they essentially demand that the theatre artist engage the volume or risk producing a limp, enervated production that does not relate to its spatial surrounding.

Using height on an open stage has a greater effect on the spectator than in a proscenium theatre. Because the audience in a thrust or arena theatre is grouped closer to the stage than in a proscenium theatre of equal capacity, the use of height is more likely to physically involve the spectator. Simply put, if you are close to the stage and the action moves up significantly, you will have to raise your head to follow the action. On the other hand, if you are far from the stage, merely shifting your eyes will account for the angle of change. Even though the actual height of the upward movement onstage may be the same, the spectator is more physically involved in the open stage than in the proscenium.

It is also important to match the theatre's volume with the size that is appropriate for the given play. Tony Tanner believes that every play has an implicit size, which the director should discover and use:

> In every show there is an inherent thing that you might call a theatrical gesture, and the size of that gesture varies tremendously from one show to another. *Aida* with elephants is one thing, and Pat Carroll as Gertrude Stein is another. Both of them can be equally

enthralling, but it's terribly important to be in the right kind of real estate.

## EFFECTS OF VOLUME ON PERFORMANCE

### Inflate the Production

One response to a space with a large volume is to conceive the production in a large scale, with an epic, pageant-like performance. Obviously, this approach will work better for a play that is inherently large in scope; for a smaller, more intimate drama, the director and designer should try to conceive the production with a large style that can still support the nature of the play, or simply decide not to produce the play in such a theatre. Unfortunately, large theatres have long production records of small plays failing because they were puffed up to suit the large volume, or were lost in the vast space.

Many theatres suffer from the problem of too much volume, with the result that designers often fill the space with scenery. John Lee Beatty cites the Mark Taper Forum as a "scenery swallower":

> A piece of scenery has to be about a third again as big as you would normally choose to make it, because the room is large. Even though it's a fairly small theatre, the room is large and it tends to shrink scenery. Something that you think would be too big or too tall actually looks pretty normal when you put it up.

Karl Eigsti notes that the Cincinnati Playhouse in the Park "is so large that you don't have any contact with what's going on. It's like being in the third balcony." As a result, Eigsti feels that his most effective designs have been "giant sets that came out into the house, that somehow tried to limit that inhibiting factor. The more you can challenge that space with large statements, the more the space accepts it, because it's such a large space anyway."

The Vivian Beaumont is frequently cited as a theatre in which the stage and auditorium spaces are simply too big, with deleterious effects on performance. The vast volume results in a lack of

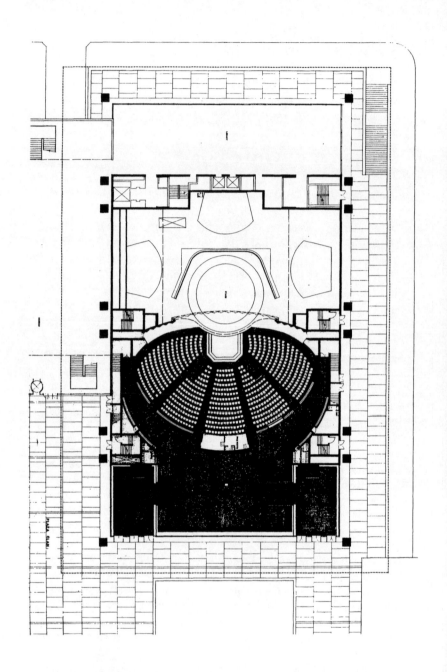

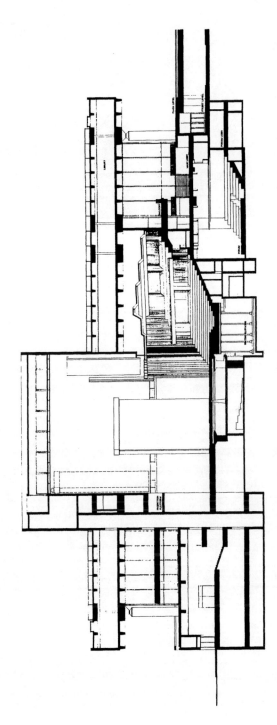

17. Plan and section of the Vivian Beaumont Theatre, New York City. Architect: Eero Saarinen. Consultant: Jo Mielziner. Reproduced with permission of Kevin Roche, John Dinkeloo and Associates.

18. View of the Vivian Beaumont Theatre, New York City (without the lighting grid currently above the stage). Reproduced with permission of the Lincoln Center Theater.

audience intimacy with itself and with the actors; the cavernous auditorium makes the stage and actors appear minuscule; and the large volume enervates productions, dissipating their power and reducing their effect on spectators.

A common response to the Beaumont's large volume has been to fill it with spectacle—scenery, actors and dazzling effects. Designers and directors tend to build up the production to the scale of the theatre. Douglas Schmidt explains the designer's dilemma: "Either you designed a gigantically over-scaled set or you designed a real-scale set that looked like a postage stamp in this great void." According to Robert Brustein, "Directors feel compelled to fill the stage with bustle and movement, designers are tempted to overproduce, and actors to stress their points more emphatically than necessary."[1]

Over the history of production at the Beaumont there are countless cases of performances that were criticized for being overproduced, presumably for the purpose of filling the vast volume. Critics complained that *Beggar on Horseback,* by George S. Kaufman and Marc Connelly, had been inflated with excess scenery and choreography in order to make a relatively simple comedy fill the Beaumont stage. Martin Gottfried wrote that the set "only emphasizes the Vivian Beaumont's problem (a roof so high it dwarfs the stage)," and concluded, "The script itself is almost buried beneath the overproduction and overdirection."[2]

For *Macbeth,* designers Herbert Senn and Helen Pond placed a catwalk spanning the downstage area 14 feet above the stage, which could be reached by two rolling staircases, one straight and the other spiral. The designers report that the catwalk and stairs were a response to the height of the theatre, as well as to provide additional downstage playing areas. But critics questioned the effectiveness of this use. Walter Kerr generally praised director Sarah Caldwell's composition, but remarked, "The staircases gradually become gratuitous, contrivances introduced simply to make use of vertical space,"[3] and Brendan Gill called the set "a desperate attempt to fill up the big and hollow-seeming Beaumont stage."[4]

Each management of the Beaumont has come to the opinion that large plays with an emphasis on spectacle work best in this theatre. Jules Irving described the plays for one season as having "a common theatricality and sweep, ideally suited to the size and scope of the Beaumont stage."[5]

Later, Joseph Papp announced that he would produce "plays that can benefit from vastness" at the Beaumont.[6] In fact, when Papp initially presented new American plays, reviewers criticized them for not adequately filling the space. John Simon wrote of one such play, "A sofa's worth of play looks even more pitiful on the vast Beaumont stage."[7]

Richmond Crinkley, the next director of the Beaumont, agreed that a "big play with an oversized performance" is best for this theatre: "You have to give an impression of something that's larger than life—of great size and scope, of high emotion. The space is too big for American naturalism, comedy of manners or drawing room comedy."

## Engage the Volume to Benefit the Production

Volume need not be looked at as an obstacle to be overcome, however; the height of a space can enhance a production. Gerald

Freedman "loves" height in a space because "it makes for a sense of theatrical size. The actor feels he's acting in a real volume, not in a basement or a small theatre. It's great for the spirit." The height of the Anspacher Theatre enhanced a production that Mel Shapiro directed: the play was "very tight and contained, a sort of constipated play—very terse," and the stage volume "added a kind of lyricism, which the play needed."

John Conklin feels that ample volume in an open stage can be helpful, because the architecture imposes itself less onto the production; the walls and ceiling are simply farther away and not as much in sight: "Blank bigness—height and space—is a neutral statement. The space doesn't say anything, but it allows you to say anything: be dynamic, be boring, be unfocused, be totally focused, be tiny, be big."

If there is significant volume over the stage, the designer and director should find a way to engage that space. That may mean tall scenery, or it may entail some subtler way of engaging the volume. Even if the designer uses only low scenery, he or she has "dealt with" the volume, in that masking or the back wall will be visible and won't simply "go away." If the volume is left open and empty, it has been, in a sense, dealt with. Schmidt maintains that engaging the volume over the stage is essential, because "it just looks naked if you don't do something." Karen Schulz, a designer, agrees: "The high space demands attention. You need to consider the vertical space in your design."

Designers and directors have found ways to use the Beaumont volume to their benefit. Two productions stand out for exploring the entire volume: *The Three-Penny Opera* and Aeschylus' *Agamemnon,* directed by Richard Foreman and Andrei Serban respectively, and both designed by Schmidt. For *The Three-Penny Opera,* the stage was opened as far upstage as possible, but could be closed off by a 30′-tall wall that rolled up- and downstage. Metal bridges extended from the stage into the auditorium and partially over the audience, providing a dish effect to the overall playing area. Schmidt says that this huge scale was "justified" because of the nature of the theatre: "*Three-Penny Opera* looked like it was meant to be in that theatre."

Schmidt's design for *Agamemnon* "completely reorganized the space in ways the theatre was never intended." The forestage elevator was lowered to the basement, leaving a vast, 20′-deep pit between the first row and the stage. A triangular, steel-mesh platform partially extended over the pit, with a chasm in front, so that spectators could see into the pit below, where a large cage contained the Chorus. To replace the seats lost to the basement, Schmidt placed movable bleachers on the stage itself, turning the space into an arena. The two bleachers "jack-knifed" during the course of the production, forming either a flat bank facing the auditorium, or splitting at the center to open up and allow for the full use of the stage. The bleachers were closed, according to Schmidt, for "intimate" scenes and then opened up for "spectacle." The opened stage revealed scenery behind, such as a high platform for the herald or a large wall depicting the House of Atreus. Gottfried described the result:

> The Aeschylus tragedy . . . unfolds this plant to its cavernous bowels, sending actors to the floor beneath its stage, to the final rear wall, to scary heights; it even shifts great blocks of the audience on moving banks. . . . And it may well be the most adventurous use this house has yet been put to.[8]

## Manipulate the Volume

As was explained in Chapter 6, the audience more readily perceives the open stage as a three-dimensional volume, as opposed to the proscenium stage, which it perceives more as a picture. The designer's job, then, is to define and shape the volume of the open stage. Eigsti refers to one method of manipulating the stage space as "breaking up the cubic volume by penetrating it," which he explains:

> You have to penetrate the space with some kind of sculpture that breaks it up, that redefines the cube, or orients the cube to the figure. It is a vertical redefinition of the space.
> At Arena Stage we've found that the most successful sets are the ones that do break up the cube; in the least successful ones, the scenery ends at the height of the actors' heads, and then there's a space between that and where the grid starts—the cube remains.

Eigsti suggests that this redefinition can be as simple as "a couple of poles," in which case "the space automatically becomes more visually dynamic."

Bill Stabile says that the designer must manipulate the space and create the volume that is appropriate for the play: "It's really the empty space that counts, the volume of empty air that you create, the negative space where the actors are going to move. You create different shapes and volumes. You are in this mostly empty space."

## Suspend Scenery Above Stage Level

One way of incorporating the volume into the performance is to hang scenic units over the stage, perhaps not filling it with scenery, but at least acknowledging the volume over the stage as part of the performance space. According to Eldon Elder, it is important for the designer to use scenery over the stage in an arena because the designer has only "two principal surfaces" in which to make the "design statement" and to "create a scenic environment, an effect, or to establish place": "the floor and the overhead."

Another reason for placing scenery overhead is that, because an open-stage theatre usually has a steeply raked auditorium, the view straight ahead from the last rows is the volume well above the stage. Eigsti explains the problem and solution at Arena Stage: "What's right in front of the spectator is this void. If there's nothing there, there is a kind of space that separates the actor from the environment. One needs to tie the actor into his environment for people looking at it from the higher plane." By placing scenery overhead, the designer can "bring the eye contact down to the actor."

But overhead scenery can cause focus problems, drawing the audience's attention away from the actors and up to the scenic elements. John Jensen says that "care must be taken or such units may distract the concentration by pulling the audience's eye up into the space." Heidi Landesman found that when designing at Martinson Hall, which has a high, domed ceiling over the stage and audience, "if you try to deal with the height, it pulls your focus so far away from the stage that it's harmful." In response to the height, therefore, Landesman did not stretch the set upward, but instead deliberately kept it down and finished at the top: "The design had to be very self-contained as a unit. It had to be visually complete itself, so you as an audience member weren't tempted to look up over the top."

## Use a Grid to Control the Space

The stage volume can also be controlled by capping it with a technical grid. At the Anspacher Theater, a lighting grid was installed over the thrust stage in order to create an overhead limit to the stage space—making the volume more manageable—and to foster a feeling of intimacy. As Ming Cho Lee, the consultant for the theatre, explains,

> When you are doing a thrust or arena stage, the exciting thing about that kind of theatre experience is the fact that the performer and the spectator are sitting under the same roof, and you want to make that as clear and exciting as possible. To give the feeling that the audience is really sitting in the theatrical space, the exposed lighting grid is essential. It's large enough that the audience feels that they are also sitting underneath the same functional ceiling that's over the stage space.

The exposed grid was not just for functional purposes, but was also to create the proper theatrical ambiance, intimacy and proportion.

The Beaumont originally did not have an exposed grid; instead, all the lighting and catwalks were hidden from view behind a dark ceiling with fins pointing toward the proscenium arch. The lack of a perceptible ceiling spanning audience and performance was one reason that the auditorium and stage volume seemed too big. At the Beaumont, Ming states,

> There is nothing over the thrust, and so the minute the house lights are turned off the theatre becomes huge, because there is no limit, there is no ceiling. The floor of the thrust stage—which is not all that small—becomes totally insignificant. You feel that you're sitting in a stadium or a void, that there isn't a room within which you're seeing a performance with the performers.

Later, a permanent grid was added in an attempt to deal with this problem.

## Effects of Volume on Acting

One of the frequent complaints about a theatre with a large volume is that it can dwarf actors, diminishing their performances visually and acoustically. Herbert Blau, former co-director of the Vivian Beaumont, writes that at this theatre, "Everybody realizes now that the place is so huge that . . . if you don't take precautions to give the actors amplitude and voice they will look (as we had to learn to our dismay) not only smaller but younger, and acoustically forlorn."[9]

Actors often exaggerate their performances in an attempt to fill the massive Beaumont space. Aline MacMahon, who acted there, observes, "In a curious way the thrust stage encourages you to enlarge the scope of the part. . . . [You] feel you're playing in an enormous amphitheatre. . . . Even though the audience is very close to you, the actor feels no intimacy at all."[10]

Actors must adjust their performances and style of acting to suit a large volume. Voices need to be louder and better supported, and gestures need to be broader. In addition, the actor may need to use physical means to grab the audience's attention, and not rely solely on his or her voice. Stephen Porter describes these effects:

> Plays have to be totally reconceived for certain huge spaces. Not only is one speaking louder, but the actors almost have to raise their hands like children in class for the audience to know who's speaking. The actors have to do something; they flounce a little bit to say, 'This is me talking,' because otherwise no one's going to know.

But a large volume can also be beneficial to actors. Irving felt that the larger scale of acting required by that theatre's volume would help move American acting away from the "Method," toward a more "classical" style:

> Our open, thrust stage does demand a certain grandeur of acting style, a kind of openness and size—and it calls for a high level of technical proficiency. The demands on the actors are very different from those of the intimate, proscenium theater.
>
> Out on a thrust stage like ours an actor is in a sense naked, fully exposed to the world. He has to have security and nobility of presence. American actors have been very well trained for the kind of theater that takes place on a proscenium stage. They excel in a subjective kind of acting, involving a sense of intimacy, but they are somewhat at a loss when pushed forward onto the open stage. . . . Certainly what must be developed for our kind of stage are actors who have authority, magnitude, stature.[11]

To others, the large scale of acting for a large theatre is inherently neither good nor bad, but depends upon the nature of the play. Jerry Zaks maintains that the broader acting style necessary for the Beaumont works for plays "when the emotions are on a slightly operatic scale," but he is more concerned about intimate drama: "It becomes more of a burden to an actor in a play like *The Subject Was Roses.*"

## DEALING WITH A SMALL VOLUME

At the opposite extreme, some theatres may have a very low ceiling, with a resulting small volume. Circle Rep is such a theatre, with its 14′ ceiling. When a 2′ platform is used, as is generally the case, the available height is further reduced to 12′, about 18″ of which is consumed by lighting instruments.

Because the Circle Rep space is so small and the audience is so close to the stage, the designer must employ different techniques than in a proscenium theatre, which has more separation and distance. According to Beatty, "You can't do scene painting of an illusionistic nature; no backdrops for instance. The audience is so close, everything gets examined closely, so everything has to look real from close-up—like 2′."

Masking must also be different because of the close audience proximity. Beatty states that masking "doesn't become a black void like it would in a proscenium theatre; it stays black velour." Beatty finds that black velour in this small space

> is very intrusive, because you are never far enough away to have it disappear. It always ends up looking like a black velour drapery, and you have to ask yourself, 'Why is a black velour drapery hanging in the middle of an exterior in the deep South? What's it doing out there in the woods?'

Beatty's solution has been to make the scenery "self-masking," i.e., the set is designed so that the scenic units themselves provide any masking that is needed. Any additional masking is usually made to look like the black-painted brick of the rest of the theatre.

Even though the scenery tends to be restricted to the stage area, the fact that there is so much detailed scenery in a small volume makes for an environmental effect: the audience feels surrounded and inundated with scenery. When Circle Rep is used in the end-stage configuration, the theatre is architecturally divided into equal halves by brick pilasters on either side and a ceiling beam running between the audience and the stage. Beatty frequently designs his sets such that only half the room is depicted onstage, implying that the other half would include the area where the audience is seated. The total size of the implied, half-depicted room would therefore be the size of the entire theatre, making the spectators feel that they are in the room with the performance. For example, for *A Tale Told,* by Lanford Wilson, Beatty enhanced this effect by hanging a chandelier between the audience and the stage, implying that it was in the middle of the living room.

•

A large volume can swallow a production or create exciting theatricality. A small volume can be cramped or intimate. A large production can be over-inflated or grand. There are no absolutes in the effect or use of a space's volume. Only one statement can be made for sure: the volume and the production must be in harmony for the audience to experience the play as intended. The director and designer must therefore manipulate the volume, whether grossly or subtly, breaking up and/or defining the space over the stage. Whatever the theatre space, the stage and auditorium volumes—whether small or large, horizontal or vertical— significantly affect the nature of the performance.

## NOTES

1. Robert Brustein, *The Third Theatre* (New York: Alfred A. Knopf, 1969) 179.
2. Martin Gottfried, "Beggar on Horseback," *Women's Wear Daily* 15 May 1970, in Performing Arts Library Scrapbook: n. pag.
3. Walter Kerr, "Caldwell's 'Macbeth' More Show than Sense," *The New York Times* 1 Feb. 1981: 12.
4. Brendan Gill, "Supping on Horrors," *The New Yorker* 2 Feb. 1981: 62.
5. As quoted in Taper 15.

6. As quoted in Neal Ashby, "Joseph Papp: Play Producer for the People," *Lithopinion* Fall 1972: 74.

7. John Simon, "Mert and Phil," *New York* 18 Nov. 1974: 122.

8. Martin Gottfried, "'Agamemnon' Off the Wall, *New York Post* 16 May 1976: 7.

9. Herbert Blau, *Take Up the Bodies: Theatre at the Vanishing Point* (Urbana, Ill.: U of Illinois P., 1982) 44.

10. As quoted in Saraleigh Carney, "The Repertory Theatre of Lincoln Center: Aesthetics and Economics, 1960–1973," diss., City U. of New York, 1976, 363.

11. As quoted in Bernard Taper, "Time, Talent and Money: An Interview with Jules Irving," *Lincoln Center Journal* Nov. 1967: 15.

# CHAPTER 13

# FLEXIBLE THEATRES

A flexible theatre is one in which the stage and seating can be rearranged. The theatre may be "multiform," with the flexibility limited to a few predetermined configurations, often with mechanized means of moving the seating and stage units. Or the theatre may be a "black box," in which interchangeable seating and stage modules can be placed into a theoretically infinite variety of configurations.

The premise behind flexible theatres is that the audience-performance relationship is determined by the production; that is, by the play and the style of performance. If one makes the assumption that every play has an ideal performance space, then the theatre should be able to conform to that space. Liviu Ciulei, for instance, states, "Each play demands another space, another air, so the stage must be flexible."

The ideal flexible theatre would be "neutral," and within that neutral space one could arrange different theatrical configurations. Each configuration would have its own set of effects on performance, but the building itself—a neutral background—would have none. All the effects would be transient, lasting only as long as that configuration. Since the theatre space must suffice for many different configurations, any striking architectural statements would tend to limit the theatre's flexibility; what might be striking in one arrangement might be inhibiting to another. In addition, everything in the theatre used to establish each configuration, from the seating and stage units to masking panels, must be movable.

A flexible theatre can serve to free the director/designer's imagination. According to Jack Garfein, any permanent architectural features, such as stage and seating, limit the director's imagination:

> The moment you walk in and the chairs are there, you immediately think, 'The audience is here and that is where the event is to take

place.' The threat is that what is already set up makes the director, without even being aware, make certain decisions. Things that might ordinarily come out of him will not come out, because he's already sitting in a certain space with certain proscribed ideas.

Garfein believes that a flexible theatre is advantageous to a director because he or she should have "no boundaries" and "no limitations"; only "an open space and his mind."

But flexibility also adds extra complications and problems. The director/designer has to design the entire space, operating, in effect, as an architect. As Hugh Hardy observes: "It puts the burden on the director—or whomever—of being an architect, because they have to make choices about the use of space, moving people around and legal matters that they're not equipped to handle."

A common problem with many flexible theaters is that they become frozen into one configuration, most often end stage. According to Hardy,

> Some people have the energy and the knowledge to constantly change the theatre, but most theatre groups don't. Even if they have that ability they tend to settle for a format of presentation that suits them. How many black boxes have you seen that were all gussied up, and you ask them how often they change it: 'Well, two years ago we did push this over there.'

The needs of the proscenium or end stage are well-known to architects and consultants, and the technical considerations (sight-lines, acoustics, etc.) are easier to handle than in a thrust or arena theatre. The arrangement that usually works best in a flexible theatre, therefore, is the end or proscenium, and so it is used the most. But the habits and expectations of directors and designers are also responsible for this common use. All too often flexible theatres wind up as *de facto* permanent end or proscenium stages, at a cost far exceeding a comparable fixed-form theatre.

Advocates of flexibility criticize the fixed-form theatre for the limitations it imposes, but others maintain that without limitations they would be adrift in a sea of possibilities. Austin Pendleton prefers working in a fixed-form theatre because "the actual architecture and the actual arrangement of the place are part of the challenge and part of the meaning of what you're doing."

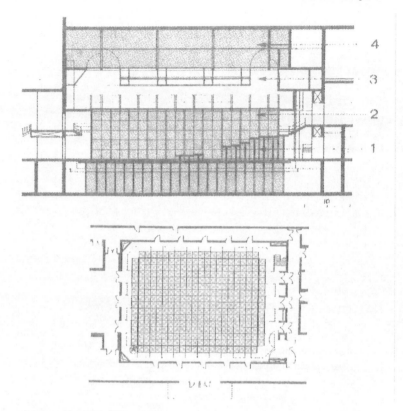

19. Plan and section of the Modular Theatre, California Institute of the Arts, Valencia, Calif. Theatre designers: Jules Fisher Associates. Reproduced with permission of Jules Fisher Associates.

Some forms of flexibility may work better than others. For instance, a theatre may be transformable between thrust and arena without encountering serious complications; in both forms the audience encircles the stage, and the only difference is the degree of encirclement. Sections of seating can therefore be added or subtracted. Both forms have a "radial" geometry, in that the sightlines radiate out from the center of the stage. But the radial geometry of the open stage may be fundamentally incompatible with the geometry of the proscenium or end stage, in which the sightlines are "axial," or along the long axis of the roughly rectangular space. If there are permanent seats for radial sightlines, in the proscenium arrangement the spectators will be facing each other, not the stage; if there are permanent seats for the proscenium along the main axis, in an open-stage arrangement the side seats become token, inferior seats.

## CHOOSING THE CONFIGURATION

The most important issue in using a flexible theatre is choosing the audience-performance configuration. This choice usually emerges from the interpretation of the play. Heidi Landesman asks, "What is most comfortable for the play?" John Lee Beatty looks at the "demands" and "structure" of the play.

While the configuration is usually determined early in the production process, Garfein suggests that ideally this decision should not happen until the play is well into rehearsal. In other words, the configuration should not be based simply on an interpretation of the text, but rather on how that text has come to life with the given cast, director and designers. According to Garfein, "The audience should be put there at the end, rather the beginning. I think one should create the reality of the play, and then ask, 'What is the best way for this audience to experience this play?'"

The first step in choosing the configuration should be to determine in general the audience's relationship to the performance; that is: should the audience be involved or separated, intimate or distant? etc. One needs to determine how the audience and performance should confront each other. In a sense, choosing the configuration starts with determining the line of the first audience row and the edge of the stage, and then works outward from there in both directions.

Jack Gelber asks such questions as, "Is the play a prize fight? Is it a fight in which I want the audience to feel that they are looking down on a ring? Is the audience at home? Do I want them to have more than one role?" George Ferencz determines the configuration by examining the relationship between "the piece and the people." For instance, "If it's a Chekhov play in which there's a fourth wall, it's quite different than if it's a play where there's a dialogue going on with the audience."

Performing the play in the configuration for which it was

20. Black Box Theatre: View of a model of the Modular Theatre, California
Institute of the Arts, Valencia, Calif. Photograph by Tom Brosterman.
Reproduced with permission of the California Institute of the Arts.

written is a common choice. Historical accuracy is often considered to be important in academic theatre, and it is no coincidence
that adaptable theatres are most often built at colleges and
universities. Scripts are chosen from the full range of dramatic
history, and the plays were originally performed on widely
divergent stage forms. Michel Saint-Denis maintains that a training theatre should allow the director and student to "closely
approximate the presentational style of all historical periods."[1]

Another impulse for choosing the configuration may be the
sheer desire for innovation—to do something different. When
Marjorie Bradley Kellogg designed *Fathers and Sons,* by Thomas
Babe, in the Susan Stein Shiva Theater, at the Joseph Papp Public
Theater, the director told her that he was bored with the space's
usual thrust arrangement, so they sought "to arrange that seating
so that it felt less like a conventional theatre space."

In a theatre with a large subscription or returning audience,
spectators may have predetermined notions of how the space is

used. They may know the theatre well and know its typical arrangements. A configuration that defies the audience's expectations of how the space is conventionally used, or how that play is conventionally performed, can startle the audience into looking at the space, play and production in new ways.

When faced with an empty space, theatre artists too often think in terms of conventional theatrical configurations: proscenium, thrust, arena, etc. Ironically, one reason for this response is the architectural rigidity of many "flexible" theatres. In many conventional black-box theatres, the configurations must be based on predetermined grid patterns, for instance with 4' by 8' platforms. Hardy believes that this restriction is artificial and arbitrary:

> Nothing in the world is organized in a four-by-eight grid, except a plywood factory. The armature that you're shaping this stage with is false. It's a geometric assumption that's made up in somebody's head for technocratic reasons. It isn't an armature you can use to construct an illusion for the real world; it's unreal. Starting with something that unreal seems to me hopeless. It's tyrannical, because you can only repeat those same patterns over and over and over again. And then on the fifth production, you finally figure out how to make a diagonal—Rejoice!

Roger Morgan, a theatre consultant, asks, "How many fascinating designs can you make with a series of squares? The real answer is none."

Many directors and designers suggest that one should experiment with more organic, free-form configurations. Adrian Hall, former director of Trinity Square Rep (Providence, R.I.), recommends, "Do ten plays where you don't let the audience sit down for the first half of the play, and then your mind begins to open up a little bit. You realize that maybe arranging all the seats facing one way is not the most interesting." Hall observes that spectators will naturally find their own relationship with the performance:

> Have you ever been at a party where the room is crowded, and somebody starts to strip, and you can't see it all entirely, yet you can hear the music and you know what's happening, and you see the bra go in the air and then suddenly the panties. People are screaming. You're into it. You're really caught up into the excitement. The whole room is throbbing with the madness. Certainly not all of you in that room are arranged so that you can see exactly what is going

on, and yet the act of theatre is happening. Something is going on
between the audience and the actor.

A flexible theatre is often built into a found space that had a
previous non-theatrical function. There may be remnants—
"ghosts"—of that previous life. The space may also have dimensions that are unconventional—even difficult—for use as a
theatre. Instead of viewing these architectural features as impedi-
ments, the designer and director may be able to find ways of
arranging the space in order to exploit the given architecture.

Loren Sherman arranges the theatre so that the set can "exploit
certain dimensions" and "make a virtue of the dimensions." He
asks, "Which element of this room—is it the length, is it the
height, is it the width—that we want to exploit? Which one will
help this particular play the most?"

According to Ming Cho Lee, designers and directors should
examine the space closely before arranging the theatre. Rather
than simply choosing an "ideal" audience-performance configuration for the text, they should pay attention to how the play will
reverberate in the space in which it will be performed:

> The director and the designer should go into the space, feel the
> space, and see how they would like to do the show in that space.
> One of the basic questions may be, 'How do you want the people to
> look at the action? Do you want the action to happen in the midst of
> the audience? Do you want the audience to look this way and that
> way, which entails some kind of environmental design?'
>
> The director and designer should start their approach in the
> person of the actor, saying, 'How would I like to play in that space?
> How would I like to get in touch with the audience?' And then put
> themselves in the audience's point of view, saying, 'How would I
> like to hear this play? How would I like to look at this play?' Let
> that inform how you use the space.

Ming maintains that the director and designer should not make
these decisions "without going in there and seeing the space—the
height, the size."

Often practical requirements will determine the configuration.
Thomas Lynch says that quite often the arrangement is based on
economics—"getting enough seats into the space." In other cases,
he notes that being able to have a "bulk of scenery" in one place

that does not block sightlines may determine the arrangement. David Jenkins points out that easy access for the actors and the audience is sometimes paramount: the designer must solve such traffic problems as fire safety laws, entrances, exits and a crossover. He recalls one case, probably not unique, in which the configuration was determined solely by "logistics": "It had nothing to do with whether or not it was the best way to do the play."

## EXAMPLES

The flexible spaces in the Joseph Papp Public Theater provide interesting histories of how configurations are chosen. The Susan Stein Shiva Theater is the most flexible of the three, in that it is the most nearly square (39′ by 60′), and thus more configurations are feasible. Like all the spaces in the Public, it is bedeviled by columns, which form a square in the center of the room.

These columns give character to the space, but also limit the workable configurations. Three configurations cope best with the columns, and most productions use one of these: 1) A long stage with the audience along the opposite long wall; 2) A more traditional "end stage," with the stage along the shorter wall; or 3) A thrust stage.

According to Bill Hart, the long stage has been the most common configuration, because this is the only conventional configuration without columns in the playing area. Richard Foreman, for example, used this arrangement for his play *Egyptology*. His aim, he explains, was "to get the most space possible" for a production in which he wanted the effect of having "the play seem much bigger than the audience."

Wilford Leach believes that the thrust is the best use of the Shiva, based on the inherent attributes of the space, which he considers to be "dark, intimate, and improvised." According to Leach, "The space lends itself more to a gathering than spectators looking on; it's a sense of community rather than a sense of the movies. It's more like people coming over to your house."

Other less conventional arrangements, unique to the given production, are also possible in the Shiva. For example, Kellogg

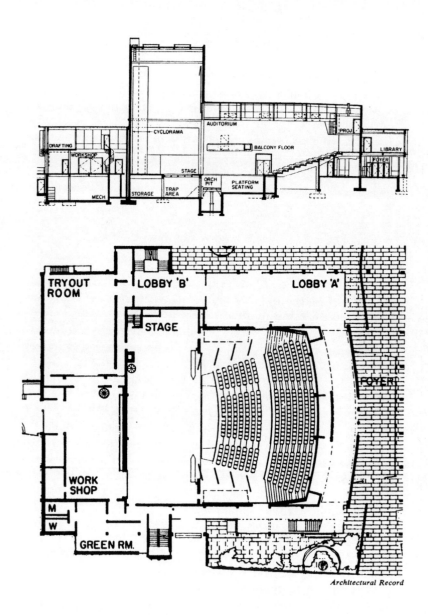

21. Multiform Theatre: Plans and section of the Loeb Drama Center, Harvard University, Cambridge, Mass. Architect: The Stubbins Associates. Consultant: George Izenour. Reproduced with permission of The Stubbins Associates, Architects.

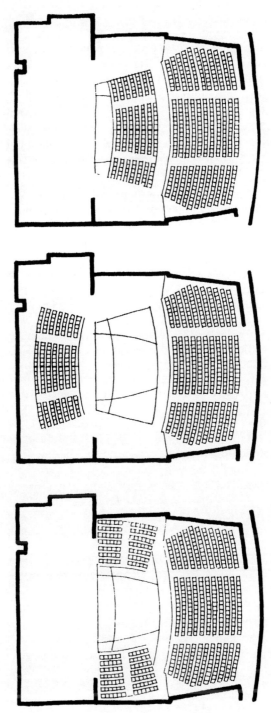

placed the stage across the center of the space, and Sherman set the stage on a diagonal across the room; both had the audience on opposite sides of the stage. But according to many who have been associated with the Public over a long period of time, the columns make such arrangements rare and difficult. In addition, it is expensive to rearrange the seating for individual shows, and this cost must be included in the budget. A production might therefore be in the position of choosing between rearranging the theatre or obtaining other scenic effects. Such non-conventional configurations may be a good use of the space, but the designer and director must be prepared to contend with the cost, ubiquitous columns, oddly shaped stage and seating rows, and tricky sightlines.

Because the Shiva is small and "neutral" in color (brown), it lends itself well to being wholly transformed for environmental productions. Kellogg, for instance, turned the entire theatre into a saloon. For *Egyptology,* Foreman created magical effects throughout the space. Frank Rich remarked that upon entering,

> you may think you've wandered into an old-fashioned tunnel-of-horrors ride in a 1950s amusement park.
> The room is a black crypt, with creepy displays in every corner: a dingy bar . . . an antiseptic hospital room that reeks of terminal illness; a cobwebbed piano with a skeleton for a player.[2]

The Shaliko Company presented an environmental production of *Ghosts,* with the performers and spectators scattered about. Walter Kerr wrote that the production

> not only dispenses with the proscenium arch, but . . . makes it virtually impossible to locate the actors *anywhere.* . . .
> Actors and/or props are going to be directly over your head, beneath your feet and crawling narrow railings that straddle your knees. . . .
> Scenes are played in small raised pockets of space at the far corners of the miniature auditorium or on a balcony.[3]

LuEsther and Martinson Halls, which are long, narrow spaces, make thrust or arena arrangements tricky: if the width is cut down by audience rows along the sides, the resulting stage is too narrow. These theatres tend therefore to be used in an end-stage or two-sided configuration, with the stage along the short axis of the room.

*The Normal Heart,* by Larry Kramer, used the two-sided configuration in LuEsther Hall, and the relationship was particularly appropriate for a play that deals with the AIDS crisis. The play was performed against a background of spectators who often became participants in the emotion onstage. Hart, who directed the transfer of the production to the Anspacher, describes the performance:

> One part of the audience could see the other side of the audience putting their hands over their mouths or holding their heads. An incredible amount of crying would go on in that play. The configuration was chosen with that in mind—for the audience to confront itself.

Martinson Hall was used occasionally in open-stage arrangements in its early years, but was then set up as an end stage and has remained that way for years. Before the configuration became permanent, Andre Gregory directed a production of Chekhov's *The Seagull,* which used different, successive stages and audience areas during the course of the production. Clive Barnes reported:

> 'The Seagull' may seem to be the epitome of the proscenium-arch play; Mr. Gregory has provided it with an intriguingly environmental look. . . . Mr. Gregory has devised three separate playing areas, each with its own seating arrangement. The audience is gently ushered, act by act, to the right setting. It is a novel device, and, through offering different perspectives, a useful one.[4]

Circle in the Square (Uptown) was designed as a thrust theatre, but subsequently changes were made to allow for the possibility of an arena. Bleachers were placed upstage of the portal line, creating a fourth side to the auditorium. Designers and directors can now choose between performing in the original thrust or the converted arena configuration.

Realistic plays with many sets and scenes provide an interesting conundrum in choosing the configuration at Circle in the Square (Uptown). While a proscenium theatre is well equipped to change from one realistic setting to another, a thrust is not: the scenery may be hard to change, and if it is not changed, the set may not be appropriate for the next scene. Ironically, the arena, architecturally farthest from the proscenium, may be best for such

22. Multiform Theatre: View of the Loeb Drama Center, Harvard University, Cambridge, Mass. Photograph by Richard Feldman. Reproduced with permission of the American Repertory Theatre.

plays: there is no possibility for large, localizing scenic units, and so the stage is more "placeless." While the thrust may inhibit a fast-paced, multi-scene play, the arena can support one.

In the case of *Once in a Lifetime,* the first production to use the arena configuration at Circle in the Square (Uptown), each scene was localized only by furniture and props. By using the arena configuration, Theodore Mann maintains, "the multiple scene changes could move more rapidly." Mann also cites Shaw's *Man and Superman,* in which many outdoor and indoor locations were needed: "So the stage area became whatever we wanted it to become by putting something on the deck, rather than putting it on a wall."

Several designers have found, however, that the shape of the Circle in the Square (Uptown) stage is not conducive to fluid arena staging. Most arenas have round or square stages, so that spectators on each side of the stage are approximately equidistant from center stage. Kenneth Foy points out that on this long, narrow stage, "the two ends are too far away. An actor in the middle is far away from the ends. If you play at one side, you're miles from the other side." Zack Brown observes that in a roughly symmetrical arena theatre, spectators on each side would see a comparable performance; at Circle in the Square (Uptown), on the other hand, "the people at the two longer ends' perceptions of the performers and the piece itself are completely different from the people on the sides."

The Performing Garage was designed as a flexible theatre, and it remains so. But the choice of configuration reflects the widely divergent artistic purposes of the two groups that have inhabited it. The Wooster Group inherited the Performing Garage from the Performance Group and its leader, Richard Schechner, who used it as an environmental theatre (see Chapter 14). Elizabeth Le-Compte, who directs most of the productions for the Wooster Group, has maintained the space as a flexible theatre, but the use and artistic policies are quite different. Schechner's configurations entailed non-frontal performance, with action occurring behind and amidst the spectators, in order to engulf and involve the spectator in an environment, breaking down the distinction between audience and performance. The Wooster Group's performance pieces, on the other hand, maintain a more formal separation, using an end-stage, frontal arrangement.

David Savran, author of a book on the Wooster Group, explains that LeCompte, "is more formal. She assumes a separation between the audience and the performers. She 'presents' material; the performer is in the position of 'showing,' 'holding up'; it's very Brechtian." According to Savran, LeCompte "hates, is mistrustful of, letting the audience share the experience. It's very important that they maintain their identity as spectators, that there be no confusion of this." There is, therefore, a "spatial separation maintained" between audience and performance.

Though the space is always used as an end stage, the Wooster Group still rearranges the Performing Garage for each production. The configuration is rotated within the space and the vertical relationship of the audience and stage shifts drastically (see Chapter 11). The end-stage arrangement supports the idea of spatial separation: material is presented directly to the audience, without engulfing them in a shared experience.

•

The examples in this chapter show that the idea of a flexible theatre that does *not* affect performance is, presently and probably in future, a chimera. The theatre space's permanent elements are not, and probably cannot be, neutral. Architectural neutrality in a theatre is impossible: the elements are there and will affect performance. But the theory and practice of flexible theatres are not thereby negated. Instead it is necessary to be aware in planning and using a flexible theatre that its permanent elements *do* make an architectural statement. A flexible theatre need not be a neutral background into which one can insert any configuration, but a theatre in which one can alter the theatre's effect on the performance by using a combination of fixed and flexible elements.

## NOTES

1. As quoted in Thomas deGaetani, "The Adaptable Theatre in the American University; and the Loeb Drama Center," *Adaptable Theatres,* ed. Stephen Joseph (London: Association of British Theatre Technicians, 1962) 19.
2. Frank Rich, "Theatre: 'Egyptology' by Richard Foreman," *The New York Times* 18 May 1983, in Performing Arts Library Scrapbook: n. pag.
3. Walter Kerr, "A Kung Fu Version of Ibsen," *The New York Times* 13 April 1975: 3.
4. Clive Barnes, "Theater: Gregory Stages Chekhovian 'Sea Gull,' " *The New York Times* 9 Jan. 1975: 49.

# CHAPTER 14

# ENVIRONMENTAL AND PROMENADE THEATRE

In environmental theatre, the performance surrounds the audience to a greater or lesser degree. The performance is not restricted to a stage in front of the audience; instead, spectators and performers may be anywhere in the space. Arnold Aronson defines environmental theatre as "nonfrontal":

> Proscenium, end, thrust, alley and arena stages are all frontal in that a spectator observing a performance rarely has to look more than forty-five degrees to the left or right in order to view the whole production. . . . In all cases the audience is facing 'forward' and is generally focused on the same space and action. Any performance of which that is not true—in which the complete *mise en scène* or scenography cannot be totally apprehended by a spectator maintaining a single frontal relationship to the performance—must be considered non-frontal or environmental.[1]

According to this definition, any theatre space—including proscenium—could be used environmentally.

Promenade is a form of environmental theatre that emphasizes one element: the actors and spectators move, or "promenade," as they follow the performance from one place to another. The audience's movement may be within one architectural volume, to different rooms of a building, or even between remote locales.

Environmental and promenade theatre have become very popular, and not just in the avant-garde. There is, of course, an important history of experimental environmental productions, including Richard Schechner's Performance Group, the Living Theatre, and Bread and Puppet Theatre, to name only a few. But popular Broadway shows, such as *Cats, Starlight Express, The Life and Adventures of Nicholas Nickleby* and *Phantom of the Opera,* have also employed environmental techniques. In popular

169

Off-Broadway productions, such as *Tamara* and *Tony 'n' Tina's Wedding,* audiences have walked around a variety of performance areas. Throughout the country, outdoor theatres producing civic "pageant drama" implicitly incorporate the natural environment. Theatre groups have also experimented with "site-specific" theatre, performances that specifically employ permanent aspects of the architecture or landscape.

Ever since environmental theatre emerged as an identifiable form, many critics and artists have pointed out long-existing events that fit its criteria, including amusement parks, street performances, festivals, parades and carnivals.

## DESIGN THE ENTIRE SPACE

In an environmental production, the designer needs to think in terms of designing the entire theatre space, not just the stage area. John Napier describes his approach as "non-pictorial," which he defines as "one that treats the space, and the performance happening in it, as a place that doesn't have a beginning and an end. The audience and the performance are in the same space." To Napier, this approach is "the opposite of Brechtian," in which there would be a clearly defined separation between audience and performance.

According to Jason Barnes, the production manager at the Royal National Theatre's Cottesloe Theatre, the promenade designer must think about the look and feel of the entire space, in that a spectator may be anywhere looking at anything. At the Cottesloe Theatre, a spectator

> might have one scene going on next to him, then another thirty feet away, which he views over the heads of the crowd, and then he might have something happening behind and twenty feet above, in one of the galleries. Any space in the whole room that's not occupied by a member of the audience in a fixed chair is open to act in from time to time. Even the foyer: as you come in, hang up your coat, go to the lavatory, there's an actor doing something to you as you go in. You could decorate the lobby as well as the performance space.

Barnes advises the environmental designer, "Don't be bound by any conventions. Either throw them all away or challenge them."

Taking an environmental approach in a conventional theatre may mean disrupting the original architecture. When *Road* moved from the upstairs studio space of the Royal Court Theatre in London to the main, proscenium theatre, the latter space had to be altered in order for the audience to promenade. The original production occurred in a single room, and the unity of the space implicitly allowed the audience to roam freely. But the bifurcated space of a proscenium theatre was not conducive to this freedom. The solution was to build a floor over the orchestra seating area, creating a large promenade area joining the stage and floored-over orchestra. Those who wished to remain seated throughout could sit in the first rows of the galleries and see the action on the floor below.

Designing the entire space need not mean covering everything up with scenery; the designer can also use the existing architecture of the theatre. Paul Brown incorporated the architecture for the original design of *Road* because of the "texture and age" of the theatre space, as well as the small production budget. For instance, a window in the space was used as a window for the play.

## THE PROCESS OF ENVIRONMENTAL THEATRE

For Schechner, environmental theatre is as much a process as a theatre form. The process need not have the text as the starting point, however, as in more conventional theatre. According to Schechner, "Work on an environment may begin long before a play has been selected or a script assembled."[2] Schechner's ideal method, though, is for all elements to be created in tandem, each affecting the other, but with no single element having primacy: "Text, action and environment must develop together. . . . The event, the performers, the environmentalist, the director, and the audience interacting with each other in a space (or spaces) determine the environment."[3] The environment is not the static creation of the set designer, but an evolving creature altered by the performers in rehearsal and the audience in performance.

23. Environmental Theatre: View of the Performing Garage, New York City, during a performance of *Dionysus in 69*. Photograph by Fred Eberstadt. Reproduced with permission of Princeton University Libraries.

The design may evolve through a process of "negotiation": the environment is developed during the course of rehearsals, while performers, director, designers, text and space "negotiate" with one another in a process of give and take. Rehearsals may begin with the environment more or less complete; as the performance piece develops in rehearsal, changes may be needed in the environment, causing further changes in the performance piece, and the cycle begins again. Schechner explains, "The rehearsal itself changes what's needed for the space. It's an interaction between the emerging action of the *mise en scène* and what the space can yield."[4]

The audience may also be involved in the creation of the environment. For *Commune* Schechner gave the audience colored chalk to draw with on the walls. In a promenade production, the spectators actively participate in the creation of the environment insofar as they choose where to stand or sit. The spectators "create" the audience area by standing or sitting somewhere, just as they implicitly create a performance area by the space they surround. The spectators are free to roam about the environment, choosing their own orientation toward the performance, from relative detachment to extreme involvement. Instead of the architect or designer choosing the spectator's orientation, it is up to the individual on a moment-by-moment basis (within the limits established by the environmental designer).

Schechner offers a series of questions that the environmental designer should ask:

1. What movement is possible in this space? What do I have to build to facilitate movement?
2. Can a spectator get from *any* one place to *every* other place? If not, is that limitation meaningful in terms of the play?
3. Are there at least two ways in and out of every space?
4. Are there 'secret' ways around the space so that each obvious route is matched by at least one secret route?
5. Are there ways of going over and under as well as around and through?
6. Are there areas for focused performing and for private performing?
7. From each area how much is hidden?
8. What is the acoustic map of each area? Other sense maps?
9. Does the whole mass of the environment express the play?
10. Does the rhythm of the environment express the play?
11. Does the material out of which the environment is made express the play?
12. Are there efficient means of upward–downward movement?
13. Would I like to live in this place? If so, where? Why? If not, why not? Are my answers in keeping with the play?
14. Can every surface and supporting member support as many people as can fit on it? Is the whole environment safe?
15. Can spectators see each other, or hide from each other?
16. Can the spectators recline, sit, stand, bunch, find isolated places—and in other ways determine for themselves their body attitudes and relationships to each other and the performers?[5]

## WHY USE ENVIRONMENTAL THEATRE?

### For a Play with Many Locales

A play with many scenes and locales may be suitable for environmental production. A conventional production might require a different set for each scene with lengthy scene changes in between, thereby disrupting the flow of the performance. By building a complete environment that contains all the "places" of the play, one can avoid these lengthy scene changes. If an entire environment is built and the audience promenades from one area to another, the only "delay" is the length of time it takes the audience to move, which they will not perceive as "empty" time since they are busy moving. Simon Curtis chose to direct *Road* as a promenade for this reason: "When I read the play, I didn't want to do a play which was about a lot of scene changes." Robert Kalfin also says that an environment was built for *Candide* (book adapted from Voltaire by Hugh Wheeler; lyrics by Richard Wilbur; additional lyrics by Stephen Sondheim and John Latouche; music by Leonard Bernstein) "to solve the problem of many locations and get rid of the overlay of tons of scenery."

### Environmental Theatre May Be the Best Use of the Space

Aspects of the theatre space may also suggest to the designer/ director that an environmental approach may be best for the production.

The small theatre space at Circle Rep has encouraged a number of designers to use an environmental approach. The environmental aspect has been limited, however, to surrounding the audience with scenery. For *Harry Outside,* by Corinne Jacker, the theatre was arranged with the audience on four sides of the stage, which represented a clearing in the woods. John Lee Beatty placed trees not only on the stage, but also in front of and amidst the audience. Beatty "put in obstructions to make the audience feel more a part of the action." *The Harvesting,* by John Bishop, was performed in the end-stage configuration, but a photo mural covered all four walls of the theatre. The play was about a town, and designer Loren Sherman "felt that the audience should feel as if they're in this town."

David Mitchell believed that the thrust stage at the Long Wharf

Theatre encouraged an environmental approach for a production of *The Gin Game,* by D. L. Coburn. Mitchell considers the thrust theatre to be an implicitly unified space, in that the stage penetrates the audience; the designer should try to enhance, rather than negate, that effect. If the set stops at the edge of the stage, "your sense of that environment can become very contrived, because you see where the set ends—it's cut off."

Tony Straiges used an environmental design at Circle in the Square (Downtown) because the entire space was oddly appropriate for *Diamonds,* a musical revue about baseball. Like the Uptown theatre, the auditorium is an elongated "U" shape, with a bank of seats on each side, which suggested a stadium to Straiges. He turned the entire theatre into a baseball stadium, making the "horrible space," as Straiges terms it, "perfect" for this production.

## Environmental Theatre May Be Expensive

Critics of environmental theatre charge that it is too expensive to be practical: the entire theatre space has to be transformed, and the expense goes into things the audience hardly notices, such as the floor, leaving little money for more conventional scenic effects that might enhance the play. Heidi Landesman observes that "nobody really wants to spend" the time and money necessary to "decorate the auditorium."

Paul Brown says that *Road* was not expensive in its original studio production, in that much of the material was borrowed or scavenged: "It's easier to chop down a tree than to build one." But when the production moved to other theatres, the production costs soared. At LaMama Experimental Theatre, "it was a highly expensive production, and no more successful."

# ENVIRONMENTAL THEATRE'S RELATIONSHIP TO THE AUDIENCE

## Engage the Audience

One reason for using environmental and promenade techniques is to engage and involve the audience in the performance. Jerry Rojo explains:

In a more traditional theatre experience, the production is appreci-
ated from outside, in a world especially created for the relatively
passive observer. In the environmental experience, on the other
hand, appreciation generates from within by virtue of shared
activity. Each environmental production generates a sense of total
involvement on the part of the audience and performer.[6]

Involving the spectators need not mean getting them out of their
seats or getting the actors into the auditorium. Subtle environmental touches can also include the audience's space in the
performance. For instance, in Circle Rep's most frequent end-
stage arrangement, spectators enter the theatre behind the set,
walking along the side of the stage on the way to their seats. The
audience is within inches—touching range—of the set. Given the
realistic style of most productions there, designers don't want the
audience to see black draperies or the back of unpainted scenery.
The most common solution is to complete the back of the set, so
the audience sees what would be "outside" the set depicted
onstage. If the set is an interior, the audience might see the exterior
as they enter. As David Potts explains, "When you enter the
theatre, you enter the play." Beatty describes this artistic approach
as "the experience of the actor is the experience of the audience,"
i.e., the audience should become sufficiently involved that they
experience the drama in the same way as the actors. The characters in the play would not see "unfinished scenery" or "black
masking," so neither should the audience.

Napier believes that involving the audience is essential to
environmental theatre, and should be the basis for deciding
whether or not an environmental approach is appropriate. He
designed an environment for the Royal Shakespeare Company
production of *The Life and Adventures of Nicholas Nickleby*
because the play contained narration, direct address and interaction with the audience. Napier wanted the performance to declare
from the outset that interaction was essential, so that actor-
audience interaction later would not seem like a gratuitous effect:

> If it had just been a kind of a frame, with the performers spending an
> enormous amount of time behind that frame, and then breaking it,
> coming out and interacting with the audience, then the audience
> would have been in a completely different state of mind. But to start

in a reverse way, to have the actors pervade the whole atmosphere with those catwalks, it got the production off on the right foot. It got them to interact with each other, particularly during the pieces of narration, which were very much part of the production.

Napier felt that it was important for *Cats* (music by Andrew Lloyd Webber; additional material by Trevor Nunn and Richard Stilgoe; based on *Old Possum's Book of Practical Cats,* by T. S. Eliot) to have an environmental design in order to state at the beginning that this was not another musical about animals, "in order for it not to be pantomimic, in order for it not to be 'twee,' like children's book illustrations."

For *Starlight Express* (music by Andrew Lloyd Webber; lyrics by Richard Stilgoe) it seemed to Napier that "it would have been very boring if a bunch of actors on roller skates rolled around in a circle on a proscenium stage for two hours with nowhere to go." Having the actors skate out into the audience was "just using the dynamics of the building to get some excitement."

Environmental techniques can be particularly effective for engaging young people. Before Adrian Hall tried such techniques at Trinity Square Repertory, he saw that young people were not interested in theatre, and so he decided to "find a way to keep the little fuckers in their seats." For an adaptation of Melville's *Billy Budd,* he "built a runway through the middle of the auditorium," patterned after the Kabuki and burlesque theatre. He staged a sea battle in the midst of the audience, with sailors running up and down the aisles. The effect was "closer to a circus and a carnival, but we kept them there!" For *The Taming of the Shrew,* as the audience was arriving at the theatre, each actor

> would corner fifteen or twenty people. They had a three-penny song sheet and we would teach them this dirty little ditty. While you were waiting for the performance to begin, the actors were teaching the audience these little dirty Elizabethan songs. Finally everybody began to sing it in rounds. As your group started to sing, you would rise and move to the next part of the auditorium and join that group. Then we went totally around this little stage and everybody ended up back where they began. Of course, chaos ensued. But the audience was just screaming and having such great times, and people were in the wrong seats. And then out of that the play just began.

The Living Theatre has long been famous for involving the audience in the performance. For instance, one part of *Prometheus* consisted of a re-enactment of the storming of the Winter Palace, as it had been re-enacted annually in Leningrad as a public spectacle. In the Living Theatre production, performers recruited spectators into the battle as terrorists, Tolstoyan pacifists, White Guard and Red Army. There were twenty minutes for rehearsal in different areas on the building, and then the battle was reenacted. Rolled-up paper was used for guns, the anarchists threw bombs and the pacifists pleaded for peace. Finally, as Judith Malina reports, the audience ran up onto the stage to take the Winter Palace, with "an incredible ecstasy, and the whole room would go berserk." Then Lenin, played by Julian Beck, walked out and said, "You can go back to your seats now," thus stilling the revolutionary spirit.

In another section of *Prometheus,* the Living Theatre led the spectators to the nearest prison and asked them to "meditate on the end to punishment." According to Malina, the purpose was to "take the spectators out of the enclosed theatre space in which it is safe, take them out into the street, into a situation in which they're not safe." Neither the spectators nor the police knew what might happen. In this case, the spectator

> is being drawn into a hostile space, facing this building about which you feel equivocal. The criminals are over there, and you're over here. You're not one of the criminals, but the police are suspecting you of being somebody that maybe should be over there, because you're here as a potential troublemaker. Any minute you could be taken inside.

Simply by being there *en masse,* "we had transgressed, so that we had already broken that barrier."

## Audience Positions

Conventional theatre architecture dictates the spectator's physical position and movement. In the conventional theatre, one is able to choose a seat, subject to price and availability. One is then obliged to sit in that one spot throughout the performance.

Schechner finds these limits detrimental to the kind of theatre he wishes to create:

> Orthodox auditoriums strictly regulate roles and distribute energies evenly. The rows of seats absolutely prevent both mass movement and individual movement. . . . Evenly spaced, separate seats keep people locked into their individuality. . . . There is no development of a group feeling, a communal consciousness.[7]

In environmental and promenade theatre, the spectator is free to choose his or her own relationship to the performance, place in the theatre and physical position. According to Schechner,

> Spectators are given the choice of sitting, standing, leaning, or stretching out. They can lay on their stomachs or backs, and orient themselves in any direction, even completely away from the action. People can be alone, with another person, or in groups.[8]

The designer/director can create the environment in such a way that the spectator has a choice of a number of different physical relationships to the performance and fellow spectators. Schechner describes the various possible areas of an environment:

> Within the theatre are *jumping-off places,* from which spectators can easily enter the performance. These are usually low areas opening onto focused performing spaces. Higher, there are some *regular places* where spectators can sit more or less as in an orthodox theatre. These places are provided for those who find environmental design too shocking and threatening to accept immediately. But of course this enclave of orthodox seating is itself a halfway house. It is part of a larger environmental framework. Still higher are *observation places,* where a few people can look down on the performance and on other spectators. At the highest points are *pinnacles* where the most adventurous spectators can dangle into the space; or where performers can hang like gargoyles or eagles. At every level are indentations, cubby-holes, and pueblos where 2 to 8 persons can sit or recline together, their bodies touching.[9]

Similarly, in most promenade productions the audience may choose to walk and sit on the main floor with the performers, or to sit in chairs in galleries overlooking the action.

## The Audience Has a Kinesthetic Response to the Performance

When viewing a frontal performance, one sits facing front. To a certain extent, one's body reacts to the tension of the performance: leaning forward with interest and excitement or leaning back in relaxation or boredom. One also reacts physically to the other spectators, as one may have to crane for a good view of the stage. But this movement is limited significantly by the constraints of the chair.

In an environmental performance, on the other hand, there may be no chair to sit in, and the "front" can shift to the side or behind the viewer, so the spectator must shift his or her body accordingly. In this way, the spectator's movements become a corollary of the performance itself. Schechner describes the "audience's actions" as "a version of the action of the play." According to Schechner, "the audience is living through the *mise en scène* in a metaphoric way." He feels that when spectators shift body positions, they are not just trying to get comfortable, they are responding to the performance: "From one point of view every performance offers two dances to the wholly detached observer: the intensive and pre-scored dance of the performers, and the reflective, improvised dances of the spectators."[10]

In a promenade production, the spectator's physical response to the performance is even greater. If well planned, the spectator's movement should be a symbolic version of the play itself. Curtis believes that *Road* is "about taking you on a journey to visit this town," and in his production "the promenade enacts that in a unique way. At the end of it you feel like you've been on a journey and met a few people. You like some, you've hated others, but you've actually learned from the experience."

For Schechner's production *The Tooth of Crime,* the spectators had to move around the space in order to follow the action, "thereby becoming groupies following the stars." Schechner saw the play as being about "how one charismatic figure loses his following and another gains." In this case, "the audience pays attention to the winner with their bodies, not just their minds."

## Promenading the Audience

One of the most difficult aspects of promenade performance is planning the audience's movements, i.e., how the spectators will be manipulated to move from place to place. The designer for a promenade production must "design" the audience area for each scene, as well as the performance area. According to Paul Brown, the designer has to "control the audience" in their promenading. For *Road*, he and Curtis "went through the play to see where the scenes could happen and where the audience would go."

The goal in promenading an audience should be to achieve a varied rhythm of movement, keeping the action fluid but not hopping. As Brown explains, "You get your audience into a tight space for a very quiet scene. Then the following scene needs people to be more dispersed, so you drive a shopping cart through the middle of them."

In addition, the director needs to ensure that the audience is actually "promenading" from scene to scene, and not just sitting in one place and swiveling. Curtis suggests that the director has to "be bold in changing the focus as often as possible" in order to "train the audience to get up and down and move with the focus." His goal was to

> change the focus as much as possible, because if you do one scene there and another scene right next to it, everyone will just stay where they are. You need to stage things in such a way that it divides the audience as much as possible, mixing long scenes and short scenes.

For instance, in one short transition scene, as a man was getting dressed for an evening of dancing, he closed his eyes and imagined dancing with his partner. He danced through the middle of the spectators, creating an alley in the middle for the next scene. The audience moved out of the way, because they could see that his eyes were closed; if they didn't move, he would run into them.

On a few occasions, stagehands would have to move reluctant spectators from the spot where a scene was about to occur, but Curtis says that generally, "when the lights came up on a scene, the spectators would move out. When you shine a light on people, it's surprising how quickly they move." If light was not sufficient to move a spectator, the actors could, in character, "tell them to shift their arses," or simply proceed with the spectator in place. For instance, "in the scene where the woman seduces the soldier on the bed, there were times when someone was still sitting on the bed when she threw the soldier on it. I encouraged the actors to keep the scene going on top of the member of the audience."

In some cases promenade productions may force the spectators to move through more insistent means, such as creating situations in which if they do not move they will be injured. For a production of *Entertaining Strangers,* by David Edgar, at the Cottesloe Theatre, bridges rolled back and forth across the space at head height. The audience could choose between moving or being decapitated.

A Spanish performance group also forced the audience to move through invasive means. La Fura dels Baus performed *Suz/O/Suz,* and *The New York Times* reported: "The spectator's main role is to flee. . . . Actors clad in shirt, tie and jockstrap pilot carts at high speed through the audience swinging heavy, wheeled machines and hurling flour-filled slings and pieces of sheep's offal at one another." According to Javier Cereza, one of the performers, "When two young warriors fight each other from atop tall, speeding carts, the audience must dodge and follow."[11]

Spectators may also be encouraged to move by less drastic measures; in fact, the movement may seem so natural that they are unaware of any theatrical manipulation at all. For *Tony 'n' Tina's Wedding* the two primary performance places were site-specific, and the audience's movement between them was quite customary: the audience gathered at a church for the "wedding," and then moved *en masse* to a restaurant a few blocks away for the "reception." Even the audience's movement within the spaces was so "natural" as to go perhaps unnoticed: spectators arriving at the church were ushered in by "members of the family" and asked whether they wished to be seated on the bride's or groom's side. At the restaurant, spectators sat at assigned tables, but then moved about in order to get food and drinks and to dance and mingle. In other words, in both spaces, their movements were very close to what they would be at an actual wedding and reception.

In *Tamara,* by John Krizanc, the spectators gathered at the grand staircase of New York City's Park Avenue Armory, where they were introduced to each of the characters by the butler and instructed to choose one character to follow, and to stick with that character wherever he or she went. The characters then ran pell-mell in every direction, each accompanied by his or her band of followers. Two or more characters then met in a room, spectators in tow, and performed a scene together, the spectators finding any available nook or cranny from which to watch. At the conclusion of the scene, the characters left in different directions, sometimes at breakneck speed, to join with other characters and spectators in yet another room. In this way, each spectator would see a "different" play, depending on whom he or she followed; spectators were assured that no matter whom they followed, a coherent "story" would emerge.

•

Some theatre artists may be attracted to environmental and promenade theatre for aesthetic, political or social reasons, and may choose to adopt this approach consistently. But for others, creating an environment or promenading the audience is one of many techniques to choose from, depending on the nature of the performance. In the latter case, the designer and director should consider the nature of the play and its relationship to the space and the audience. In creating the environment, the designer should consider how the permanent aspects of the space can be used, and how to transform the pre-existing architecture in the created environment. The director needs to plan the production in such a way as to keep the actors and/or audience moving throughout the environment.

## NOTES

1. Arnold Aronson, *The History and Theory of Environmental Scenography* (Ann Arbor, Mich.: UMI Research P., 1977) 2.
2. Richard Schechner, *Environmental Theatre* (New York: Hawthorn Books, 1973) 12.
3. Schechner, *Environmental* 28–30.
4. Schechner, "Design" 397.
5. Schechner, "Design" 390–91.
6. Jerry Rojo, "Some Principles and Concepts of Environmental Design" *Theatres, Spaces, Environments,* Brooks McNamara, Jerry Rojo and Richard Schechner (New York: Drama Book Specialists, 1975) 14.
7. Schechner, "Design" 389–90.

8.  Schechner, "Design" 392.
9.  Schechner, "Design" 391–92.
10. Schechner, "Design" 389.
11. William Bryant Logan, "From Spain, Street Theater with Fire-
    works," *The New York Times* 9 June 1991: 36.

# CHAPTER 15

# TRANSFERRING A PRODUCTION

The effect of the theatre space on performance is especially evident when a production transfers from one theatre to another.

Sometimes the transfer can help a production, or at least allow new aspects of the play to emerge because of its new surroundings. Melvin Bernhardt points out that most transfers consist of an "upgrading," for instance from a workshop to a full-fledged production, "and generally at that point there is a little more money to spend on the physical production, so that you are able to fulfill your concept a little more fully. You're able to execute things in a better fashion." According to Robert Kalfin, the production often gains technical capability not present in the previous, smaller theatre.

For example, Tony Straiges recalls that when *Sunday in the Park with George* (book by James Lapine; music and lyrics by Stephen Sondheim) moved from Playwrights Horizons to Broadway, "we could do whatever we wanted to do," including the use of a fly system, traps, etc. *The 5th of July,* by Lanford Wilson, was also redesigned to exploit the greater capabilities of a Broadway theatre. John Lee Beatty wanted "the feeling of children playing in the ruins of their forebears' house," but was not able to achieve that large-scale effect for the original production at Circle Rep, because of the theatre's low ceiling. He was able to add height to the set for the Broadway production, which "gave the illusion of a large house."

But transferring a production may also have a negative effect. The production may have been, to a greater or lesser extent, inspired by or married to the original space, and the production may no longer be suited to the new theatre. Zack Brown maintains that a designer creates scenery "for a particular space. The way the production sits onstage and operates is for a particular place, and I really don't think it can just be taken anywhere."

Bernhardt suggests that the director should advise the producer regarding what will and what will not transfer well:

You have to say to producers sometimes, 'You can't take this and
drop it on your stage. It won't work. You have to redo this. You
cannot take this and put a lot of black drapes around it and set it
down on a Broadway stage and save a buck. You're cheating
yourself in the long run.'

## PROBLEMS IN TRANSFERRING A PRODUCTION

### Production May Be Less Imposing in a Big Theatre

One of the problems is that a transfer is usually from a smaller to
a larger theatre. While the change in scale may help some productions, in other cases it may be disastrous. What may have seemed
intimate and "just right" in a small theatre, may be lost in a larger
one. If the scale of the original production is maintained, it may be
dwarfed in the larger theatre. If the production is inflated to meet its
new surroundings, it may ring false. Marjorie Bradley Kellogg reports that size is the biggest problem in a transfer: "You scale objects and conceptions to the space that you're working in. It's about
the size of detail." According to Joseph Papp, a play "in a small loft"
may look "terrific there," but "you move that same play into a 300-
seat theatre with a proscenium stage and it looks less enforcing."[1]

### Different Expectations When a Production Transfers

The expectations set up by the theatre space are especially
noticeable—and even crucial—when a production transfers from
one theatre to another. Most often, the transfer is from a smaller,
less polished space to a larger, more elegant one. If the production
benefits from the more impressive space, or if the production is
adapted well to meet the higher expectations, the transfer will be
an improvement. All too often, however, the success of the
original production was related to the intimacy and "rough and
ready" quality of the first space; the production then seems lost
and unfinished in the grander theatre. In addition, the smaller
theatre may have been more intimate and involving, setting up a
non-judgmental atmosphere, while the larger theatre may be more
distancing and imposing. Kalfin has found the latter to be the case

when a production moves from a "basement" to Broadway: "The moment you are in that large commercial environment, people are wearing a different pair of glasses to look at it."

Comparing a small, Off Broadway space to a Broadway theatre highlights this distinction in expectations. Circle Rep, like many other small theatres, is not designed for spectacle and generally doesn't provide it; audiences expect that and accept it. Spectators arrive with low expectations for scenery and spectacle. They sit in a 42' by 50' black brick room, sharing the space with the set, the actors, the lights and the technical booth; everything is visible and apparent. There is no attempt at lavish interior decoration; the walls are bare and everything matches, as closely as possible, the stark blackness of the walls, including the hard plastic seats, audience risers and exposed pipes. The stage itself has no hidden areas for the creation of theatrical magic. There are none of the peripheral spaces of a Broadway theatre: wings, flies or traps. The entire playing area is visible to the audience and any magic must be created in full view.

This space differs sharply from a Broadway theatre, which has differentiated, specialized areas. On Broadway, the audience sits in a discrete large volume created for viewing the performance, which is decorated with gewgaws that serve to please the spectators' eyes. The play takes place in its own separate volume, equipped with more or less elaborate machinery for the creation of illusion and spectacle, and with more or less sufficient space for scene shifting. Broadway theatres, with their architecture, prices and tradition of "a Broadway production," set up the expectation of an extravaganza.

Brooks Atkinson describes how this difference can affect a critic's reception of a performance:

> I did have different standards when I went downtown, but it wasn't done with a slide rule. If you walk into a small tawdry theatre, where you are only five feet away from the actors, you are naturally in a different frame of mind than when you go to Broadway. . . . So, although I never consciously adjusted my standards, I know I did it unconsciously . . . inside the theater.[2]

John Falabella feels that a "nontraditional space makes you accept somewhat non-traditional writing. You walk in and your expectations are a great deal different than walking into one of those gilded proscenium houses." This difference became especially important, and detrimental, to a production of *Safe Sex,* by Harvey Fierstein, that Falabella designed. The production was originally produced at the LaMama Experimental Theatre and later moved to Broadway. Falabella comments: "It should have been a dirty space; it should have been an unfinished space. Walking into LaMama, you have an expectation that is completely different than walking into the Shubert."

When a play transfers, it may need to be altered, to a greater or lesser extent, because of this difference in expectations. For instance, Beatty cites the difference between seeing the lighting instruments in a Broadway theatre as opposed to an Off Broadway theatre: "Off Broadway, you learn to ignore them. But on Broadway, it says, 'Oh! We're doing a play!' " For instance, in the Circle Rep production of *Knock Knock,* by Jules Feiffer, the lights were exposed—by necessity. The designers decided to leave the lights exposed and unmasked when the production moved to Broadway, a decision Beatty now feels was a mistake: "A Broadway production should have been slicker."

When Michael Yeargan designed the Sheldon Harnick adaptation of the French film *The Umbrellas of Cherbourg* at Martinson Hall, there was no attempt to mask the architecture: the columns were visible, and the audience was seated at small tables. According to Yeargan, the production implicitly stated, "Okay, we're in this room, and we're going to do *The Umbrellas of Cherbourg* for you." The audience was "in a nightclub watching this surreal experience happen at the end of the room." But when the production moved to Broadway, the audience's experience was quite different: "The minute you had to put your coat and tie on, buy a ticket, sit in a theatre seat, watch it and take it seriously, there wasn't enough material, enough depth to it." In a proscenium theatre, the audience "took it too seriously."

Beatty transferred several productions from Circle Rep to Broadway largely intact, but decided with *The 5th of July* that the design should be altered to acknowledge the different expectations: "We started hiding lights and doing it like a real Broadway show. It's different, and we acknowledged that it's different, rather than pretending that we could make a Broadway theatre into the Circle Rep, which it isn't." Beatty knew he "had to compensate for the Broadway experience," in which the theatre lacks the intimacy and close audience proximity of Circle Rep, and so the scenery was "more aggressive. It came out toward the audience and grabbed them more. There were pieces of scenery sticking out toward the audience, and the proscenium was covered with greenery over the audience's heads to get them to feel they were in the set more."

## Acting Problems

One of the major adjustments a production must make when transferring is in the nature of the acting. In some cases, the acting can be subtly or grossly enlarged to fill the larger theatre, but the larger style may not be appropriate to the play as it was created in the smaller space.

John Caird has found with the Royal Shakespeare Company that changing the scale of the acting for a transfer is not enough. Instead, the actors have to re-explore the text itself:

> What you discover in rehearsal relates to what the size of the theatre is.
>
> Most directors and actors working in classical texts will try to do as much detailed work as they can, and they want as much of that detail as is possible to be communicated to the audience. That's easy to do in a very small space, but difficult to do in a very large one.
>
> If you have a group of actors who have played in a very small space, they're used to all the details being appreciated by the audience. If you move into a big theatre, you're really requiring the actors to select the two things they're doing in every line rather than the five things, because you're asking them to project their voices, to act physically in a broader way, to get across the void. Once you've increased in size what you're doing inside a single Shakespearean line, you've got to say farewell to the details within that line.
>
> The converse is also true. If you're in a big space, you're used to doing two things in a line. If you bring it down to a small space, you bring the volume of your performance down, the physical size, and you're left with a feeling of emptiness, vapidness. There's nothing to work with. You have to reinvestigate the text, use much more detail through each line, and re-explore things, especially relationships between one character and another on the stage.

Bernhardt used such a technique when the Broadway cast of *Crimes of the Heart,* by Beth Henley, performed the play at the Ahmanson Theatre (Los Angeles), which is larger and less intimate: "I tried to broaden the strokes. I eliminated a lot of little stuff, in terms of blocking and physicalization. I tried to make stronger moves—fewer and stronger moves, make the business simpler but larger—in order to fill that space."

## HOW SHOULD A PRODUCTION BE TRANSFERRED?

### Reconceive the Production

When a production transfers from one theatre to another, it may have to be reconceived for the new theatre space. Caird says that if the production is "changing in size," the designer "really has to start again."

Austin Pendleton recommends that the director should "totally abandon everything from the first production. You don't try to hang on to any values or any moments. You completely let go and start over again, so that it develops its own logic in terms of the theatre space that you're now in."

### Only Adjust the Production

In other cases, one need only adjust the production to suit its new surroundings, while maintaining the overall tone of the performance. Tony Walton changed the scale, but tried to maintain the same effect, for the transfer of *The House of Blue Leaves* from the smaller Mitzi Newhouse to the larger Vivian Beaumont. Almost everything was enlarged in order to fill the new theatre:

> We tried to see whether you could take the same form and enlarge it so that the size seemed to be in appropriate proportion to the volume of the theatre, to just subtly readjust the proportions of everything onstage. We were hoping that anybody who saw the two productions wouldn't know that anything had happened, but we did in fact change the size of everything that the cast played with.

The "meaning" of the play, as conceived by the director and discovered by the cast through the rehearsal process, may not have to be changed if the production transfers. Instead, one can adjust the expression of that meaning to suit the new space. Gregory Mosher, while maintaining that in a transfer it is best to "marry" the production to the new space, stresses not to "throw out what you did, because it represents months and months of work." According to Arvin Brown, "A play means a certain thing to me, and that meaning, once developed through the rehearsal process, will not fundamentally change, but the expression of that meaning will change."

## Don't Reconceive the Production

It may not be possible to reconceive a production for a new space, in that the production's very conception was based on the original space. Jonathan Miller states,

> Usually the idea of reconceiving it is probably misplaced. There's no such thing as reconceiving a design that itself is constitutive of the production. You undertake the production for that particular form. To reconceive it is really another way of saying that you've settled for something less than perfect.

Instead, Miller's approach is simply to "disown" the later production.

Reconceiving the production for the new space may also be impossible for the practical reasons. Jules Fisher says such a process is "too expensive." The transfer is usually made for "economic reasons," and therefore the producer "doesn't want to spend lots more for a new production." In addition, Fisher points out that it is difficult to reassemble the artistic staff for a complete overhaul of the show. David Jenkins observes that from a "practical point of view," a designer tends to think in terms of "shoehorning" the production into the new theatre, for several reasons. First, "probably you don't have the kind of director who wants to totally rethink a show." Second, "the producer is anxious to reuse as much scenery as possible." Third is the "time factor" of the transfer, which is usually "minimal," with the result that "you don't have the time to change things around very much." Fourth, the designer has probably "lost interest in it, and probably it's moving because of purely financial gain, so you lose the spirit of the adventure."

## TRANSFERRING TO A THEATRE WITH A DIFFERENT AUDIENCE CONFIGURATION

One of the greatest challenges is to alter the performance to fit a new audience-performance configuration. In some cases, it may be possible to adjust the stage or auditorium slightly in order to maintain certain characteristics of the original production. Walton subsequently transferred *The House of Blue Leaves* from the Beaumont thrust to the Plymouth proscenium, and tried "to get some of the virtues of the thrust into a conventional proscenium" by extending the stage out as far into the auditorium as sightlines would allow. Walton cites a rule of thumb in a proscenium theatre, that one can thrust out to the far edge of the orchestra pit: "If you have an orchestra pit, the likelihood is that the audience upstairs can see the hands of the conductor and can see the conductor when he turns and bows." Walton also tried to incorporate other aspects of the thrust into the proscenium production: "We tried to replace the convenience of the vom with an exit that skidded along the outer edge of the forestage and wrapped around the wall underneath the boxes on the audience right, so there could be entrances in front instead of all from behind the proscenium."

When a production moves from a thrust to a proscenium, the director must also adjust for the different sense of movement and focus in the two theatre forms. The problem, according to Arvin Brown, is that

> stillness can't simply be imposed on actors. You can't take the production you've done in three-quarters, which involved a certain amount of vital, physical interaction in order to encompass all sides of the stage, and simply remove that. That becomes negative directing. You have to find the ways in which the stillness that the proscenium demands becomes positive values in terms of character and dramatic meaning of the scene.

You also have to guard against the stillness itself taking over, so that what was fluid in one medium becomes static in another. Movement is vital in the proscenium, and if you are doing a piece of naturalism, the movement should seem to spring from a sense of motivation and knowledge of the demands of dramatic action. And it must have the same energy and the same flow that it had in three-quarters, but very much translated.

But some directors and designers maintain that proscenium and open-stage forms are so inherently different that the original production must essentially be scrapped and a new one created. Paul Weidner reports that for productions he transferred from Hartford Stage to proscenium theatres, "I just forgot about what I had done at Hartford, because it was completely different ground-plans, completely different circumstances." His approach was to "start from scratch."

Ming Cho Lee warns that if a designer tries to transfer a set from a proscenium theatre, "the initial starting point probably is wrong for the arena stage or thrust stage, because you constantly have to refer back to your experience as a pictorial set designer, and then try to make it work for the thrust stage." He suggests that the designer look back to his or her original reaction, "to find the intrinsic look that informs the play." He cautions that no matter how much one tries to think of the play anew for the different theatre, one's "initial encounter with the play and with the space" will color all subsequent designs.

•

Ideally, any production should be well-matched to the theatre space in which it is being performed. In theory, therefore, an ideal production could not or should not be transferred, because the new theatre cannot be identical to the old. But the actual practice of theatre is very different from theory. In some cases, the production may not have been well-matched to the original space, and a new theatre may enhance it. Or the business of theatre may dictate a transfer, in which case theatre artists may need to accept compromises for the greater glory and money of a larger, continuing production. If the new theatre is similar to the old, one may be able to subtly adjust the production. If the new space is radically different, one needs to consider an essentially new production, or make the best of what time, money and energy allow.

# NOTES

1. As quoted in "Learning from a Performer: A Conversation with Joseph Papp," *Gamut,* in Performing Arts Library Scrapbook, n. date: 19.
2. As quoted in Howard Greenberger, *The Off-Broadway Experience* (Englewood Cliffs, N.J.: Prentice-Hall, 1971) 168.

# CHAPTER 16

# TWO PLANKS AND A PASSION

The second half of the twentieth century is a rare period in theatre history, with its myriad forms of theatre architecture and drama. In most eras there was a single kind of theatre building, but a "theatre" today can refer to anything from Broadway to a massive domed arena, to a loft. Spectators may view the performance from one or all sides, from above or below. In addition, there is no dominant style of drama, and theatres commonly draw on a worldwide array of plays from the past 2,500 years.

This situation necessarily raises the issue of compatibility: what plays are appropriate for what theatres (and vice versa)? Can the play be performed in any space? Is there a "right" space for any given play?

Many theatre artists hold fast to the idea that any play can be done in any space. They are not blind to the complications and problems, but believe that the inherent flexibility of this approach is healthy. According to Ming Cho Lee, this belief is important to hold, because, "otherwise one gets dogmatic and gets stuck. Your first instinct is to say, 'Why do this play in this space?' But I would like to think, 'Well, isn't it interesting that this play is normally associated with that space? Let's see what happens.' "

Alvin Epstein points out that "history proves" that any play can be done in any space:

> So many plays, certainly recently, have been produced in types of theatres for which they were not conceived, and in which you might think, 'Well, that couldn't possibly work.' But I don't believe that a play requires one and only one kind of space—any play can adapt to a variety of spatial arrangements.

Joseph Papp, quoting a theatre maxim, declares, "In the theatre you can do anything, anywhere, any place, if you have two planks and a passion."[1]

Robin Wagner offers the challenge: "I would defy anyone to tell me that there was a space in which you could not do a play." He believes that "plays are written to fit anywhere." According to Wagner, there is no single "space equivalent" for each play; any space can work for a play, because "the play contains its own space." Wagner cites his designs for big Broadway musicals, which would seem to require a large theatre with a proscenium, wing space and flies; but Wagner maintains that the adaptation of one of these designs to a theatre with none of these attributes is a "minor fix." For instance, adapting *A Chorus Line* (Book by James Kirkwood and Nicholas Dante; lyrics by Edward Kleban; music by Marvin Hamlisch) to an arena "is a minor adjustment." Wagner says he spent only about three hours on the changes, because the musical is simply "about entrances and exits." Similarly, he adapted *42nd Street* (Book by Michael Stewart and Mark Bramble; lyrics by Al Dubin and others; music by Harry Warren) for an arena stage with a 16′ ceiling, which he calls another "minor adjustment."

Wagner stresses, though, that the performance will be different in each theatre. He is often asked by producers if a given show can be put into a given theatre: "And the answer is always the same: 'Sure, it will fit anywhere you want. But you're going to give up certain things and you're going to make certain adjustments, and you may think of them as compromises.' "

Matching a play with an unconventional choice of space may offer startling revelations, as Jonathan Miller suggests:

> While you thought the period or the genre demanded one space, you can surprise yourself by discovering that another space liberates and releases certain qualities that are inherent in it which you had previously not seen.
>
> In many cases what you're doing is trying to arrest the audience's attention by making sharp contrast with what they expect. They've gotten used to seeing it in a deep space, and you say, 'Have a look and see what happens when it's all squashed flat.' Each of those releases things that are unforeseen, and often you're just making a sharp break with an accepted spatial tradition. I don't think there are any unbreakable generic rules about that.

Gregory Mosher points out that young directors work most frequently in small, shabby theatres, but suggests that they should not be put off or discouraged by such spaces. According to Mosher, "There's no Shakespeare play that can't be done on a patch of grass, and there's no Mamet play that can't be done in a room."

A play can be made to work in any space provided the creators find a concept appropriate to that space. Bill Stabile believes that one can perform any play in any space "provided everybody is flexible and open to solving it in new ways." He says that if the director and designer "come into the space with preconceived ideas, based on some other way, you're going to be beating your head against a brick wall."

While one can do any play in any space, there still may be better and worse theatres for a given play. Performing the play in a less appropriate space is possible, but the production may not be as good. According to Melvin Bernhardt, "If you want to do a play, and this is the space you have to do it in, then you find a way to do it." But he also maintains that "there's no question that certain plays work better in certain environments than in other environments."

But some take an even less positive tone, saying that the play will suffer measurably in a space that is less than appropriate. Liviu Ciulei observes, "Any play can be done mediocrely or badly on any stage."

While one might be able to present any play in any space, the effort may be too great, the compromises too many, or the end result simply not worthwhile. Robert Kalfin advises,

> Energy gets drained into torturing space into trying to work for you. Sometimes that drains energy from the production, because you're working so hard at trying to make something work that really isn't supporting what you're trying to do. It's very hard to recognize that when you're passionate about a work. You just want to get it on anyway.
>
> Where is the point where you say, 'Wait a minute. I love this play, but it would suffer here. It would not be what it could be, because the problems are going to fight it.' That's hard to do when you're passionate about something.

In effect, all the issues presented in this book can be seen as a series of questions that the theatre artist should ask in order to use space creatively. The answers are, in a sense, unimportant. What is important is to engage in the process of discovery and exploration that asking these questions entails.

The first question is: What is the nature of the theatre space? This examination needs to be conducted neutrally, without preconceptions and in as relaxed a manner as possible. What does the space suggest? What is the nature of the audience-performance relationship? Where is the focus of the space? What is unique to this space?

Next, the theatre artist needs to ask: What should be the performance's relationship to the architecture? To answer that question, ask: What is the nature of the architecture and the play? Should the production be in harmony with the architecture? In an oppositional dialogue with it? Ignore it? But keep foremost in mind: What is the fundamental artistic, theatrical purpose?

How can architectural features that impose on the production, such as columns or dominant architecture, be dealt with? How can the "problems" of the theatre be turned into positive advantages for the production? Can the problematic features be accentuated? Can unique aspects be incorporated? Can existing architecture be echoed in the design? Can the very production itself be based on the space—its style, what it represents, etc.?

To what extent should the audience be involved in or distant from the performance? How can the involvement or distance be achieved? How should the audience's relationship to the performance be manipulated to achieve the desired result?

Consider that theatre forms may implicitly call for different styles of production. A performance in an open stage theatre is not the same as a performance in a proscenium theatre. But to what extent those differences rule the production is up to the theatre artists involved.

Whatever the theatre space, it should be understood and honored in the production process. No theatre, however "simple," should be taken for granted. The proscenium theatre, no matter how much theatre artists are accustomed to it, has conventions that should be recognized, and can create moments that are unique to that form.

If the performance is to occur in an open stage, consider the unique production demands of the thrust or arena. These characteristics should be viewed not as hurdles, but rather as inherent qualities.

For instance: What degree of realism is desired for this production? How can the design opportunities of the open stage be exploited fully? Can the stage shape be manipulated? How should the floor be designed? How can levels define and break up the space for this production? How can the portal be exploited for scenery or action? Or how can it be effectively eliminated?

For the director: How can the play be made available to the entire encircling audience, without the actors' movement seeming arbitrary? How can diagonal and curving blocking patterns support the world of this play? How can this play be seen in a dance-like, three-dimensional style? How can the unique architectural qualities of the open stage, such as the vom and the moat, create unique effects?

How can the director and designer create an environment that will permit the flow and pace of action needed for the production?

Is the stage raised, sunken, or level in relation to the first audience row? How steep is the auditorium rake? What implicit relationship is established between audience and performer? What are the implications in terms of "power" and intimacy? Can the vertical relationship be adjusted?

If the volume of the theatre space seems large, can the production reach up to the size of the space and maintain its inherent validity? How can the volume be manipulated so as to create a space more hospitable to the production?

If the theatre is flexible, what configurations are possible? What audience-performance configuration will best suit the play, the style of performance and the space itself?

Is the play appropriate for an environmental or promenade production? Does it have many locales? Will the greater degree of audience movement and involvement support the play? Is the space appropriate for environmental or promenade theatre?

If the production is transferring to a different theatre, why is it being moved? The answer to that question may determine the degree to which the production is reconceived or shoe-horned. What are the expectations set up by each theatre? How can the new expectations support, rather than undermine, the production?

Theatre space need not remain in the background, serving only as a neutral frame for the production. The space can be exploited so that it serves as more than a handmaiden to the drama. With an awareness of the space, theatre artists can create a performance that is in tune with the surroundings, celebrating the space.

If theatre artists accept the idea that theatre space can be a constructive, positive element in the creation of a performance, these and many more ideas can be put to use in theatrical production. But the first step is to free our own minds—to see theatre space as an area for exploitation, negotiation and creativity. To see the space as theatrical.

## NOTES

1. As quoted in Harold C. Schonberg, "Beaumont: Must It Be Remodeled?" *The New York Times* 1 Sept. 1983: 15.

# INDEX

(Numbers in italics refer to illustrations)

*Agamemnon* 146–47
Ahmanson Theatre (Los Angeles) 190
Alabama Shakespeare Festival (Birmingham, Ala.) 93
Anspacher Theater (Joseph Papp Public Theater, New York City) 25–26, 108–09, 132–33, 134–35, 146, 149
*Antigone* 26, 129
*Anything Goes* 39
Arena Stage (Washington, D.C.) 76, *78, 79,* 86, 87, 147, 148
Aronson, Arnold 169
Asolo Theatre (Sarasota, Fla.) 52
Atkinson, Brooks 187
Ayckbourn, Alan 119

*Bacchae, The* 41, 86
Barbican Centre (Royal Shakespeare Company, London) 133
Barnes, Clive 26–27, 165
Barnes, Jason xv, 170–171
Beatty, John Lee xv, 45, 23, 24, 27–28, 47, 52–53, 54, 55–56, 64, 66–67, 72, 73, 74–75, 76, 79, 89, 97, 100, 116, 123, 141, 151–152, 157, 174, 176, 185, 188–189
Beck, Julian 178
*Beggar on Horseback* 145
Berkowitz, Gerald M. 110
Bernhardt, Melvin xv, 52, 185–186, 190, 197
*Billy Budd* 177
*Birthday Party, The* 78, 130
Blau, Herbert xv–xvi, 28, 150
*Bohême, La* 108–109
Bosco, Philip xvi, 120

Bouffes du Nord (Paris) 23
Bread and Puppet Theatre 169
Brook, Peter xvi, 23
Brooklyn Majestic (New York City) 24
Brown, Arvin xvi, 5, 50, 63–64, 88–89, 104–05, 190, 192–93
Brown, Paul xvi, 171, 175, 181
Brown, Zack xvi, 71, 122, 167, 185
Brustein, Robert 144
Buch, Rene xvii, 110
Burris-Meyer, Harold 49

CSC Repertory Theatre (New York City) 78, 130
Cacoyannis, Michael xvii, 41, 86
*Caine Mutiny Court Martial, The* 42
Caird, John xvii, 43–44, 133–134, 189, 190
Caldwell, Sarah xvii, 145
Call, Ed 80
*Candida* 88, 174
*Cats* 169, 177
Cereza, Javier 182
Chekhov, Anton 72, 157
*Cherry Orchard, The* 23
*Chorus Line, A* 196
Christie, Agatha 72
Cincinnati Playhouse in the Park 141
Circle in the Square (Downtown) (New York City) 31, 175
Circle in the Square (Uptown) (New York City) 21, *22,* 41, 42, 55, 74, 79, 85–86, 88, 103, 105, 111–112, 118, 119, 120, 121, 122, 165–167, 175

Circle Repertory Theatre (New York
City)   23, 24, 66, 151–52, 174,
176, 185, 187, 188–189
Ciulei, Liviu   xvii, 101–102, 197
Cole, Edward C.   49
Comédie Française   15
*Comedy of Errors, A*   39
*Coming of Age in Soho*   26
*Commune*   172
Conklin, John   xvii, 4, 77, 101, 146
Cottesloe Theatre (Royal National
Theatre, London)   170–171, 182
Coward, Noel   118
*Crimes of the Heart*   190
Crinkley, Richmond   xvii, 145
Curtis, Simon   xvii–xviii, 44–45,
174, 180, 181–182

Dana, F. Mitchell   xviii, 12–13
*Danton's Death*   99
*Days in the Trees*   21
Delacourt Theatre (New York City)
30, *30*
Denver Theatre Center   7
*Design for Living*   85
Detweiler, Lowell   xviii, 7, 17, 64,
65, 71–72, 93
*Diamonds*   175
*Drinks before Dinner*   38

*Egyptology*   161, 164
Eigsti, Karl   xviii, 3, 12, 16, 18, 19,
38, 56, 59–60, 66, 67, 85, 88, 93,
115–116, 123, 141, 147, 148
Elder, Eldon   xviii–xix, 1, 15, 64–65,
115, 116, 148
*Emperor, The*   21
*Endgame*   105
*Entertaining Strangers*   182
Epstein, Alvin   xix, 42, 104, 106,
125, 195

Falabella, John   xix, 25, 42, 75, 76,
94–95, 187–188
*Fathers and Sons*   158
Ferencz, George   xix, 137–138, 157
*5th of July, The*   185, 188–189
*Figaro's Marriage*   41, 85

Fisher, Jules   xix, 9–10, 190
Fitch, James Marston   35
*Floating Light Bulb, The*   97, 118–
119
Folger Theatre (Washington, D.C.)
24
Foreman, Richard   xix, 2, 6, 14, 15,
16–17, 29, 39–40, 146, 161, 164
*42nd Street*   196
Foy, Kenneth   xx, 87, 88, 124, 131,
166–167
Freedman, Gerald   xx, 131, 135,
145–146
*Front Page, The*   99–100, 125–126
Fura dels Baus, La   182

Garfein, Jack   xx, 6, 36, 154–155, 157
Gassner, John   60–61, 77, 110–111
Gelber, Jack   xx, 72, 130, 157
Gersten, Bernard   xx, 98
*Ghosts*   76, 77, 164
Gill, Brendan   145
*Gin Game, The*   174–175
*Glass Menagerie, The*   65
*Good Woman of Setzuan, The*   87
Goodman, Robyn   xx, 84
Goodspeed Opera House (New Had-
dam, Conn.)   52
Gottfried, Martin   72, 120, 145, 147
Gregory, Andre   xx, 165
Grosbard, Ulu   xx–xxi, 77–78, 97,
104, 118–119, 120–121
Gruenewald, Thomas   xxi, 5, 52,
122–123
Gunter, John   xxi, 17
Guthrie Theatre (Minneapolis, Minn.)
7, 42, 60, 65, 68, 70, *71*, 73, 79–80,
92, 104, 113
Guthrie, Tyrone   xxi, 10, 33–34, 37,
49, 61, 76–77, 80, 103, 113

Hall, Adrian   xxi, 159–160, 177
Hamburger, Richard   112
*Hamlet*   24, 41, 43, 96, 136
Hardy, Hugh   xxi, 10, 24, 36, 87,
112, 155, 159
Harrison, Rex   120
*Harry Outside*   174

Hart, Bill   xxi, 133, 161, 165
Hartford Stage (Conn.)   5, 44, 80–81,
    *82, 83, 84,* 94, 96, 101, 124, 128,
    135, 193
*Harvesting, The*   174
*Heartbreak House*   120
*Henry V*   113
*House of Blue Leaves, The*   50, 100,
    190, 192

*Iceman Cometh, The*   31
*Importance of Being Earnest, The*
    105
Irving, Jules   145, 150
Irwin, Bill   xxii, 10, 20–21, 28–29
Ivey, Dana   xxii, 118
Izenour, George   xxii, 61

Jackness, Andrew   xxii, 132–133
Jenkins, David   xxii–xxiii, 5, 13, 24–
    25, 27, 53, 117, 161, 191–192
Jensen, John   xxiii, 3, 28, 59, 60,
    73–74, 80, 92–93, 100, 101, 107–
    108, 125, 148
*John Gabriel Borkman*   111–112
Jones, Robert Edmond   36
Joseph, Stephen   5, 63, 67, 106, 135–
    136
Joseph Papp Public Theater (New
    York City)   16, 25–26, 133, 161,
    164–165
Jourdan, Louis   74
Juilliard Drama Theatre (New York
    City)   86–87, 94, 101–102, 112,
    130–131, *131, 132,* 132, 135

Kahn, Michael   xxiii, 94, 131
Kalfin, Robert   xxiii, 48, 120, 174,
    185, 186–187, 197
Kellogg, Marjorie Bradley   xxiii–
    xiv, 4, 5, 46, 79, 81, 92, 98, 100–
    101, 121, 122, 158, 161, 164, 186
Kerr, Walter   85–86, 145, 164
*King Lear*   43, 136
Kissel, Howard   30
*Knock Knock*   188
*Kool Aid*   130
Kroll, Jack   38, 99

*L.S.D. ( . . . Just the High Points . . . )*
    137
Lagomarsino, Ron   xxiv, 44, 51, 80
LaMama Experimental Theatre Club
    (New York City)   13, 137–138,
    175, 188
Lamont, Rosette C.   27
Lamos, Mark   xxiv, 56, 44, 67, 80,
    94, 96, 104, 112, 121, 128, 135
Landesman, Heidi   xxiv, 6–7, 13, 16,
    21, 30–31, 54, 87, 94, 148, 157,
    175
Landwehr, Hugh   xxiv, 7, 46, 54, 65,
    80–81, 84
Langham, Michael   xxiv, 98
Langton, Basil   xxiv–xxv, 40, 74
*Largely/New York*   20
Leach, Wilford   xxv, 26, 37, 108–
    109, 134–135, 161
Leacroft, Richard   133
LeCompte, Elizabeth   xxv, 167
Lee, Eugene   xxv, 24
Lee, Ming Cho   xxv, 3, 4, 6, 59, 60,
    61, 149, 160, 193, 195
Lesser, Gene   xxv, 135
Leverett, James   136
Levy, Jacques   xxv–xxvi, 37, 62
Lincoln Center (New York City)   15,
    29
*Little Foxes*   54
Living Theatre   31, 169, 177
Loeb Drama Center (Harvard Univer-
    sity, Cambridge, Mass.)   *162, 163,
    166*
Long Wharf Theater (New Haven,
    Conn.)   5, 27, 50, 55, 84, 174–
    175
Loquasto, Santo   xxvi, 7, 24, 29–30,
    61, 69–70, 81, 121–122
*Lucky Stiff*   11
LuEsther Hall (Joseph Papp Public
    Theater, New York City)   133,
    164–165
Lyceum Theatre (New York City)
    55
Lynch, Thomas   xxvi, 25, 26, 53, 54,
    61–62, 85, 86, 88, 92, 96–97, 119,
    160–161

*Macbeth*   118, 145
Mackintosh, Iain   xxvi, 35–36
MacMahon, Aline   xxvi, 150
*Major Barbara*   42
Malina, Judith   xxvi, 31, 178
Mamet, David   197
*Man and Superman*   166
*Man Who Came to Dinner, The*   71
Manhattan Theatre Club (New York
   City)   23
Mann, Theodore   xxvi–xxvii, 31, 32,
   103–104, 166
*Map of the World, A*   38
Mark Taper Forum (Los Angeles)
   89, *90*, 141
Marshall, E.G.   111–112
Martinson Hall (Joseph Papp Public
   Theater, New York City)   26, 27,
   148, 164–165, 188
*Medea*   85–86
*Memorandum, The*   26
Memorial Theatre (Royal Shakespeare
   Company, Stratford-upon-Avon,
   England)   133
*Midsummer Night's Dream, A*   30,
   87, 132
Mielziner, Jo   51–52, 93
Miller, Jonathan   xxvii, 21, 40–41,
   51, 134, 190, 196
Milwaukee Repertory Theatre   28,
   112
*Misanthrope, The*   111
*Miss Margarida's Way*   29
Mitchell, David   xxvii, 48, 99, 124,
   129, 174–175
Mitzi Newhouse Theater (New York
   City)   121, 130, 190
Modular Theatre (California Institute
   of the Arts, Valencia, Calif.)   *156,*
   *158*
Moiseiwitsch, Tanya   80
Montresor, Beni   xxvii, 85
Morgan, Roger   xxvii, 159
Moro, Peter   48
Mosher, Gregory   xxvii, 2–3, 5, 39,
   55, 104, 105, 121, 190, 196–197
*Mousetrap, The*   63
Murphy, Rosemary   111–112

Murray, Brian   xxvii–xxviii, 4, 7,
   103

Napier, John   xxviii, 170, 176–177
*Nayatt School*   136, 137
Newman Theater (Joseph Papp Public
   Theater, New York City)   29, 38
*Nicholas Nickleby, The Life and Ad-
   ventures of*   43, 169, 176–177
*Night of the Iguana, The*   122
*Normal Heart, The*   133, 165
Novick, Julius   118

*Oedipus*   137
*Oh, Calcutta!*   62
Ohl, Ted   xxviii, 94
Olivier Theatre (Royal National The-
   atre, London)   17
*Once in a Lifetime*   85, 166
Ontological-Hysteric Theatre   14
Orton, Joe   89
Other Space (Royal Shakespeare Com-
   pany, Stratford-upon-Avon, En-
   gland)   133
*Our Town*   18, 55

Papp, Joseph   xxviii, 145, 186, 195
Park Avenue Armory (New York
   City)   182–183
Pendleton, Austin   xxviii, 1, 2, 14–
   15, 54–55, 56, 111–112, 155, 190
Performance Group   10, 167, 169
Performing Garage (New York City)
   136, 137, 167, *172*
Perloff, Carey   xxviii, 78, 88, 107,
   130
*Phaedra*   130
*Phantom of the Opera*   169
Pinero, Arthur Wing   99
Pinter, Harold   78
Pit (Royal Shakespeare Company,
   London)   133
*Play Strindberg*   130
Playwrights Horizons (New York
   City)   11, 185
Plymouth Theatre   28, 50, 192
Pond, Helen   xxviii, 145
Porter, Stephen   xxix, 21, 23, 40, 42,

50, 103, 105, 106, 107, 111, 124–125, 150

Potts, David   xxix, 10–11, 18, 47, 85, 176

*Present Laughter*   118

*Pretenders, The*   42

*Prometheus*   178

Quintero, José   xxix, 110

*Real Thing, The*   28

*Regard of Flight, The*   28

Repertorio Espanol   110

Rich, Frank   25, 119, 164

*Road*   44, 171, 174, 175, 180, 181–182

Rojo, Jerry   175–176

Royal Court Theatre (London)   171

Royal National Theatre (London)   17

Royal Shakespeare Company   43, 133–134, 176–177, 189

*Safe Sex*   188

Saint-Denis, Michel   60, 158

*Salonika*   132–133

Savran, David   xxix, 137, 167

Schechner, Richard   xxix, 6, 10, 44, 137, 167, 169, 171–173, 179, 180

Schmidt, Douglas   xxix–xxx, 26, 86–87, 96, 129, 130, 135, 144, 146–147

Schreiber, Terry   7

Schulz, Karen   xxx, 146

*Seagull, The*   165

Second Stage (New York City)   24, 84

Senn, Herbert   xxviii, 145

Serban, Andrei   xxx, 41, 146

Shakespeare, William   104, 112, 117, 124–125

Shaliko Company   164

Shapiro, Mel   xxx, 146

Shaw, George Bernard   42

Sherman, Loren   xxx–xxxi, 26, 95, 98, 122, 160, 174

*Short Eyes*   24

Simon, John   145

*Six Characters in Search of an Author*   18

*Six Public Acts*   32

Skelton, Thomas   xxxi, 85

Southern, Richard   36, 48–49

*Spring's Awakening*   101–102

Stabile, Bill   xxxi, 1, 12, 13–14, 21, 118, 134, 137–138, 148, 197

*Starlight Express*   169, 177

Stephen Joseph Theatre in the Round (Scarborough, England)   119

Straiges, Tony   xxxi, 23, 175, 185

Stratford Festival Theatre Thrust Stage (Stratford, Ont.)   *34, 35,* 76, 94, 98, 113

*Streetcar Named Desire, A*   72

*Subject Was Roses, The*   151

*Sunday in the Park with George*   185

Susan Stein Shiva Theater (Joseph Papp Public Theater, New York City)   158, 161, 164

*Suz/O/Suz*   182

Swan Theatre (Royal Shakespeare Company, Stratford-upon-Avon, England)   133–134

*Swing Shift*   23

Symonds, Robert   xxxi, 99

*Taking Steps*   119

*Tale Told, A*   152

*Tamara*   170, 182–183

*Taming of the Shrew, The*   177

Tanner, Tony   xxxi, 50, 63, 74, 123, 140–141

*13 Rue de l'Amour*   40, 74

*Three-Penny Opera, The*   29, 146

*Three Sisters, The*   76, 77

Tillinger, John   xxxii, 44, 53, 89, 101, 110, 124

*Tony 'n' Tina's Wedding*   170, 182

*Tooth of Crime, The*   137–138, 180

*Treats*   112

*Trelawny of the 'Wells'*   99

Trinity Square Repertory Theatre (Providence, R.I.)   159, 177

*Turning the Earth*   31

*Umbrellas of Cherbourg, The*   188

*View from a Bridge, A*   77
Vivian Beaumont Theater (New York
   City)   5, 29, 39, 50, 51, 87, 97,
   98–100, 105, 118–119, 121, 125–
   126, 129, 133, 141–145, *142, 143,*
   *144,* 146–147, 149–151, 190, 192

Wagner, Robin   xxxii, 11–12, 17, 47,
   62, 76, 118, 133, 195
*Waiting for Godot*   105
Wallace, James Dale   80
Walton, Tony   xxxii, 28, 38, 75, 99–
   100, 105, 122, 125–126, 190,
   192

Weidner, Paul   xxxii, 4, 10, 87, 89,
   101, 109, 116, 124, 193
Weiss, Marc B.   xxxii–xxxiii, 12
*White House Murder Case, The*   28
Whitehead, Robert   117–118
Wooster Group   136–137, 167
Worth, Irene   111–112
*Woyzeck*   104

Yeargan, Michael   xxxiii, 4, 18, 27,
   59, 81, 97, 124, 188

Zaks, Jerry   xxxiii, 5, 11, 37, 50, 53,
   111, 125, 151

## ABOUT THE AUTHOR

William F. Condee is Associate Professor of Theater and Chair of Undergraduate Studies at Ohio University. His articles on theatre architecture have appeared in *Journal of American Theatre and Drama, Architectural Review, World Architecture, Western European Stages, Theatre Design and Technology, Themes in Drama* and *Theatre Insight*. He has also worked as research assistant for *Theatre Projects*, a theatre consulting firm in London. In the professional theatre, he was dramaturg for the London Young Vic—West End production of *A Touch of the Poet* with Vanessa Redgrave and Timothy Dalton, directed by David Thacker. Dr. Condee received his Ph.D. from Columbia University, where he studied under Dr. Bernard Beckerman. He received his A.B. and M.A. from Vassar College, where he was elected to Phi Beta Kappa. Dr. Condee has also taught at the University of Wales College of Cardiff, where he was Honorary Visiting Lecturer, and at Vassar College. He received the Citation for Teaching Excellence and the Teaching Recognition Award from Ohio University.